Evidence, Politics, and Education Policy

Evidence, Politics, and Education Policy

Lorraine M. McDonnell

M. Stephen Weatherford

HARVARD EDUCATION PRESS

Cambridge, Massachusetts

Paperback ISBN 978-1-68253-516-5
Library Edition ISBN 978-1-68253-517-2

Library of Congress Cataloging-in-Publication Data

Names: McDonnell, Lorraine, 1947– author. | Weatherford, M. Stephen, author.
Title: Evidence, politics, and education policy / Lorraine M. McDonnell,
    M. Stephen Weatherford.
Description: Cambridge, Massachusetts : Harvard Education Press, [2020] |
    Includes index. | Summary: "In Evidence, Politics, and Education Policy,
    political scientists Lorraine M. McDonnell and M. Stephen Weatherford
    provide an original analysis of evidence use in education policymaking to help
    scholars and advocates shape policy more effectively—Provided by publisher.
Identifiers: LCCN 2020027725 | ISBN 9781682535165 (paperback) |
    ISBN 9781682535172 (library binding)
Subjects: LCSH: Education and state—United States. | Education—Research—
    United States. | Education—Political aspects—United States. | Educational
    accountability—United States. | Policy sciences. | Educational change—
    United States.
Classification: LCC LC89 .M334 2020 | DDC 379.73—dc23
LC record available at https://lccn.loc.gov/2020027725

Published by Harvard Education Press,
an imprint of the Harvard Education Publishing Group

Harvard Education Press
8 Story Street
Cambridge, MA 02138

Cover Design: Wilcox Design
Cover Image: Kieran Stone/Moment via Getty Images

The typefaces used in this book are Jenevers and Open Sans.

To Colin and Theo,
students of the Common Core,
learning about evidence

Contents

1

Evidence Use from a Political Perspective

We're actually one of the better groups when it comes to using evidence. But you often see evidence falling on deaf ears, because it doesn't comport with a particular ideology or point of view.

—*Executive director, education interest group*

We talk a lot about polarizing ideology, but in the actual meetings where the work gets done, it has not been my experience it's about that. It's much more data-driven . . . When data is there, people are using it, when it's not there, people are going off on their own.

—*Obama administration official*

I don't want to appear anti-academic or a Luddite, but research isn't where I ground my arguments. I happen to believe that all meaningful legislation takes place based on an anecdote. Now the best combination is to have the human face in front of ten tons of research, but I never lead with the research.

—*Former governor*

THESE COMMENTS FROM prominent members of the education policy community capture an increasingly serious paradox: the wide acknowledgment that research can usefully inform policy decisions, but a recognition that other types of evidence often take precedence and even occasionally sideline research in policy deliberations. For researchers committed to producing work that can inform education policy, the dilemma has only grown sharper with two recent contradictory developments. One is the federal directive in the Every Student Succeeds Act (ESSA) that programs and interventions be "evidence-based." Although judgments about quality are left to individual states, the legislation assumes that "evidence-based" means showing a statistically significant relationship between interventions and student outcomes.[1] At the same time, the polarization of national politics has resulted in questions with settled scientific answers being reopened for partisan debate, with a senior presidential adviser advocating the use of "alternative facts" when documenting observable and quantifiable events. As research has become more politicized even within the education policy community, inconsistent or incomplete findings that were once seen as contingent and subject to further study have become fodder in ideologically charged debates over issues such as school choice and curriculum content.

The current situation is only the most recent manifestation of the tension between calls for research-based policy and challenges to scientific legitimacy. One consequence has been to reinforce perceptions that partisanship and ideology inevitably drive the selective use of research in advancing particular agendas. While we don't reject this claim, we take an explicitly political perspective in this book and argue that blaming the nonuse or misuse of research on ideology is an incomplete explanation for how evidence is applied in the policy process, and it inhibits thinking about ways to increase effective research use. Analyzing research use through a political lens leads us to focus primarily on the information needs and incentives of policymakers and the groups that provide such information, and also on the context of policymaking. By doing so, we hope to provide researchers, typically most concerned with the educational implications of their studies, with a better sense of the political environment in which the policy implications of that work are debated.

THE CENTRAL ARGUMENTS

The use of research and other evidence in education policy is best understood by viewing it as a part of the larger process of formulating policy and predicting its outcomes. Consequently, in building a theory of evidence use we draw directly from political science and policy analysis research, in both the questions we pose and the concepts we apply in addressing them.[2] We make two arguments. First, the use of research-based evidence in the policy process cannot be understood without considering other types of evidence that policymakers draw upon in their decisions.[3] The "what" of evidence use includes peer-reviewed research, but it goes beyond that, including statistical data, judgments based on professional expertise, the personal experience of policymakers and practitioners, and appeals to values articulated through stories and symbols. Evidence serves multiple roles in the policy process. It can function as analytical information providing assessments about the scope, distribution, and probable causes of identified problems; the conditions under which different policy options are likely to produce their intended effects; and their technical and resource requirements.

Different kinds of evidence may also provide political intelligence about the preferences and strategies of major actors, and about who wins and who loses under different policy options and institutional rules. In many cases, moreover, the strategic uses of evidence may be more central than its analytical functions. In using the term *strategic*, we are referring to the intentional use of evidence in pursuit of a policy or political objective (such as winning an election or enacting legislation). It is done in a context where the accomplishment of the actor's goal depends on the reactions of others, so that it is rational for the actors to anticipate those reactions and shape their argument accordingly. At their core, policies reflect ideas about what societal goals should be pursued, how those goals are most effectively attained, and what lessons from past policy successes and failures can inform policy. The strategic use of evidence reflects the reality of political decision-making, where even solid, well-accepted ideas are transformed through negotiations and compromise. Such transformations introduce the risk that validated inferences will be short-circuited before they can influence practice, and that evidence will be distorted and manipulated.[4]

Recognizing that evidence use in policymaking is strategic has several implications. It means that the capacity of researchers to address questions relevant to policymakers in forms that are understandable to them is an insufficient condition for the use of their work. Similarly, policymakers' use of research depends only indirectly on their ability to process and understand that information. What is crucial, rather, are the incentives of those who supply and use a variety of evidence, and the broader institutional and political context in which policy decisions are made. Incentives that often crowd out research in favor of other types of evidence can include the credibility of conventional sources or the familiarity of conventional ideas, the promise of political support or financial contribution, association with new ideas, and options customized to a local area or constituency. In chapter 2, we elaborate our concept of the "what" of evidence use, distinguishing the different types of evidence by comparing the scientific warrants and political attractiveness of research versus others kinds of evidence.

Our second argument elaborates the primary conditions accounting for variation in the use of evidence: the incentives of those supplying and using different types of evidence, and the context that constructs the occasion for the political choice among policy alternatives. In chapter 3, we identify the "who" as participants in the policy process—elected officials, their staffs, and the interest groups and policy entrepreneurs who seek to persuade them— and we detail their incentives for producing, transmitting, and using research evidence. In chapter 4, we examine the "how" by analyzing the way the purposes for which evidence is used vary across stages of the policy process and institutional arenas. Simply stated, the theory presented in this book assumes that the types of evidence used in policymaking depend on the incentives of those supplying and using that evidence, and on the stage of the policy process. In examining these factors, we highlight three concepts:

Policy learning describes how policy actors apply evidence from past experience to guide and improve subsequent decisions. Peter May summarizes the literature on policy learning, pointing out that, although policymakers often strive to learn from the impacts of policies—writing formal evaluations into authorizing legislation, for instance—it is the experience of policy failure that most strongly and regularly motivates policymakers to rethink the formulation of the problem and seek to generate a wider range of solution alternatives.[5]

Policy entrepreneurs are advocates willing to invest their time, money, and reputation in promoting a particular position or policy agenda. Policy entrepreneurs bring new ideas into the policymaking arena (and the ideas are nearly always grounded in research), but entrepreneurs use evidence more strategically than researchers in trying to persuade legislators that enacting these ideas will be feasible and will solve an acknowledged problem;

successful entrepreneurs rely on social skills, as they build trust in their preferred alternative and construct the political coalition to pass the new policy.[6]

Policy feedback is the process by which policies, once enacted, generate costs and benefits, motivating political responses by affected groups. Those, in turn, influence future policies. The concept of policy feedback reverses the conventional aphorism that "politics creates policies," investigating how "policies create politics" by redistributing political resources and creating incentives for previously advantaged interests to mobilize to reclaim the status quo ante, and for newly recognized interests to defend the policy change. For example, standards-based accountability policies begun in the states were reflected in the federal No Child Left Behind legislation, and dissatisfaction with that law energized and focused the movement for the Common Core State Standards (CCSS).[7] For a policy to be politically sustainable over the long term, its proponents must generate positive feedback in the form of policymakers and the public acknowledging its benefits and providing support sufficient to counter negative feedback from opponents.

The remainder of this chapter establishes the groundwork for these arguments by briefly describing the cases, the research design and data collection, and the analytical approach.[8]

STUDY APPROACH

In constructing the model of evidence use, we draw on empirical material from our extensive investigation of the formulation of the Common Core State Standards. It might appear that a single case study would provide a thin foundation for building a political theory of evidence use. This concern is not unusual—the social science methodology literature has discussed the trade-offs between the depth of information in a case study versus the breadth in a larger sample. We draw on that literature and our knowledge of education policymaking to address the concerns about case study research in several ways. First, the Common Core is a historically important policy reform, impacting the status quo both in its depth (envisioning corresponding changes in curriculum, teaching methods, and learning) and in its scope (proposing common standards in place of wide variation across states). The significance and magnitude of the reform make this case a prime locus for observing the process of policy change.[9] Second, we designed our study to take advantage of the qualitative research dictum that even in examining a single case, the potential for evaluating theory is significantly enhanced by increasing the number of observations of the process viewed from different vantage points. Complex changes constitute multiple processes, and participants in different contexts view the process from valuably different local vantage points and personal perspectives.[10] Our investigation rests on data collected from research producers, from intermediary organizations that translate and communicate research, and from a broad range of users within the policy community, including federal and state officials, agency administrators, and interest group representatives. The number of observations is also increased because we examine the Common Core's development over more than a decade, beginning with how the policy problem was initially defined, its subsequent design and adoption, and its early implementation. In addition to multiple categories of participants at the national level, we closely examine the use of evidence relevant to the adoption and implementation of the Common Core in four states.

Third, we strengthen the approach of earlier studies of research use, which have tended to rely on retrospective self-reports by policymakers, typically well after the decision, a method known to be susceptible to selective recollection and bias. Although our interviews did not occur in real time, they did take place soon after the standards were formulated and thus minimized the effect of retrospection. More importantly, we studied and coded a large number of documents *before* we began conducting interviews, giving us a prior basis for validating self-reports and the context for probing interviewees about the reasons why some sources were used and not others. Fourth, in developing a political theory of evidence use, we seek to move beyond past studies that focus narrowly on research. Our focus is on the entire policy process, taking in the use of multiple types of evidence and also the different ways that evidence is combined and communicated. This study design allows us to examine evidence in-depth through a case that represents a major change in contemporary education policy and allows us to evaluate our theory in multiple contexts and at different levels of analysis.

Finally, we address the limitations of case study research for theory building by systematically comparing a secondary case that examines evidence use in the Children's Health Insurance Program (CHIP). CHIP shares the focus on services for children, so that designing effective policy raises many of the same sort of research questions posed in K–12 education. On the other hand, Congress was the primary locus of deliberation over CHIP, while the states were the focus of evidence use with the Common Core. Chapter 6 describes the use of evidence in the enactment and implementation of CHIP, and depicts the similarities and differences between these two cases.

THE COMMON CORE STATE STANDARDS: AN ILLUMINATING CASE OF EVIDENCE USE

Not only does the Common Core represent a major change in US education policy, with its goal of K–12 mathematics and literacy standards shared across multiple states, but it also provides a unique opportunity to examine the use of varied types of evidence among a range of policy actors in different institutional venues and stages of the policy process. The group of policy entrepreneurs who advanced the idea of common standards and oversaw their development learned from previous policy: they explicitly promoted the CCSS initiative as "research and evidence-based," and established procedures to encourage the use of research in drafting and validating the Common Core standards. The resulting process combined research from the full range of specialties in education scholarship, but it also drew upon the expert judgments of state administrators and politicians, and the active engagement of practitioners with classroom experience teaching mathematics and English Language Arts (ELA).[11] The product of this process was endorsed in the low-key adoption of the CCSS by forty-six states. Yet soon after its implementation began (to the surprise of its initial supporters), the Common Core was attacked from both the ideological right and left, mirroring to some extent the broader tensions in US politics, where polarized ideological competition has undermined evidence-based policy. Although this opposition was intense and attracted considerable attention, its policy effects were limited to a handful of states; forty-one of the original forty-six continue to implement the CCSS a decade after their initial adoption, while those that have made changes have typically retained the essential elements of the Common Core.

    Policy feedback is apparent in the use of evidence. Even before opposition to the Common Core became visible, it was clear that evidence was used strategically in developing the standards, as a resource much like money or reputation. By focusing on the strategic use of evidence, we show how the formulation of the Common Core benefited from policy feedback. By the mid-2000s, state academic standards as the central component of an assessment-based accountability system had a twenty-year history, culminating in the federal No Child Left Behind (NCLB) program.[12] Although standards and student assessments specific to each state were well institutionalized, policy feedback, particularly from NCLB, was becoming increasingly negative. Early expectations that standards-based accountability would narrow achievement gaps between affluent white students and low-income students of color went unrealized; at the same time, NCLB-mandated testing was narrowing the curriculum. There was little agreement about how NCLB should be revised. Influential groups, such as the national teacher unions, were mobilizing in opposition to the strong emphasis on high-stakes testing; yet several former governors and their allied interest groups continued to believe in the potential of standards-based reform, and sought to preserve the policy idea by redefining it in a new incarnation.

Acting as policy entrepreneurs, they promoted academic standards designed to prepare students for college or entry-level careers, and to replace individual state standards with shared standards common across the states. Their strategy for advancing these new standards placed evidence of multiple types front and center. The leadership of the Council of Chief State School Officers (CCSSO) and the National Governors Association (NGA) asserted that the development process:

> is being driven by evidence and research. In the past, standards were largely based on personal judgment. By allowing personal judgment to determine what concepts are in or out of standards, the process often becomes a negotiation, rather than a reflection on what the evidence and research tells [sic] us about the connection between K–12 experiences and success in higher education and promising careers.[13]

This approach reflected a commitment to research-based evidence, but as one leader of the process described it: "I would argue that the standards development was primarily a political process informed by evidence."[14]

Leaders of the CCSS initiative acknowledged that their commitment to ground the effort in research and evidence was a strategy to avoid past ideological debates stemming from the "curriculum wars" of the 1990s. In essence, reliance on research operated to depoliticize the standards development process. This strategic use of evidence is a prime example of policy learn-ing. However, that learning extended beyond avoiding a repeat of past ideo-logical battles. The commitment was to research *and* evidence, and, as we discuss in chapter 2, multiple types of evidence were used. These included: research syntheses published by organizations such as the National Research Council (NRC); expert panels convened by federal government agencies and national subject-matter associations; scholarly journal articles, chapters, and conference presentations; reports by Achieve, ACT, and the College Board, based on faculty surveys and analyses of the relationship between student performance on admission tests and grades in first-year college courses; and reviews of international test data and the standards of high performing coun-tries. The standards writers also reviewed existing state standards and the National Assessment of Education Progress (NAEP) frameworks.

In short, the process of formulating the CCSS entailed vigorous use of many kinds of relevant evidence. Part of the reason for including evidence beyond traditional peer-reviewed studies was the limited supply of relevant research. When asked why the standards documents emphasize "research and evidence," a leader of the development effort replied, "we wanted to be able to cite non-peer-reviewed research because there's not enough research available, and often the findings are inconclusive."

But the scarcity of directly relevant research was not the only reason Common Core advocates drew on other types of evidence. The failed efforts of the George H. W. Bush and Bill Clinton administrations to introduce lim-ited forms of cross-state standards and assessments provided another source of policy learning. As a civil rights organization executive who served in the Clinton administration noted:

> We learned our lesson—from the VNT [Voluntary National Test] and other attempts to introduce assessments. This cannot be top-down. If we had gone to more trouble to build information and support, those [prior initia-tives] would not have had so many problems.

In drawing lessons from past attempts to establish national standards, the Common Core policy entrepreneurs recognized that states would not accept such standards if they came from the federal government. Consequently, CCSSO and NGA, as groups representing state policymakers, took the lead in developing the CCSS, and what they had originally referred to as "national standards" were quickly renamed "common standards" with "state" as one of the primary identifiers. A longtime congressional staffer and executive of a Washington education organization summarized this policy learning:

> Whoever conceived of the process of drafting the standards—bringing in groups, getting feedback—must have been aware of what had happened, and they did it more comprehensively and more thoughtfully than it had been done before . . . There were no virgins in this process; they had been around. They drew on this experience to avoid the pitfalls . . . And then they assiduously tried to stay away from the federal government. Leaders repeatedly told [Secretary of Education Arne] Duncan, "Keep your mitts off this; don't even talk about common standards." The leaders didn't succeed completely in making sure that Washington was seen to be not involved, yet they basically succeeded.

One especially salient lesson, perhaps the most important form of policy learning in the CCSS process, was the value of wide and genuine consultation. In addition to bringing in the work of expert researchers on teaching and learning, the standards writers consulted with state education agency personnel, classroom teachers representing the American Federation of Teachers (AFT) and the National Education Association (NEA), and civil rights organizations concerned about the education of low-income students of color, especially English language learners. Those consultations brought to the table a variety of valuable perspectives beyond formal research, including systematic reviews and reflections on existing state standards, and the judgments of professionals and practitioners, for instance, about when in students' development particular standards should be taught.

If wide consultation strengthened the process, a too-narrow conceptualization of the conditions for successful implementation led to what is arguably the largest mistake. Policy learning requires not only analytical evidence about how to improve upon past policy choices, but also strategic evidence to inform calculations of what changes will be politically acceptable. One lesson the Common Core entrepreneurs could have drawn from the past twenty years of standards-based policy is that if high-stakes accountability systems are implemented without commensurate system capacity, the policy will fall short of its goals.[15] Initially, proponents gave very little attention to teacher training, appropriate curriculum, and instructional materials. Instead they focused on assessment design, even before curriculum aligned with the Common Core was widely available, and they accepted federal funds for test development. This choice of emphasis was not out of ignorance, for both experts and practitioners emphasized the importance of planning for implementation. The explanation for why such evidence might be acknowledged but not acted upon stems from the proponents' attempt to take into consideration the political context. The promise of Common Core–aligned assessments was critical to persuading governors to support the CCSS and encouraging states to adopt the standards, because maintaining test-based accountability systems was a high priority for states. Without federal financial support, the development process would likely have been less efficient or taken longer. The proponents of CCSS, political entrepreneurs who were well aware of the short duration of a window of opportunity for policy change, opted to link the standards to assessment at an early stage, even though they knew from experience that testing would likely become the dominant focus, leapfrogging the multiple steps involved in building system capacity sufficient to move the CCSS effectively into classrooms. Predictably, the early turn toward testing interfered with capacity-building for implementation. The optimistic policy entrepreneurs assumed that the timetable for actually using the tests to hold schools and teachers accountable could be revised in light of experience, but that it was important to get the standards written and adopted by states before the opportunity for policy change disappeared. The early emphasis on testing undermined teacher support in some places, but the entrepreneurs were surprised at the vehemence of opponents' attacks on the CCSS reforms as a whole, charging that the role of national government money for test development signaled federal overreach.

The theory we develop specifies the conditions under which a set of factors—the what, who, and how—are combined and used strategically. Because we have selected two cases representing major changes in youth policy and involving a diverse group of policymakers and interests across multiple governmental levels, the theoretical framework is applicable to other major youth policies that pass through several levels of the federal system. Our theoretical framework, however, stresses correlations and policy-process connections; it makes no claims about causal relationships between policy actors and their use of different types of evidence. Nor should the conceptual framework be directly exported from this study of education policy to practice. The use of evidence by school administrators and classroom teachers should be quite different, given different time frames (typically longer for practice than for policy arenas), central tasks (such as creating new policy versus interpreting enacted policy and adapting it to local circumstances), and types of interme-diary organizations (for example, the dominance of advocacy organizations in policy versus consultants and private providers in practice).

DATA SOURCES

Evidence use is a process that extends from those who produce research and other types of evidence to those who translate and communicate it, and finally to members of the policy community who decide if and how to use the evidence. In the case of the Common Core, that process included education researchers, policy entrepreneurs promoting the CCSS, representatives of national and state organizations supporting and opposing the Common Core, members of CCSS working groups who developed and vetted the standards, foundation staff, state elected and appointed officials, and third-party pro-viders who developed Common Core curriculum materials and worked with educators. To understand that process, the incentives of the different partici-pants, their use of evidence, and their decisions, we conducted 117 interviews between May 2011 and June 2013. Potential interviewees were identified through multiple sources, including a large database of documents related to the CCSS and its development (described below), consultation with staff at the James B. Hunt Jr. Institute for Educational Leadership and Policy who were active participants in the CCSS process, and additional names of infor-mants offered by interviewees. In examining Common Core evidence use at the state level, we focused on four states: California, Indiana, Massachusetts, and Tennessee. They were selected to provide regional variation and different political contexts, and to include representatives from states receiving Race to the Top funding and those not receiving it. Sixty-four of the 117 interviews were conducted in the four states. A detailed profile was prepared for each of the four states based on the interviews and documentary sources. Each profile summarizes the governance and politics of the state as they relate to education policy, the state's past experience with standards policy, the CCSS adoption process, plans for CCSS implementation, and the use of evidence in support and opposition to the Common Core. These profiles were updated as the CCSS process progressed from adoption to implementation.

The interview guides were customized for each category of respondent, with questions tailored to Common Core participants based on their unique roles. To facilitate comparability, however, the core of the interview consisted of a similar set of questions about the interviewee's involvement in the CCSS: what prompted it; what types of evidence they provided or used, and the reasons for those choices; what arguments for or against the Common Core they found to be most persuasive; and how they rated the significance and effectiveness of findings from research as compared with other types of information. We also asked a set of general questions about what types of evidence interviewees have found to be the most convincing to elected officials and other relevant policy audiences, what formats they have found to be most effective in communicating with them, and the extent to which they have to translate or interpret research findings in their work. As a final question, we asked our interviewees what advice they would give those interested in ensuring that research-based evidence is considered and used appropriately in education policy.

To ensure greater reliability and validity of the interviews, we coded a large number of documents before we began conducting interviews, so that we would have a sense of how key actors were actually using evidence in public presentations such as speeches, testimony, and legislation. We collected 1,655 artifacts that were produced between 2004 and 2011. These include research reports, policy briefs, speeches, blog posts, press releases, and congressional testimony related to the CCSS. They were collected and archived from the web sites of fifty-three nongovernmental organizations, along with the US Department of Education, the Obama White House, and the Senate and House Education and Labor Committees. The organizations were identified iteratively with the first set based on prior research on standards-based reform, the work of a National Research Council (NRC) committee examining the implications of state standards policies for common standards, and consultation with Hunt Institute staff.[16] As new groups became involved with the Common Core, their documents were added to the database. Media articles published during this time period by the *New York Times*, *Washington Post*, and *Education Week* were also collected. In addition, two other types of documentary data were collected. To understand how evidence was used in the actual writing of the mathematics and ELA standards, we collected the successive drafts produced as the development process moved from the initial College and Career Ready (CCR) versions to the K–12 standards that map back from the CCR standards to the grade-by-grade standards, specifying what students need to master to graduate from high school ready for college or a career. We also collected information on CCSS-related grants from private foundations, since most organizations' use of evidence and participation in the CCSS process was facilitated by private funding. (The interview and documentary data are described in the appendix, on page 206.)

ORGANIZATION OF THE BOOK

Chapter 2 focuses on the types of evidence used in the policy process. We array the types of evidence along a continuum indicating how each type is situated in the canon of scientific procedure. Even if research knowledge must compete for attention with other types of evidence, how the legitimacy of peer-reviewed research is grounded in the scientific method represents a useful starting point for considering other types of evidence. The reason is simple: for any type of evidence to be effective in policy argumentation, whether it be anecdotes or statistical data, its intended targets must view it as credible, valid, and generalizable in comparison with the other evidence available to them. This chapter compares other types of evidence and their sources of legitimacy with the scientific canon that defines peer-reviewed research. In addition to research-based observation and analysis, we also examine three other categories typically used in policy deliberation: professional judgment, comparisons with past and current policy, and values-based arguments and stories. We discuss the threats to credibility that are endemic to each type of evidence when used in highly politicized venues.

In analyzing the conditions under which different types of evidence are combined for persuasive purposes, we consider the special case of policy ideas that link research results with normative values (for instance, linking studies of how students learn with calls for greater educational equity). Concepts such as school choice and standards-based accountability are closely linked with abstract philosophical ideals—for example, market efficiency or democratic accountability—but their role in education policy conversations hinges on academic researchers presenting some type of research-based evidence supporting the concepts and working out the application of the concepts to new policy domains. This process, more appropriately understood in terms of building an argument than as the mere translation of research findings, plays a crucial role in policy change.

In chapter 3, the diverse array of policy actors who produce, translate, and use evidence is analyzed, focusing on how their institutional roles and policy goals condition their use of research. Two groups receive special attention: policy entrepreneurs and intermediary organizations (IOs). Policy entrepreneurs are central to understanding evidence use because, in their efforts to advance a policy agenda, they typically take the lead in framing a policy idea, determining what will be the most effective way to support it and arguing persuasively for its adoption. But they face political dilemmas that often cannot be neatly resolved. For instance, several former governors played crucial roles in the development of CCSS, and they were aware that the concerns of the potential audience for such an ambitious policy change would be diverse and often hold inconsistent views. Learning from the mistakes of past proponents of standards-based reforms, their framing and the process of formulating the standards anticipated the sort of objections likely to come from governors and teacher unions—for example, concerns based on states' rights, local control, and professional autonomy. Those concerns led to a development process focused on policy elites and largely invisible to the general public. The result was an efficient development and enactment process, but it left CCSS proponents open to charges of secrecy and lack of public transparency.

Intermediary organizations have become the predominant channel through which policymakers learn about relevant research. Although IOs are often lumped together, we distinguish three categories—disseminators and translators, policy advocates, and hybrids—and compare each category to research producers.[17] IOs engaged primarily in *dissemination* interpret and customize research to the needs of specific types of users. These IOs include third-party providers (e.g., ASCD, McRel, Learning Forward) and government agencies that address an audience that includes policymakers and practitioners (e.g., state education departments and the National Center for Education Statistics). Compared to research producers, these IOs are more oriented toward policymakers and practitioners, and because they are concerned with maintaining their reputation for trustworthy advice, they generally adhere to the canons of scientific method and are cautious about making inferences far beyond their data. Quite distinct from these are IOs that *advocate* group interests in the policy process (e.g., Association of Test Publishers, National Education Association, National Alliance for Public Charter Schools, American Legislative Exchange Council). Their use of evidence is driven by short-term effectiveness at modifying current policy, and research is one among several instruments (also including ideology and campaign contributions). Although they are wary that competing groups or policymakers will publicize unwarranted exaggeration, they are not bound by scientific canons. A third category, *hybrid* IOs, are similar to advocacy groups in that they seek to advance a policy alternative (although typically aiming at a purposeful and inclusive goal, such as standards-based reforms or children's health, rather than particular material benefits). These groups act as disseminators in interpreting research to policymakers (e.g., the Ford or Gates Foundations), and the fact that credible research findings are a central component of their identity and reputation makes them attentive to scientific considerations such as validity and generalizability.

The fourth chapter details how evidence varies systematically across four stages of the policy process: problem definition and promoting a solution, policy design, enactment, and implementation. For example, during the problem definition stage, Common Core policy entrepreneurs used research evidence in how they framed its rationale, strategically emphasizing global competitiveness because it carried great appeal among governors concerned about the economic health of their states—even though educators were less persuaded that this was a compelling reason for major curricular change. During this stage, advocates focused on the particular set of inferences relevant to national competitiveness, among the many that could be drawn from research and indicator data, in such a way as to persuade key policy audiences that common standards were the best solution to rectify pressing educational and economic problems. In contrast, we know from policy analysis that the implementation phase leads to more diffuse evidence use across the distinct local sites where the new policy is introduced into agency routines, and to a proliferation of anecdotal evidence stemming from many actors and different local contexts. This type of evidence is often disseminated informally among educators and through media accounts, and it is sometimes dismissed as idiosyncratic and unscientific, but we describe how it augments more formal evidence derived from research.

While chapter 4 examines evidence use over stages of the policy process from a national perspective, chapter 5 focuses on the adoption and implementation of the Common Core in the four case-study states. Officials in California, Indiana, Massachusetts, and Tennessee engaged in similar tasks as they considered CCSS adoption and began to implement the standards. All used research, current policy, and professional judgment to inform their decision. The extent to which research-based evidence has helped guide Common Core implementation has partly depended on the capacity of state institutions, particularly state education agencies, to produce and disseminate that information. However, even where that capacity is strong, negative policy feedback can jeopardize the political sustainability of the Common Core, with value-based arguments challenging research and other types of evidence for public support. Such challenges can be exacerbated if the state's educators feel unduly burdened by accountability policies linked to the standards.

Chapter 6 takes up our comparative case study of the enactment and implementation of the Children's Health Insurance Program. We rely on the secondary literature and a close reading of the testimony at relevant congressional hearings from 1997 to 2017. As in the case of the Common Core, we document the variety of evidence use, depending on the policymaking stage and the institutional roles and policy goals of the advocates. The CHIP case study mirrors our investigation of the Common Core in tracing how evidence use in the deliberation over both programs responded to the changing balance of political ideology and resources; the use of evidence is not a smooth process, because it tracks discontinuous changes in the political context. This chapter highlights two significant shifts in the use of evidence over CHIP's twenty-year history: the transition from federal agencies supplying most of the evidence in the early stages of enactment to the states providing the bulk of the evidence as the individual state programs were implemented; and the shift from the emphasis on enrollment of low-income children to the analysis of evidence about health outcomes, in response to conservatives' critiques.

The final chapter continues to build on the focus of the book, outlining recommendations for strengthening the use of research-based evidence, with particular attention to creating political incentives in the policy process. We discuss three leverage points for improving evidence use: policy ideas, policy design, and the training of policy analysts. Although we are under no illusions that the paradoxical nature of research use—valued but often sidelined—will be resolved in the near future, our analysis offers a better sense of the political environment in which the policy implications of the use of research evidence are debated.

2

The "What"—Types of Evidence Used in the Policy Process

Standards writing is an art; it's not a science. You have to begin with the best evidence you have, and then you have to add a layer of professional judgment over that. Having said the process is an art, I do want to emphasize that we always came back to the evidence; it wasn't just what people thought, it was up to what the evidence said. The research evidence was the important driver, but experience and professional judgment played a very important role as well.

—*Member, Common Core standards development team*

RECENT EFFORTS TO INCREASE the use of research in policymaking focus on knowledge generated according to well-defined norms of scientific inquiry and subject to expert review. The scientific method specifies clear procedures for production of research and strong norms for the transparency and frankness of criticism. Scientific research does not yield certainty, but its rules specify the best procedures for identifying errors and correcting them quickly.[1] The standards for peer-reviewed research require that it be clear and explicit as to method (e.g., data collection sites and techniques, analytical procedures), the causal mechanism connecting inputs to outputs, and the logic of inference for generalizing from the research site and sample to other situations. Research findings are disseminated to a scientific community in which norms encourage public criticism that is structured to be constructive and substantive. The dialogue between researchers and critics

19

begins when researchers share their findings and invite criticism; critics are bound by norms that their judgments focus on evidence and reasoning (not ad hominem or partisan censure), that they support their arguments with evidence, and that alternative interpretations be formulated precisely enough to be tested empirically against the original results.

Yet for a variety of reasons, ranging from intellectual limits on current scientific knowledge to political pressures, peer-reviewed research is never the only body of evidence informing the policy process. Policymakers need answers to pressing problems in real time, so they inevitably muster other types of evidence. In this chapter, we compare types of evidence to the ideal of peer-reviewed research, showing how the kinds of evidence span a continuum defined by how closely they comport with five characteristics integral to research-based evidence:

- explicit, detailed description of methods and the logic of inference
- wide sharing of research findings (and, increasingly, data)
- criticism focused on evidence and logic
- criticisms substantiated with explicit evidence and argument
- alternative interpretations that are empirically falsifiable

We distinguish four types of evidence. *Research-based evidence* provides the best grounds for predicting the consequences of a given policy change; its controlled comparison of the outcomes from different treatments allows the observer to say which is more effective at solving the problem. The prospective orientation of research-based evidence is complemented by the *investigation of current policy*, structured to identify strengths and weaknesses of procedures as they have been implemented in a given context. *Professional judgment and practitioner experience* fill out the first two categories by recognizing that reflection by knowledgeable actors can frame inferences that build on existing research, and can yield insights that an investigation of rules and procedures might miss. Our fourth category is both the furthest from the canons of science and the most political. *Normative appeals and personal stories* lend an emotional charge to problem definition, and they frame policy change as contributing to a better future. As long as their advocates are open to evidence and argument, they constitute a legitimate component of the policy debate.

Some aspects of the institutional and political context in which evidence was used in the CCSS process are shared by most major education policies.[2] They include federalism with multiple participants across governmental levels—each with distinguishable roles and interests in the policy process—together with politicians' need to move quickly before opportunities for policy action disappear. Other elements, such as the explicit commitment to standards based on research and evidence, and a design process largely shielded from public view, are unique to the Common Core.

TYPES OF EVIDENCE

Research-Based Evidence

Several categories of studies fall within research-based evidence (RBE). The first is *empirical research* that meets the standards of scientific inquiry. For some studies, the findings can be immediately applied in settings such as schools and classrooms. Others, however, may not have immediate or direct practical applications. Examples of the latter category include basic research on cognition, learning theory, and human development. *Policy analysis* is a second form of RBE that meets the standards of scientific inquiry and has immediate application in addressing public problems. In response to policymakers' need for systematic studies that assess the costs, political and administrative feasibility, and trade-offs associated with different policy options, policy analysis has developed over the past fifty years to meet the informational demands of increased policymaking at the federal and state levels. As questions emerged about why the operations of federal and state policies often vary significantly from one locale to another and do not always reflect legislators' expectations, policy analytic studies expanded to examine how policy is implemented and to identify the factors shaping that process. Also included in the general category of policy analysis are evaluation studies that assess the extent to which policies and programs have produced their expected effects and analyze the factors explaining the outcomes.

A final category of research-based evidence consists of *statistical data*, describing the status of social systems, such as the demographic characteristics of a particular population group or the performance of public- and private-sector institutions. Statistical data are often collected by governmental agencies, such as the US Census Bureau and the National Center for Education Statistics (NCES), for the purpose of describing and comparing groups over time and location, or for administrative purposes, such as tracking financial outlays or monitoring regulatory compliance. As such, statistical data differ from other forms of research-based evidence because, although they may have been collected for purposes other than scholarly research, the data often subsequently provide the evidence base analyzed in research studies. Statistical data share the properties of peer-reviewed research to the extent that the data are based on clearly and objectively defined concepts, and indicators are measured by a transparent and replicable process. In use, statistical data may come to resemble research even more closely, as when data on several variables that comprise a causal system are brought together to show relationships, or when a time series or multiple indicators of a target phenomenon are presented and compared in a systematic way.

The College and Career Ready (CCR) standards that constitute the anchor for the Common Core provide a good example of how research-based evidence is used. The design of the Common Core was a two-step process. The first phase focused on developing CCR standards representing the mathematics and literacy skills and knowledge that students need by high school graduation; the second phase mapped back from the CCR to specify what students should know at each K–12 grade level in order to meet the end-of-high-school CCR standards. The CCR standards are based on more robust research than the K–12 standards, whose development and implementation depended on a mix of formal research studies and professional judgment.

In describing the evidence base, those responsible for developing and reviewing the standards drew upon peer-reviewed syntheses of research in mathematics and English language arts (ELA), surveys of college faculty and employers conducted by ACT and the College Board, standards of high achieving countries, and a variety of student test data. The ELA standards include a forty-page appendix that describes the research supporting the standards. Although the math CCR standards lack such a detailed account, the final version contains a list of a "sample of works consulted," and an earlier version of the math CCR standards included a short essay explaining how evidence from high performing countries and college admissions test data were used in selecting which mathematical skills and knowledge would be expected of students at the end of high school.[3] Research evidence on the learning and teaching of reading and mathematics was prominent in the documents that went into the writing of the CCSS, because the new standards were intended to elevate text complexity and nonfiction reading over literary content, and to integrate new thinking about the teaching of fractions and the number line. The experts whose work had produced the new knowledge were active participants in the oral deliberations over formulating the CCSS, and a variety of organizations synthesized extant research and mapped the relevance of academic findings to specific policy questions. The Educational Testing Service (ETS), for example, carried out a quantitative analysis of research on reading and authored a report directed to the question of learning progressions in the ELA standards. ACT's research on literacy skills combined information on US students' performance with data on student course-taking to address questions about group differences. The National Council of Teachers of English used research evidence to criticize the Common Core standards for grades K–2, arguing that research on early childhood showed that the literary skills required by the new standards were inappropriate for the early grades. Research-based evidence on mathematics learning is illustrated by the meta-analysis of the research literature on mathematical problem-solving produced by the American Federation of Teachers (AFT), which identified where the evidence about teaching and learning is strong or weak, and by Achieve's analysis comparing CCSS to the National Council of Teachers of Mathematics' "focal points" approach to teaching math.[4]

Reflection from several participants illustrate how such research-based evidence was used:

> We looked at test results. We looked at ACT's *Reading Between the Lines*, and this report showed what made a difference in students being ready for college classes and not. And that's where we got the whole notion of text complexity, because that seems to be the key characteristic that was differentiating between students who are ready and those who are not—whether they can handle the complexity of the text, which was very new, by the way, compared to the standards any states have ever had before.
>
> . . . [W]e thought about evidence broadly, but also concretely and specifically—we would sit with the college faculty surveys, and we would see that literary terms were not high on their list as something that is critical for students to come to college knowing. On the other hand, students having an academic vocabulary was critical, so you'll see in the standards that

those kinds of emphases began to come through. We actually spent a lot of time, initially, looking at the research and evidence about what made a difference for the students from any number of remedial courses to being prepared for credit-bearing courses. In the workplace, it's a little hard to get hold of that information—we did have some employer surveys, but they are not nearly as detailed as college faculty surveys. And of course, we looked at the testing that goes on. We looked at the ACT tests and what they found in terms of students being ready for classes or not and also the National Assessment of Educational Progress [NAEP].

What those actually told us was some very detailed information—they told us text complexity was important; they told us marshalling arguments was important; they told us academic vocabulary was important; they told us informational text was important. So, in a way, evidence framed the emphases of the standards.

—Member, ELA standards development team

———■-■-■———

ACT had great databases and would be able to answer questions in their database about student achievement. So, we were looking at the quadratic formula for completing the square—sort of a critical moment in high school mathematics. Should this be required for all kids graduating from high school, which would be a consequence of putting it in a certain place? We were able to ask this question: What students who graduated successfully from college who got a B or better in college mathematics (these would be non-STEM majors: political science, English, business) . . . What percent of them got the quadratic formula for completing the square items on the ACT correct when they were in high school? . . . Incidentally, it was less than 20 percent. So basically, you could go to college and major in some non-STEM field without having learned it. That evidence told us . . . the way we treated it, we called it an "expensive item." When it's in the curriculum, it's expensive in terms of teacher time, kid time, and realism in terms of the kids. In this case, we kept it in. But there were some items that we took out because they were expensive and not important enough as expensive as they were.

—Member, mathematics standards development team

Comparisons to Current Policy

Participants in the CCSS process repeatedly mentioned turning to international and state standards as a source of evidence. Part of the reason was political. The policy entrepreneurs promoting the standards understood that the CCSS would be viewed as more legitimate if they were similar to those of countries whose students ranked highly on international mathematics assessments. An even stronger political rationale dictated that the new standards should not fall below the most robust current state standards, thus certain state standards served as a source and an essential criterion. One of the math standards writers explained:

> [T]he states that signed on to CCSS essentially said, if the standards are good, we'll adopt them. Well, some states thought they have very high standards (and they did)—for example, Massachusetts, Minnesota, and California. NGA and CCSSO said to the states, you will not have to lower your standards to adopt the Common Core. So, we had to be constrained by that promise. We needed to make sure we had standards that were up to that level of high standards.

However, there were also solid instrumental reasons for considering standards that were well regarded and seemed to be working as expected in the student learning process. For example, one of the ELA standards authors described why the team turned to state standards for guidance:

> That whole progression piece, we certainly relied on the faculty surveys, but also on some of the model state standards: California, Massachusetts, Indiana . . . Several of those had really strong progressions in their standards and were highly thought of. We would then go back to those standards and take a look at how they had put their progressions together. It doesn't mean we just copied it and put it in, but it does mean we considered that very carefully.

Promoting a set of standards that differed from many existing state standards, and seeking to reach across multiple states, was an ambitious goal whose promulgation and persuasion hinged on evidence that shared standards were feasible. Current policy provided this crucial piece of evidence. The America Diploma Project (ADP) illustrates this function. In 2001, Achieve, in collaboration with the Education Trust and the Fordham Foundation, established the ADP to ensure that high school diplomas signified that students are prepared academically for entry into higher education and the workforce. These standards were based on surveys of higher education faculty and businesses, indicating what knowledge and skills students needed to pass college-level courses and workplace training programs.[5] Sixteen states agreed to align their high school graduation requirements with the benchmarks derived from the surveys. Subsequently, fifteen states agreed to develop a common assessment in Algebra II, and later five states agreed to develop and administer an Algebra I exam. As one organizational representative involved in the effort noted, "The ADP was the existence proof that you could get common standards." Documents tracing the history of the American Diploma Project were an important part of the institutional memory of the evidence base for the CCSS. A second policy example was the New England Common Assessment Program (NECAP), a collaboration among New Hampshire, Rhode Island, and Vermont. The state education agencies in those states developed shared grade-level expectations and test specifications in reading, writing, mathematics, and science with the first assessment administered in 2008 and results reported on a common scale. Peter McWalters, at that time the Rhode Island commissioner of education, argued that one of the most important benefits of the program was the political cover it provided for tensions that inevitably arise when any state attempts to raise expectations for its students.[6]

Research comparing the new standards to current state standards and to international benchmarks predominantly focused on variation in how standards were implemented, especially on the rigor of the high school curriculum. Brookings Institution researchers authored an early study showing that the robustness of the curriculum covaried with student achievement. ACT and CCSSO analyzed data from the National Curriculum Survey in ELA and math; the AFT replicated the approach of the Trends in International Mathematics and Science Study (TIMSS), measuring opportunity to learn mathematical content. Working with the American Institutes for Research (AIR) and the National Center for Education Statistics (NCES), CCSSO correlated the alignment of state standards with the subject-area themes tested in TIMSS and PISA (the Programme for International Student Assessment), showing that closer alignment of the curriculum with the topics regarded as central in international tests covaried with higher student achievement.[7]

Research on current policy complements the evidence of theory-driven research in that it reflects the specifics of real-world situations. Offered in a context of critical deliberation, it is a type of evidence from which policy-makers can draw inferences. The staffs of organizations representing state officials are particularly sensitive to the need to provide their constituents with examples from current policy:

> When talking to elected officials, the most effective sort of evidence is information about what has worked, especially in other states (it could even be a district that has scaled up). So, what has worked, and why has it worked. Was it unique—did they just get a lot of money to do the project? What policy was in place, what sort of program was it?

This type of evidence is especially useful when the lessons learned from current policy are clear and consistent and (in some cases) validated by findings from research. Just as current policy can inform questions about feasibility, it can also suggest what is not working and point to alternatives. One example relates to how the US mathematics curriculum compared with that of other countries:

> [T]he findings from international comparisons . . . [t]here are a lot of things there. But one of the robust findings is that the American curriculum was "a mile wide and an inch deep" [from] Bill Schmidt, but from many others, as well as from the TIMSS studies. This was combined with a category of evidence called "lessons learned," meaning lessons learned from three decades of standards-based accountability. So, the lessons learned had some policy research, but mostly it was anecdotal and sometimes the anecdotes were a chorus. And one of the things that is almost universal—every teacher you spoke to and everyone who listens to teachers—there was too much to cover. The standards have too much.

Professional Judgment

The role of professional judgment is well illustrated by the process of moving from the CCR standards to K–12 grade-by-grade ones. The academic researchers advising the standards development teams recognized that the research base for this mapping was considerably weaker than for the CCR standards. A noted reading researcher explained the difference in this way:

At the level of the college and career readiness standards, it's really easy to see the mapping from the anchor standards to the research traditions that I mentioned earlier [Kintsch's construction-integration model of reading comprehension, NAEP, the RAND report on reading comprehension]. It's a little trickier when you get down to what a standard looks like in fifth grade and how it changes from fourth to fifth or fourth to fifth to sixth.

. . . I think that we would be hard pressed to find any sort of research evidence that the gradations of difficulty are research based. But you know I'm not sure they could be. Because I can't imagine the kind of research you'd need to do to validate a scope and sequence. We've only just begun to do that as a profession in psychometrics with these learning predictions. And that's a relatively new thing. To my knowledge, nobody ever tried to validate scopes and sequences of skills in the way that psychometricians are now trying to validate learning frequencies. So maybe in another decade or so, we might actually have a research base that someone could look at.

The researcher continues, suggesting another type of evidence: "these progressions that are in the standards, I think are—they're professional judgment." When the underlying research base is incomplete or inconclusive, as in the case of the Common Core, expert judgments are useful to extrapolate validated research knowledge toward the policy question at issue. A notable example emerged in the development of the mathematics standards. Research on learning trajectories in mathematics is quite robust at the K–2 level, but not at higher grade levels.[8] Learning trajectories or progressions in the early grades are better developed for several reasons, including the ability to draw on a rich research base by developmental psychologists about children's early learning, and the relative simplicity of concepts and skills at the early childhood level as compared with the complexity of topics and how they might be related and sequenced in more advanced mathematics.[9] Consequently, the standards writers asked several researchers who study math education for their best judgments about what trajectories might look like in higher grades based on how students learn; they then used those assessments in deciding where to place topic and skill standards. As one of the standards writers explained:

I sort of relied on their expertise and their judgment on what sort of resources that they were going to draw on. I wouldn't want to make the case that those "progressions" are "learning progressions" in the technical sense, because when researchers talk about that, they have a fairly precise definition of what they mean by that. So, I just call them "standards progressions." I mean, they are not unrelated, but the standards progressions are not the product of research. They are products of synthesis.

. . . [W]e assembled the best team that we could, and we tried to get the top people in the country . . . that includes researchers, mathematicians, policy people. We wanted the best minds in the country working on this, and that was the first step. And then step two is . . . we would have a particular issue we were trying to think about and we would look at our team. We would say the right people to talk to were "x, y, and z." So, we would pull those people together in a phone conference and emails . . . and get all their different opinions and try to synthesize them.

An academic adviser to the mathematics standards team indicated how she used the trajectory maps that she had helped prepare: "the mapping I did was to see how consistent it was with the research on learning and to look for holes, so by doing the learning trajectory charts, I would say 'you missed this topic,' or 'what about this topic?'"[10] Consistent with the transparency norms of scientific research, the standards progressions that served as source documents for the mathematics Common Core were subsequently published online.[11]

In the ELA standards, text complexity provides an example of the need for judgment. While acknowledging its importance and appropriateness as a standard, literacy researchers note that "the underlying theory and research on text complexity that would support creation of state and district curricula and programs is in short supply."[12] For example, although there are numerous formulas for measuring the readability of various types of texts, text complexity refers to more than the difficulty of words; it also includes structure, genre, and demands on prior knowledge. Because current formulas do not measure all these dimensions, they cannot be calibrated to the ELA Common Core text complexity grade bands. The standards document calls for the development of new tools as quickly as possible, noting in the interim that "the use of qualitative and quantitative measures to assess text complexity is balanced in the Standards' model by the expectation that educators will employ professional judgment to match texts to particular students and tasks."[13]

Another type of professional judgment applies a theoretical or logical model to inform an empirical case. This approach was used in developing the mathematics standards. The developers were guided by three principles—focus, cohesion, and understanding—as they melded relevant knowledge from two different scholarly vantage points: the discipline of mathematics education and the discipline of mathematics. From their perspective, mathematics education research provides useful knowledge about what it is possible to teach students at different grade levels, and how it might be done. However:

> There's a lot of useful information about how to sequence things . . . that's not quite the same as having research that tells you what you must do. So, when you're writing standards and trying to write a description of the entire K–12 body of mathematics, you can't just put in everything you think that is good. Just because something is possible it doesn't mean you can put it in since there'll be too many things.

With "too many things," focus, cohesion, and understanding as guiding principles would be compromised. Consequently, the standards writers needed another basis to augment research in choosing among possible standards. They were further constrained by the emphasis in the CCR on students arriving at postsecondary institutions with a solid mastery of algebra.

As a result, the developers decided that they "had to build a ramp to algebra, which would mean putting in more fractions and taking out data and statistics at the lower grades." That decision was controversial among some members of the work team and within the mathematics education research community. Consequently, the developers looked to mathematicians and how they define the logic and structure of their discipline. Particularly important was mathematicians' extensive writing about the mathematics of fractions. The developers noted that the content of K–12 mathematics is not a subject of mathematical research. However, once they focused on the content at that level, the mathematicians who were consulted were able to produce more elegant and simplified mathematical content for articulating the standards related to fractions. Although they lacked research in mathematics education at the K–12 level, the mathematicians could draw on their discipline's axioms and theorems to address questions about content and sequencing.

Up to this point, the types of professional judgment discussed are ones that function as substitutes when research directly applicable to a particular policy is incomplete or unavailable. At the same time, the judgments rendered are based on one or more bodies of research, and are offered by researchers who are drawing inferences either from empirical data or from the underlying logic of theoretical models. However, another form of judgment is based not on formal research, but on personal and professional experience. For elected officials, their own experience frequently serves as one of several lenses through which they view policy options. Just after the first draft of standards was released for public comment, *Education Week* interviewed several Congress members who noted that framing the CCSS initiative could affect its political support. Two innovations—the commitment to value research and evidence over political preference and ideology, and the leadership by the states rather than the federal government—framed the CCSS process as distinct from conventional politics, where "historically, standards have been created in a political sausage factory, in which the most important goal is to respect each individual committee member's personal, cherished opinions." But to guard this distinction, it was important that national policymakers keep their distance. Congress members in both parties praised the states' initiative, but they "stayed out of the way [fearing that] significant federal leadership would only hinder the movement, potentially bogging it down in partisan politics." It was harder to restrain the White House, however, and the perceived link of Race to the Top and proposals to renew Title I to CCSS gave credibility to critics' accusations of "federal overreach."[14]

In addition, policymakers often turn to constituents for advice. In the case of education policy, classroom teachers and administrators can draw on their daily experience to identify what works with a degree of concrete specificity that abstract research lacks. This perspective is potentially a valuable source of information. But the vantage point of any given practitioner—whether they are elected officials, agency staff, or educators—is inevitably idiosyncratic, and not everyone is equally reflective or analytical at discerning the reasons for successful (or failing) outcomes. The process of writing the CCSS utilized evidence culled from a variety of experience, calling on the active participation of multiple, distinct sources of advice and evaluation, and melding this input in an iterated process with a good deal of back-and-forth exchange.

The major teacher organizations, the NEA and the AFT, stressed to the organizations developing the standards that their support for the Common Core would be contingent on the close involvement of teachers in the standards-writing process from the beginning, and both groups relied on delegations of teachers brought together in a way that heightened the usefulness of their practice-based insights while blunting the potential disadvantages. The AFT, for instance, convened a panel of thirty experienced teachers (half mathematics, half ELA) who had previously served locally as mentors, with each team including elementary, middle, and high school teachers, and also those working with English language learners (ELLs). The teams were brought to Washington three or four times to review successive drafts and to meet with standards writers, in addition to participating in numerous conference calls. An AFT staff member noted that "most of the teachers [on the two National Standards Review teams] have masters degrees and are familiar with relevant research [but] we asked all of them to think about the teachers they work with and how they would respond to the standards."[15] The NEA convened similar groups of experienced teachers, all National Board certified, who met in Washington with the leading staff from NGA and CCSSO, held conference calls with the standards writers, and submitted feedback on successive drafts. An NEA representative noted that the teachers involved in the process were adept at thinking "not only in terms of their own classroom but also speaking for other teachers." The types of changes that the two teacher groups suggested primarily dealt with the logical presentation of standards, with their placement in particular grade levels based on their experience teaching different age groups, and with the language of some of the draft standards, motivated by the concern that the language was too academic and would not translate successfully to the practicalities of the classroom.

Documentary accounts elaborate the role these teacher representatives played in the formulation of the standards, not only facilitating the translation of the standards into usable curriculum, but also raising salient questions about how the standards would integrate English language learners and special education students and about the relevance of research on early childhood education, and generating pressure for state policymakers to "provide greater leadership on the issues of curriculum and instructional supports." The teachers, as the AFT put it, "worked both individually and collectively to bring judgment and real-world classroom experience to bear in drafts of the standards." The teacher unions then took the resulting detailed information about CCSS and used it to distill lessons—transmitted to their members via blogs and videos—about aligning curriculum, professional development for teachers, and outreach to parents. David Coleman, one of the ELA standards writers, recalled that teachers "took the lead in shaping many aspects of the standards," and Jason Zimba, one of the mathematics standards writers, said, "There's no substitute for the kind of expertise that teacher teams have brought to the process."[16]

In addition to teachers, the standards writers called on the professional experience of state education agency (SEA) personnel familiar with how local districts and schools interpret standards as they implement them. As with the teacher unions, SEA input served both political and educational purposes. The NGA and CCSSO had to maintain support among their state-level constituents, especially given that the CCSS would have to be adopted in each state, with SEA staff serving as key advisers to the state officials responsible for adoption. Although public comments were only solicited on one draft of the CCR standards and one of the K–12 standards, state education agencies were asked to comment on multiple drafts. Six states that had highly regarded standards (California, Colorado, Florida, Georgia, Massachusetts, and Minnesota) were specifically asked to recommend standards writers and to review drafts. In states with standards that had been judged rigorous by external groups, such as the AFT and the Fordham Institute, SEA personnel reviewed the draft CCSS to ensure that they met or exceeded their current standards in terms of parsimony, coherence, and rigor (the "fewer, clearer, and higher" promised by CCSS developers). Throughout, SEA staff in all participating states were also given an opportunity to review several drafts. In exercising their professional judgment, they were most concerned about clarity and logic of presentation based on their experience organizing and formatting standards to facilitate their use in classrooms.

Professional experience served as a partial substitute when the relevant research base was inadequate, but it was also a legitimate alternative source of evidence that augmented research results by connecting the standards to the real-world context in which the Common Core would be implemented.

One group that recognized the value of such evidence were the researchers serving on the committee charged with reviewing the completed standards. NGA and CCSSO convened a twenty-nine-member committee: seventeen were university faculty, and six others worked in research positions. In addition, three teachers, two principals, and one urban superintendent served on the committee. Their charge was to review the process by which evidence was used to create the CCR and K–12 standards, and to determine whether the standards writers had adhered to a set of principles, including "a grounding in available research and evidence."[17] The committee's remit did not run to rewriting the standards, but it provided substantive feedback to the standards writers. After meeting twice in person and through email exchanges with the NGA and CCSSO staff, all but four members of the committee signed a statement certifying that the CCSS are consistent with the criteria established in the committee's charge. Those who demurred argued that the CCSS were not sufficiently rigorous, and that current standards in states such as California and Massachusetts were superior. Professional judgment was, in short, a major source of evidence for the members of the validation committee. The compressed time frame and the limits of the research base meant that they had to fall back on judgments based on inferences drawn from their expert knowledge and practical experience, rather than from a review of specific studies. One member of the validation committee described the process in this way:

> It was pretty clear from the start that nobody thought there was sufficient evidence for any of the standards ... The review process, in short, was inclusive and involved feedback from a lot of different perspectives. This is not "sufficient research evidence," but it is thoughtful professional judgment, applied systematically.[18]

The legitimacy of professional judgment as credible evidence was founded on three considerations. It was distilled from knowledge of the field and relevant research literature. It took into consideration current state standards, especially the more demanding ones, and the fact that systematic comparison showed that the CCSS were at least as rigorous as the most demanding state standards. Finally, familiarity with those drafting the standards was also a factor in the decision to validate them. Like the SEA staff and groups supporting the CCSS, validation committee members had worked with the standards writers in the past and were familiar with their reputations as researchers and professionals. Their work was known to be rigorous, and they were trusted.[19]

Value-Based Argumentation, Stories, and Metaphors

Even when they present research and statistical data, those espousing a particular policy are acting as advocates in advancing their ideological and substantive agendas. They do this through the issues they choose to highlight, what evidence they use in defining those issues, and in how they frame and interpret the evidence.[20]

In deciding whether or not value-based claims should be classified as evidence on the same continuum as the other types discussed in this chapter, we apply similar criteria. Are the underlying value assumptions transparent? Are the groups making the claims willing to subject them to criticism, feedback, and revision? Deciding whether expressions of values, ideological beliefs, and group interests belong in a typology of evidence requires a judgment call, but the criteria derived from peer-reviewed research center on the transparency of the evidence and the willingness of the claimants to debate the claim, not on the content of the claim. Purely self-interested or ideological claims, for instance, rely on premises that would not be accepted by others who did not already share that interest or subscribe to a particular ideology; they are qualitatively different from claims that are advanced as part of a scientific conversation. Claims that are not open to debate or responsive to change in light of better evidence or reasons also cannot be placed on the continuum we have outlined. However, claims based on value assumptions can be considered a form of evidence if the groups making them are willing to participate in a process of public dialogue anchored in systematic, reciprocal evaluations of the logic and information supporting those claims and to consider alternative interpretations of the evidence presented.

The promotion and development of the CCSS was not a particularly ideological process, especially in comparison with other education policies, such as school choice, or the current highly charged state of US political debate.[21] Documents in our database show that the main ideological battle was over federalism, with both sides appealing to widely shared values. Advocates made the case that local control led to variability in educational standards that both violated the ideal of equal opportunity and undermined the nation's competitiveness in the global economy. The AFT compared curricular content in a large sample of districts, showing that opportunity to learn was vastly unequal. La Raza, America's Promise, and the Campaign for High School Equity noted that local variability inevitably worked to the disadvantage of racial minorities and students from poor families.[22] If these arguments emphasized the moral issue, other advocates stressed the economics. The Hunt Institute quoted a McKinsey report that likened the current system to "permanent recession," and the governor of Tennessee acknowledged both the moral and the economic challenge in setting the agenda for his state's reform under Race to the Top. NGA summed up the case for common standards as "not only because [the change is] socially just, it's essential for ensuring that the US retain a competitive edge." Advocates drew the analogy with occupational standards, building codes, or food labeling regulations, pointing out that these establish a baseline that assures minimal quality but do not limit practices that exceed the standards. The *Boston Globe* articulated the trade-off: "local choice [is] respected where it makes sense, but teaching basic skills such as reading and math differently, however, makes no sense at all."[23] Critics such as the Cato and Pioneer Institutes did not contradict research showing variability in educational opportunity, but they argued forcefully against government intervention, appealing to the tradition of local control, the menace of centralization, and the homogenizing influence of standards, claiming that CCSS would only replicate the failed "bureaucratic approach," and painting a picture of "federal overreach . . . forcing [all students] to march in lockstep through the curriculum." They argued that common standards were educationally inappropriate, since "all kids are unique . . . education needs competition, not standards."[24]

Those active in the Common Core movement recognized that it involved values. As one executive of an interest group supporting the CCSS argued:

> Standards are always going to come down to what kind of country do we want. And in a modern, competitive, global world where a kid is as likely to go to fifth grade in Oregon as in Maine, why should their instruction in math and English be different? And if we're competing with countries that have a national curriculum, why wouldn't we want to have one too? It's almost more a societal, political rationale than a research-based one.

Even one of the academics most concerned that the standards be research-based acknowledged the role of values:

[S]tandards are a combination of values and evidence. It's not all evidence and it's not all values. They have to be a combination of both . . . I mean, standards are value statements. It's valuing what it is that the students are going to know and learn, what you think is most important, what you think the basis of learning is.

The power of values-based arguments depends not only on their content, but also on how that content is communicated. In place of statistics or other types of research findings, the mode of persuasion in support of values-based claims often centers on stories, metaphors, and other images that evoke common understandings of how the world works. Such commonsense appeals can make abstract ideas or complicated technical material more accessible to broader audiences. Particularly effective are compelling personal stories or the use of metaphors that resonate with a target audience's own lived experience.[25] They also recognize that different approaches are needed depending on the audience. For example, the policy entrepreneurs most involved in promoting the standards understood that the evidence for *promoting* them differed from what was necessary in *developing* the CCSS:

The level of rigor for evidence was highest in writing the standards. In building support for them, the evidence was largely anecdotal—including what other states were doing. But the anecdotal wouldn't have sufficed in the standards documents. We talked about it very differently in the media than we did in the actual standards. When I was on the radio, I would say, "wouldn't it be great if you and your kids knew exactly what they are supposed to learn in seventh grade math, and that there are only six things."

Not surprisingly, as skilled politicians, the former governors most responsible for advancing the Common Core tailored their approaches to the audience, and they frequently used stories and analogies to make their points. In testifying before the House Committee on Education and Labor, former North Carolina governor James B. Hunt Jr. told a story:

As governor of North Carolina for sixteen years, I conducted my share of trade missions. When visiting India, China, South Korea, and other developing nations, I witnessed countries intensely focused on educating students to compete in a knowledge-based economy. These countries knew that having a well-educated workforce was critical to building a strong economy, and even back then, they were working to reform education in ways that made sense for their future. For them, it wasn't about tailoring the system; it was about changing the system. Today, those same nations are eating our lunch.[26]

Later in the same testimony, Governor Hunt noted that "geography should not represent academic destiny" as a metaphor for stressing that common standards would be a way of ensuring equal opportunity to learn regardless of where a student lives. Another former governor mentioned the effectiveness of analogies in selling the CCSS, and the need to tailor those metaphors to particular audiences:

> The business community understands the Common Core or the need for some set of national standards because they get workers from every place. I often use the argument in talking to state legislators that the Army doesn't ask whether a soldier was trained [in Texas, North Carolina, or California]—they expect a soldier to be a soldier—and consumers don't ask whether a car was made in Mississippi or Detroit—cars, pharmaceutical products are reliable because they're built to certain standards. We need to make sure we do the same with our students.

HOW STRONG IS THE COMMON CORE EVIDENCE BASE?

The combining of evidence during the Common Core's development is quite typical of how it is used in the policy process more generally. What was unusual was the CCSS leaders' public commitment to a research- and evidence-based process. The way that promise was implemented, though, was shaped by factors, such as limitations on available research and the necessity to build political support, that are similar for most major education policies. Given the practical realities that the CCSS developers had to accommodate, how solid was the evidence base on which the Common Core rests?

Although later opponents of the Common Core would base their opposition on political ideology, early critics questioned the validity of its research base and the underlying assumptions that linked more rigorous standards to improved student outcomes:

The most important kind of information regarding CCSS that I've focused on is the evidence connecting national standards to better educational outcomes. Proponents have provided no evidence that standards lead consistently to successful outcomes. Standards are observed in countries that rank high on international tests and in those that rank at the bottom: there is no meaningful correlation between standards and test outcomes. In general, research on the connection between standards and outcomes is sparse or of poor quality.

—Researcher affiliated with an ideological advocacy group

The assertion that those promoting the CCSS had overstated the link between standards and student outcomes was not limited to groups opposed to the Common Core. Some respected researchers argued that there is no research evidence documenting a causal relationship between standards and student performance on assessments, and that there is no correlation between quality ratings of state standards and NAEP scores. States with content standards rated as weak by external bodies score about the same on NAEP as those with strong standards.[27] Using a different analytical approach, other researchers disputed this conclusion as it applies to the Common Core mathematics standards.[28] Building on techniques developed as part of TIMSS, they first compared the proximity of state standards in 2009 to the CCSS in mathematics, and after adjusting for cut points on state assessments and controlling for state demographics related to poverty, they found that states with standards more like the CCSS in mathematics had higher performance on the 2009 NAEP. These analyses represent different ways of predicting the likely effect of the CCSS on student achievement, and illustrate that even research-based evidence is subject to varying interpretations depending on the data and the design of the analysis.

However, a more compelling response to criticisms that the Common Core evidence base fails to demonstrate a direct relationship between the quality of standards and student outcomes is the simple point that such a relationship should not be expected, given all the elements needed to support it. As one researcher who has questioned some of the claims made by CCSS promoters noted:

The evidence we looked at on standards suggest[s] to me pretty strongly that good or bad standards don't have much penetration down to the classroom level because we can find no correlation between standard quality [and student outcomes]. That doesn't mean, from my perspective, that standards aren't important; it means that if you don't put them into a connected systemic approach to improving instruction, you're not likely to get much. So, it's not just the standards; it is the assessments; it is the instructional materials; it is the scope and sequence guides that teachers are going to end up working with.[29]

In other words, standards are intended to serve as the core of a network of linked elements in an aligned education system that includes curriculum, instructional materials, assessment, teacher preparation, and professional development. Consequently, it would be unreasonable to expect that simply establishing standards would be sufficient to bring about improvements in teaching and learning.[30] Rather, standards have the potential to function as a necessary, but not sufficient, condition for improved educational outcomes. Although the developers understood that the relationship between standards and outcomes is complex, they did not emphasize that as part of their advocacy. In the interests of keeping the policy spotlight on the concept of common standards, the other elements of the system were rarely discussed until the standards development process was almost complete. At that point, the assessment requirements of the No Child Left Behind legislation and state governors' interest in educational accountability had to be addressed. Soon after most states had adopted the CCSS, researchers and state education authorities turned their attention to the instructional supports that would be needed to implement the standards in schools and classrooms.

The decision to concentrate on selling the stand-alone standards as evidence-based was a strategic one reflecting the recognition that in the policy arena a simple message works best. Telling policymakers and their constituents that the process and the conditions needed to ensure a policy's effectiveness are complicated before they have bought into it lessens the likelihood of gaining their support. The CCSS policy entrepreneurs dealt with that trade-off in the way they judged best, all things considered, but their decision does raise the question of whether they still would have been successful had they been more vocal about the indirect and complex relationship between standards and student outcomes.

Several researchers who served as members of the validation committee understood this trade-off and the CCSS leaders' decision to, in effect, over-state the strength of the evidence base underlying the CCSS. But they justi-fied their decision to sign off on the standards because they judged them to be the best available and significantly better than most existing state standards. A mathematics education researcher who had serious misgivings about some parts of the mathematics standards explained her eventual support:

> I think the other thing to consider about all of it is how much of the decision-making in the end was based on a perception of the trade-off between the value of having common standards—albeit imperfect—and not having them . . . I think it [the CCSS development and validation] was a very imperfect process. That said, I also think pragmatically it might not have happened without the political savvy on the other side. It's one of those things you just say, "Most of us did the best we could with the cir-cumstances." I'm really happy that the standards made it through and did a good thing.

Another researcher member of the validation committee justified his approval based on his concern about students learning English:

> I ended up happy with the standards, but mostly because of what I thought they could deliver to linguistically marginalized students. To the extent they paid attention to research, they helped recognize that all kids need access to content-based literacy. So, paying attention to that sets up enormous challenges but it also recognizes that ELL students fall behind English speakers not because of language, but because they lack exposure to content—engaging reading, engaging text. That was a good move. The way the federal policy works around content standards: ELP [English Lan-guage Proficiency] standards under Title III are required to be aligned with state standards. So, whatever happens around the Common Core is going to set the bar for ELP standards in states. So, if you put in text-based con-tent literacy as the standard in the Common Core, then the ELP standards have to align to that.

To some extent, both the judgment of respected researchers that the CCSS were a measurable improvement over the status quo, combined with trust in the designers, lent credibility to the Common Core. Nevertheless, the political imperative to portray a direct relationship between the standards and student outcomes meant that the CCSS evidence base was presented as stronger than it is.

Other aspects of the development process and the broader context in which it occurred also undermined the strength of the evidence base. A significant one was the time constraints imposed to ensure that the CCSS policy entrepreneurs could take advantage of what appeared to be an open policy window. A participant in the process likened it to a gallop—"the incredible gallop, the insane gallop." One downside was a perception on the part of those providing feedback to the standards writers that they were not being systematic. The tight time constraints of a process that lasted less than a year meant that changes made after each successive draft were not annotated or explained: reviewers of successive drafts could see that they had been changed but could not tell precisely in what ways. The standards writers recognized the time constraints as another trade-off with its implications for responsiveness and transparency:

> Normally, in something like this, you would have the time and resources to make it more transparent . . . Ideally, there would have been some very public process where people can see all that's happening. There wasn't time for that. Basically, it's just working within a window of opportunity.

Although they were not providing systematic responses to feedback, the standards writers maintained that they read all the comments, and that they used the input in clarifying the sequencing and wording of the standards. However, despite the writers' good intentions, the time constraints meant that the nature of the evidence base was not uniformly transparent, and the reasons for using some research and evidence and not others were not widely publicized. Criticisms about either the choice of standards or the evidence base were not explicitly addressed, and opportunities for public comment were limited.[31] Consequently, the CCSS evidence base and its construction fell short of the characteristics integral to research-based evidence.

Several other aspects of the broader policy and political context shaped the CCSS development process and its evidence base. Although these political realities may have led to a greater reliance on non-research-based evidence, they also strengthened the likelihood that the CCSS would be supported by the states and ultimately implemented. The promise to states that they would not have to lower their standards if they adopted the Common Core is one example that has already been discussed. Another example was the attempt by the mathematics standards writers to balance the pedagogical preferences of different stakeholders. They maintained that they "ignored the math wars. We didn't want any math war vets. The math wars are history, in the past." Yet they recognized the necessity of accommodating the mathematics educators who supported the National Council of Teachers of Mathematics (NCTM) standards—a version of which was in widespread use in many states—while also considering approaches favored by academic mathematicians and curricular conservatives. The attempt to balance these two approaches was also an example of drawing from both empirical research on how students acquire mathematical knowledge and from the structure and logic of mathematics as a discipline. The accommodation was most evident in the use of the number line in the early grades as an alternative to the traditional way students had been taught fractions. The extent to which the number line is prominent in the standards became a subject of negotiation between the standards writers and NCTM representatives. But part of the reason it remains central in the mathematics standards is that there was empirical evidence from cognitive researchers that if students are taught how to use the number line, they will understand proportions better.

In sum, it is reasonable to conclude that the Common Core evidence base was flawed in several significant ways. Nevertheless, the process was more intentional and thoughtful and the use of research more systematic than how state standards had been set in the past. Political necessity greatly influenced the quality of the evidence base on which the CCSS rests, and it often posed trade-offs that had to be navigated to ensure success of the initiative. The need for a simple message meant that the strength of the relationship between standards and student outcomes was overstated. The compressed time frame resulted in a less transparent process with the standards development teams lacking the time to justify their decisions or answer critics and those who would be implementing the Common Core. But taking political necessity into consideration had some advantages. It required that the development teams consult a broad array of groups in areas where there was disagreement among stakeholders, and that they find a way to balance competing perspectives. Accommodating political realities also meant that research-based evidence had to be combined with other forms of evidence. That process had the benefit of bringing greater external validity to a policy whose ultimate impact would depend on a deep practical understanding of the environment in which it would be implemented.

COMBINING TYPES OF EVIDENCE:
THE SPECIAL CASE OF POLICY IDEAS

This chapter has included multiple examples of how research is combined with other forms of evidence in policy discussions. However, one special case of combined evidence requires closer attention because of its centrality to the rationale and design of major education policies. Ideas typically meld normative values with empirical evidence, the most compelling of which is often grounded in research. Despite the role of ideas as a foundation for major policies, it is frequently overlooked in examining research-based evidence because the normative component is more prominent than the research supporting it. Yet one of the most important contributions of researchers to policy discourse has been their function as a source of policy ideas.

Along with interests and institutions, ideas are the major determinants of policy. Ideas have risen to prominence in explanations of policy outcomes as scholars have shown that accounts based solely on interests are seldom complete and often invalid. The concept of ideas initially referred to conceptions of a public interest that transcends self-interest.[32] More recently, the notion of ideas has been expanded and deepened. Ideas are more than a static alternative to interest-based explanations; they are central to the dynamic of interpretation and persuasion, acting along with interests as codeterminants of policy outcomes. Even when groups seek to advance their material interests through the policy process, they must build support for their position through ideational arguments.[33] Empirical observations of the different ways that ideas intersect with institutions and interests in policy development have led researchers to conceptualize policy ideas as elaborated images that go beyond goal statements, including specific alternatives, strategies, or theories of action (e.g., test-based accountability or school finance reform), as well as the organizing principles and values in which policy proposals are embedded (e.g., democratic representation or distributional equity). In effect, policy ideas have two dimensions: 1) programmatic ideas that facilitate policymaking by specifying how political institutions and policy instruments should be organized to solve particular problems or achieve broad policy goals, and 2) frames or normative ideas that are located in the foreground of policy debates, and that are critical in legitimizing and building public and elite support for policy proposals.[34]

Policy ideas are typically grounded in causal beliefs or paradigms that serve as road maps, providing experts and policymakers with a relatively coherent set of assumptions about the functioning of social, political, and economic institutions.[35] For example, although the term *common* explicitly points to making standards more uniform across jurisdictions, many participants in the discourse over common standards subscribed to the reform because they believed (via an implicit image of the causal process) that it would lead to making standards higher or more rigorous. Because they encapsulate both desired ends and a theory of action about how best to produce those results, ideas capture normative and instrumental dimensions of policy.

Ideas, especially but not exclusively those reflecting the instrumental or programmatic dimensions of policy, are usually grounded in research knowledge. Concepts such as school choice and opportunity to learn are examples of ideas that have shaped education policy by combining normative theories about what education ought to achieve and how it ought to be delivered with empirical evidence from a variety of sources. Although these two ideas lead to quite different policy proposals, both embody the aspirational goal of making education more effective and equitable, and the strategies they espouse to advance this goal draw on bodies of research that either infer or document causal relationships between key factors and schooling outcomes. For example, the research base for the early school choice proposals was inferential, drawing on studies outside education that examined the effects of market competition and the behavior of political institutions.[36] In contrast, opportunity to learn grew out of a technical concept originally designed to measure students' exposure to instructional content as an explanatory variable in models accounting for cross-national differences in student achievement.[37] These examples illustrate how research is used to operationalize the normative dimensions of policy ideas and to develop policy strategies and theories of action.

The characteristics of the institutional context also affect the accessibility and use of research-based ideas in the policy process. For example, the rules and norms governing policymaking affect which ideas and research evidence penetrate the process by influencing the degree to which academics and other intellectuals can access policy arenas.[38]

The shift to common standards represents an updating and modification of current policy ideas. However, in the case of a new idea, requiring a major redirection in policy, an existing policy monopoly must be challenged. That monopoly is composed of a powerful and widely accepted policy idea. Nevertheless, these monopolies and the interests they represent can be disrupted, resulting in major policy change. A primary reason such changes occur is that those opposed to or excluded from the policy monopoly can be considered underutilized resources (potential allies for change, or creators of new ideas for policy). Entrepreneurs mobilize these latent resources through a redefinition of the dominant policy image, using ideas that challenge and capture the imagination of the media, policymakers, and the public.[39] Although ideas and the resulting policy images often have a basis in research, the path from research findings to an altered policy image depends on how those promoting a new idea and those seeking to maintain the status quo frame and interpret research and other evidence.

In making the case for the Common Core, the policy entrepreneurs undertook a good deal of "idea work." We summarize the themes below, and in the next chapter we turn to the participants in the policy process who supply and use evidence, with particular attention to how key actors frame evidence in mobilizing support.

Most of the policy ideas underlying the CCSS were ones that had defined the standards and accountability movement of the past two decades. They included the normative belief that as public institutions, schools should be held accountable to citizens and their elected representatives for the schools' effective operations and especially for student learning. Along with a commitment to democratic accountability, the standards movement also embodied a belief in ensuring equal opportunity to learn regardless of a student's family circumstances. A third normative value reflected in standards and accountability is that schools, as public institutions, should be transparent about the knowledge and skills students are being taught, including a clear rationale for how they are consistent with public expectations for what should be the valued outcomes of schooling.

As discussed in this chapter and subsequent ones, the values of accountability, equity, transparency, and federalism were linked to research-based evidence that included the analysis of NAEP and state assessment data; the relationship between student outcomes and demographic factors such as race/ethnicity, socioeconomic status, language status, and disability; cognitive and developmental research on how students learn academic subjects and skills; and earlier research on effective schools that examined the linkages among curriculum, instructional strategies, and school organization.

Because the initial impetus for the Common Core was the result of policy feedback—its leaders were attempting to maintain the standards and accountability policy regime in the face of opposition sparked by NCLB—it built upon the ideas already defining standards policy. However, in advancing the notion that common standards across multiple states would be more transparent and effective in promoting equitable learning opportunities, the CCSS policy entrepreneurs were acknowledging the constitutional value of federalism, while also proposing a way to overcome its downsides. As organizations representing state officials, CCSSO and NGA accepted (and promoted) the strongly held value that because states have constitutional responsibility for education, they also have the authority to determine the content of schooling in their state. At the same time, state leaders recognized—and a substantial body of research confirmed—that with each state setting its own standards, students' learning opportunities would continue to vary significantly from state to state. Not only did formal standards differ, but educational institutions were fragmented, resulting in major differences in their capacity to deliver instructional services.[40] The Common Core is an idea that respects federalism as a value while also mitigating the effects of institutional fragmentation.

3

The "Who"—Producers, Entrepreneurs, and Intermediaries

[S]ome of us were looking around, but Governor Hunt convened the first meeting; it was June of 2006. And he carried that forward. Jim Hunt deserves the credit; even if he didn't have the idea initially, he's the one who instituted it, carried it forward.

—*Former governor*

Many of the researchers who are looking at policy-relevant questions have, frankly, no insight into policy or the policy process, and so they make stupid recommendations. Most of us in the policy community, when we get to the last couple of pages of a research report and the author turns to "policy implications," we just roll our eyes. The authors have no idea about the policy implications of their research. If you want research to get legs in the policy process, give it to an organization that has a track record of accomplishments in policy. Don't shop it around yourself or expect the researchers to sell it.

—*President, hybrid IO*

THE CONVENTIONAL WAY to classify those involved in evidence use in policy venues is to distinguish between participants who supply information and those who use it. However, the distinction between suppliers and users is often blurred because the same individual or organization can serve both functions. For example, intermediary organizations supply information to target audiences, but they also use evidence produced by others. Furthermore, within-group differences among suppliers and users can be greater than between the two categories. Consequently, rather than distinguishing between suppliers and users, we highlight the two most important groups in evidence use: *policy entrepreneurs* and *intermediary organizations* (IOs). In doing so, we consider the various sources from which they obtain evidence, how they make strategic choices about what evidence to use, and whom they view as the targets of that information. We differentiate among three categories of IOs, distinguishing whether their primary orientation is dissemination, advocacy, or a hybrid of the two. Intermediary organizations include groups that link the work of *research producers* with potential users. Therefore, we also examine how research producers generate evidence and interact with the policy process. In the exposition below, we draw on policy research and organizational sociology to ground our distinctions in the salient characteristics of the organization, the purposes and incentives for evidence production and use, and the organization's target audience.[1]

THE ROLE OF POLICY ENTREPRENEURS IN EVIDENCE USE

Policy research has consistently demonstrated the critical role that policy entrepreneurs play in bringing new ideas into different policy arenas and in advancing those ideas, sometimes for many years before they reach decision-makers' agendas.[2] They are "advocates who are willing to invest their resources—time, energy, reputation, money—to promote a position in return for anticipated future gain in the form of material, purposive, or solidary benefits."[3] They can occupy a variety of formal and informal policymaking roles, but the most effective ones typically have reputations for policy accomplishment or currently occupy political leadership roles that give them claim to a public hearing, are known for their political connections or negotiating skills, and are persistent.[4]

One of the resources that policy entrepreneurs draw upon is research. Entrepreneurs are advocates, however, and they use research and other evidence strategically in defining a policy problem, framing it, and then shaping and promoting a particular solution. Although these strategic and persuasive uses of research are at odds with the rational choice models that dominated policy analysis in its early years, they represent a more valid depiction of the actual use of research in policymaking venues.[5] A simplistic version of this assumption is that policy entrepreneurs use research results selectively and even distort findings to advance their case. Entrepreneurs may certainly misuse research, but the competitive nature of the political process and the fact that credibility is the policy advocate's most important resource minimizes outright distortion. At the same time, the inevitable complexity of real-world policymaking allows ample room for uncertainty and interpretation. For instance, in some cases, such as school choice, research results are inconsistent or contested. Even in cases where the research base is solid, however, as with early literacy acquisition or the determinants of student retention, its application to problem definition and policy solution is open to interpretation and framing, depending on the context and feasibility factors such as political, organizational, and resource conditions.

How policy entrepreneurs use research knowledge also depends on who the entrepreneurs are. In some instances, they may be knowledge producers such as university researchers or think tank staff who choose to disseminate their work directly as it relates to particular policy issues and venues. Alternatively, they may be IOs that act as research brokers and translators in the course of pursuing their organizational mission (e.g., foundations, nonprofits, or interest groups). Policy entrepreneurs may be current or former elected officials, whose political status lends their advocacy an additional claim to the attention of their colleagues.

In his study of the role of policy entrepreneurs in promoting state-level school choice legislation, Michael Mintrom found that effective policy entrepreneurship requires a range of skills, all of which include social aspects.[6] Entrepreneurs bring new ideas into the policy arena, but it is not enough to offer a novel approach—decision-makers have to be convinced that it addresses a pressing problem, is consistent with their beliefs and those of their constituents, and that the idea is feasible. To meet these challenges, policy entrepreneurs have to be creative and insightful. They have to be able to frame their preferred option so that it appears to be the appropriate solution to a current problem. They also need to understand the preferences and incentives of their policymaker targets and how they define policy problems, so the entrepreneurs can speak to them in ways that are persuasive. To understand the preferences and concerns of others, Mintrom found that policy entrepreneurs need a high degree of social perceptiveness, and that one of the best ways to gain such a skill is to spend time talking with and listening to people from a range of backgrounds.[7] Understanding diverse perspectives also requires the ability to mix in a variety of social and political settings, not just with natural allies but also with potential opponents. All these social skills contribute to the two most critical skills for policy entrepreneurs: persuasiveness and the capacity to be a strategic team builder, able to discern what type of coalition is best able to promote the policy change they advocate.[8]

As they advance their ideas, policy entrepreneurs are engaged in argumentation: attempting to persuade members of the policy community that their proposal is worthy of support. In doing so, they connect values and evidence to a particular policy alternative, with the success of that effort dependent on whether those values and evidence resonate with a broad range of potential supporters.[9] The skills that policy entrepreneurs can draw upon and their use of evidence are especially central as they define a policy problem that is viewed as pressing by many other participants in the policy realm and to which their preferred option can be framed as an effective solution.

Critical to the success of policy entrepreneurs is their understanding of what types of evidence are most convincing to policymakers. Their experience working with policymakers and the staffs that support them provides insights into how decision-makers view research and why they often combine it with other types of evidence. These comments from current and former staff to elected officials are typical of the constraints that policy entrepreneurs need to consider in selecting evidence to advance their agendas:

> Most policymakers don't have the background or interest to get involved in learning about technical areas . . . When you call an expert before a congressional committee, the members will listen to the testimony, and if they know something about the person's reputation, they will have an inclination to trust that person or not. If they don't know much about the person, they will usually listen (if they're not reading the newspaper or gossiping), and they'll think about whether it makes sense for their district, and whether there is a commonality or consensus among people with different political points of view. But they don't sit there and weigh the research methodology in the way that academic syntheses do.
>
> —Former congressional staff director[10]

With the chiefs, there is definitely an interest in research, but there's always the context—how much money was spent, what were the students like, what were the parents like—so you can say, "well, in my state," and dismiss some of the research.

—*Staff to chief state school officers*

This has been our great challenge—getting legislators to trust research, to think about how it could be useful for more than just narrowly supporting their own projects, to understand that valid research is grounded differently than political or ideological arguments.

—*Staff to state legislators*

The two major policy entrepreneurs promoting the Common Core are experienced and skilled politicians. James Hunt Jr. had been the longest-serving governor of North Carolina (1977–85, 1993–2001). As early as his first term, Hunt had become known as an "education governor," establishing a Smart Start program for prekindergartners and promoting a standards-based state accountability system. As one of the earliest proponents of teaching standards, Hunt served as the founding chair of the National Board for Professional Teaching Standards. One longtime participant in national education politics described Governor Hunt's motivation for promoting the Common Core:

> He lobbied people for standards as the solution, saying "I want one last achievement before I pass. We've had so many false starts, but standards is the one place where you can do it." I think he, like so many other leaders, thought that standards were the point where you could get agreement.

Bob Wise served nine terms (1983–2001) in the US House of Representatives, including as a member of the House Education and Labor Committee. He then served a term (2001–5) as governor of West Virginia. While governor, Wise secured funding for a Promise Scholarship Program to pay the tuition for West Virginia students attending an in-state higher education institution. He also expanded enrollment in the Children's Health Insurance Program.

During their long political careers, Hunt and Wise honed the skills necessary for successful policy entrepreneurship. They have a deep understanding of education policy—how problems are framed, what types of solutions are viewed as feasible, and who the major players are. As individuals and as elected representatives, they were among those major policy actors. To extend their network of potential allies even further, each also heads an organization that gives them institutional standing. The Hunt Institute was established in 2001, first located at the University of North Carolina at Chapel Hill, and now affiliated with the Sanford School of Public Policy at Duke University. From its inception, the Institute has focused on convening and building partnerships with state policymakers, including governors, lieutenant governors, legislators, and their policy staffs. Much of this effort has emphasized connecting state officials with researchers and IO representatives working on topics relevant to their policy concerns. Wise served for fourteen years as the president of the Alliance for Excellent Education (All4Ed), a nonprofit advocacy organization focused on increasing opportunities for underserved students to graduate from high school prepared for postsecondary education and employment.

In their roles as governmental and nonprofit leaders, governors Hunt and Wise have made research and other types of evidence integral to their advocacy. In 2003, Hunt was the first recipient of the American Educational Research Association's Distinguished Public Service Award, which recognizes individuals who have worked to enact or implement policies grounded in education research. At the same time, the Hunt Institute's convening activities emphasize the role of professional judgment in encouraging state policymakers not just to interact with researchers and IO representatives, but also to bring their own experience and ideas to interpreting research findings and projecting them into concrete policy alternatives. One of the Alliance's functions as an IO is to synthesize and translate research for lay audiences on topics such as adolescent brain development and student learning. However, most of All4Ed's advocacy is based on thoughtfully selecting concepts that bridge the worlds of research and policy, and then "just trotting out statistics" (as one of the staff noted) on those indicators. For example, the organization collects comparable data and prepares state report cards that track graduation rates and the effect of improving that rate on indicators such as increased employment, tax revenue, and reduced health care costs. The Alliance staffer explained the organization's use of evidence in this way:

> I think of all this as data points rather than research [or] complicated analysis. Making this information really clear and simple is important—politicians can digest it quickly, and it carries more credibility.

For policy entrepreneurs, their skill as persuaders able to mobilize a broad network of supporters depends not just on strategic choices about which evidence to use, but also when to use it to maximize the likelihood of moving their issue onto the policy agenda. The origins of the Common Core movement can be traced back to several unsuccessful attempts two decades earlier, including efforts spearheaded by organizations representing subject-matter specialists and the National Council on Education Standards and Testing (NCEST) chaired by Roy Romer, then governor of Colorado.[11] These attempts, introduced in both the George H. W. Bush and Bill Clinton administrations, foundered, enmeshed in controversies over the curricular values underlying state standards and assessments. They were opposed in Congress by Republicans who feared possible federal encroachment and Democrats concerned about the impact of assessments on students who had not had adequate opportunities to learn the required content. However, by 2006, Hunt and Wise decided that what had seemed impossible ten years earlier was now a realistic aspiration. In their view, policymakers, educators, and the public had become accustomed to the idea of content and performance standards. Opinion polls indicated support for national standards, and state policymakers were beginning to see potential cost advantages to common standards, particularly given the requirements of NCLB.[12] Even though the CCSS policy entrepreneurs determined that a policy window could potentially be opened for consideration of academic standards that extend beyond a single state, they quickly recognized that these could not be national standards developed under the auspices of the federal government. Rather, they developed the alternative of common standards originating from the organizations representing state policymakers.

In the next chapter, we examine in detail how Hunt and Wise, joined by their NGA and CCSSO allies, used evidence to define the problem to which the Common Core was the solution. Research was a major resource in that effort. But it was used strategically to ensure that it pointed toward a match between problem definition and preferred policy option, and that it provided a sufficient rationale for support by the intermediary organizations that inform politicians and mobilize their constituents. In fact, the Common Core policy entrepreneurs assumed, at least in the early stages, that their advocacy could be focused primarily on state officials and IOs who would then serve as a bridge to a broader audience. Consequently, the entrepreneurs' efforts were essentially targeted at policy elites; the wider public was not part of their direct targeting of evidence.[13]

RESEARCH PRODUCERS AS A SOURCE OF EVIDENCE

Those who produce and fund research are typically affiliated with universities, independent policy research institutions (e.g., RAND, AIR, or Brookings), or government agencies (e.g., Institute of Education Sciences (IES), National Institutes of Health (NIH), or the National Science Foundation (NSF)). Their main purpose is to produce the types of research-based evidence described in chapter 2: basic or applied empirical research, policy analysis, and statistical data. Dissemination of results to audiences beyond other researchers is important, but it is not their primary motivation. Rather, producers are guided by the canons of the scientific method that constrain both the production of research and the framing of results. The major challenge, then, is to produce research that is valid and reliable, and that can measure up to peer review. Research producers also aspire to ground their studies in broader theoretical frameworks, testing those theories with data and discovering and elaborating commonalities across issues and policy areas.

Producers with an interest and expertise in policy will often address research questions in forms useful to policy actors. Many adopt dissemination as a significant secondary function. These include national institutions as well as organizations that operate at the state and local levels (e.g., Policy Analysis for California Education (PACE) and the UChicago Consortium on School Research). Research producers who view dissemination as part of their function strive to make their findings understandable to diverse audiences. Although the primary focus is their own work, they may synthesize other relevant research to show how their studies build upon and expand earlier research. Unlike academics engaged in basic research, those conducting applied policy research are typically experienced in policy analysis, attuned to addressing questions of concern to decision-makers, and able to identify the implications of their research for policy.

But they are researchers, not advocates. So the expectation is that their analysis of policy implications will be balanced—transparent in the assumptions and data underlying their results, clear about limitations on the findings, and explicit as to the strengths and weaknesses of different policy options. Consistent with these norms is the inability of policy research to resolve value conflicts.[14] Although research can identify the underlying assumptions of policy arguments and outline possible consequences of policy options based on differing normative values, determining how conflicts might be settled or which values should prevail is beyond the purview of research.

INTERMEDIARIES AND EVIDENCE USE

In contrast to producers with dissemination as a secondary function, the primary purposes of IOs are to understand the information needs of policymakers and their constituents and to reduce the costs of their obtaining the necessary information. Part of that effort involves locating appropriate research and other evidence, assessing the applicability of findings to particular policy issues, and then translating and communicating those findings to specific audiences. As such, IOs are instrumental in shaping the amount and type of evidence available to policymakers and practitioners. Their audiences may be clients, group members or constituents, decision-maker targets, or the general public. However, this function often involves more than translation and transmission. It may also require identifying the implications of research findings that may not be obvious to the producers, and also specifying feasibility conditions, such as cost and administrative capacity. How these tasks are designed and undertaken can vary significantly by the type of IO, its organizational goals, and its target audiences. We examine three basic categories of IOs: translators and disseminators, policy advocates, and hybrids.

Translators and Disseminators
The major functions of these IOs are the translation and transmission of research and other evidence customized to specific types of users. The audience for many of these groups is practitioners rather than policymakers, as information dissemination is often part of a technical assistance function.

Examples of such groups in education include the Regional Educational Laboratory Program (REL), ASCD, McREL, and Learning Forward. As third-party providers, these groups typically work under contract to states and school districts delivering curriculum materials, professional development, and other forms of assistance to administrators and teachers. In contrast to research producers' general focus, disseminators are more strongly oriented toward meeting the specific information needs of their clients. The challenge for them is to identify high-quality research; understand the limits of inconsistent, incomplete, and contested research; tailor the application of findings to different local contexts; and combine research responsibly with other types of evidence. The last challenge is especially relevant because often clients are more persuaded by the professional judgment and experience of peers and by compelling anecdotes. But the extent to which disseminators rely on different types of evidence varies. Several examples of evidence use by IOs, all of which have been funded by the Gates Foundation and involved in implementation of the Common Core, illustrate this variation. For example, one IO executive talked of basing much of his group's dissemination on experience, but also combining it with research and recognizing the limits on practitioner judgment:

> The evidence base we're pulling from is our years of experience doing professional development and taking it and making it effective and friendly to a practitioner. That's where our expertise is . . . It's like a quasi-literature review, where it's not us doing the research. It's almost leveraging the research and expertise that's already out there, and putting it together with our experience in professional development, and not repackaging it, but bringing them all together.
>
> The idea of "best judgment" is a potential problem area—best judgment by whom? Is it objective or subjective, and who do you trust? For instance, my mom is a kindergarten teacher in California, and it frightens me that she is not good at math. So she might not be the best person to ask, but we do need to combine research with . . . what—vetting, validation—by practitioners, but practitioners who can explain why it would work better this way, and be able to explain it not only for their grade, but outside their grade span.

An IO staffer who is delivering professional development directly in teachers' classrooms talked of obtaining mathematical content for curriculum and assessments from researchers, but needing to draw mainly on her own professional experience in designing lessons to assist teachers in implementing formative assessments in their classrooms:

> I've been involved in the CCSS from the beginning. I have spent a lot of time in classrooms, so all of the work that I do is built upon work in classrooms and learning in classrooms . . . So, how did I realize we need a new way to do PD [professional development]—it's akin to realizing do I want to keep banging my head against the wall or do I want to do something that's more effective to understand the problem? Where did I get the idea [to conduct professional development in classrooms]? I just dreamed it up! It's because I'm smart. I just noticed that we've been doing professional development the traditional way for a very long time, but teachers were coming back and saying, "I can't work with my kids" and "I can't apply what I learned in the workshop." I thought, let's go to where the problem is—the process—and we'll support the teachers. We'll watch the way teachers teach and see what teachers find challenging while working with students.

In contrast, another IO leader, also engaged in teacher professional development, mentioned by name and affiliation researchers whose work had been influential in the IO's design of professional learning standards. She then described the organization's relationship with a university researcher as one example of the IO's collaboration and ongoing relationship with research producers:

> For us, research is really critical. We have had the pleasure to be identified as an organization that bridges policy, practice, and research. A number of years ago, when we had an outside firm provide us with some constructive and critical analysis of the work that we are doing, that was one of the things they identified. So we lean on the research because it helps us think about the practice. But at the same time, we also move practice back to research . . . so we're also in close contact with a number of researchers. Linda Darling-Hammond, for example, has done a great deal of consulting work with us on a series of studies we commissioned on professional learning. We like that kind of relationship; we thrive on it. We're actually right now looking for a university that would be willing to house the center for research on professional learning.

An executive of an IO designing CCSS curriculum materials offered insightful reflection on how research complements anecdotal evidence:

> I don't think policy decisions will ever be made based on anecdotal evidence. I think policymakers like to quote statistics and quote the numbers. Unfortunately, I think anecdotal evidence, especially in education, is really critical and valuable. I just think on a policy level, you really need the data to put things into place and get things into motion . . . When you are representing a body of people, it's really hard to justify any decision or position merely on "this is what I feel," or "this is what I see happening," or "I talked to these people and this is what they told me." It's especially hard when you are talking to people who are not in the classroom and to constituents who aren't involved in education—they won't connect in that way to anecdotal evidence or approach. If you can quote the hard data or back up your position with facts, with numbers, that's what's most effective in policymaking . . . but it's very important to really go into schools and talk to teachers and parents and get that type of anecdotal information from them.

Depending on the needs and interests of their clients, then, disseminators are likely to rely to differing degrees on their own professional experience and that of the educators they assist. However, they have an incentive to use evidence responsibly. Their continuing credibility with clients requires that research-based applications be reliable and appropriate, given the nature of the situation in which the findings are being applied. In other words, when disseminators choose to use research, they usually attempt to apply it consistently with the norms of scientific inquiry.

Policy Advocates

This category of IOs differs significantly from disseminators in the incentives that motivate their work. Policy advocates are membership organizations that represent group interests in policy arenas, and do so on behalf of their members' material or ideological interests. In education, these groups function at all three levels of the intergovernmental system and represent their members' interests before legislative bodies, executive agencies, and courts. They range from teacher unions to general business groups such as chambers of commerce, and from education providers such as publishers and charter school associations to organizations representing the officials governing public education.

Policy advocates use research strategically as one resource among others, such as money and access to the media. For these IOs, research can be one part of an advocacy strategy, but seldom the most important. The scientific canons that shape the work of research producers, especially avoiding the selective use of data and making exaggerated claims, are not operative for policy advocates. Their mission is to promote their members' interests, so they have a strong incentive to ignore or downplay research evidence at odds with those interests and their preferred policy options. In his study of how research has been used in policy debates on charter schools, Jeffrey Henig draws several distinctions between researchers and advocates. He notes that good science depends on uncertainty, contingency, and time needed to reach conclusions. In contrast, those supporting a particular policy often need to move quickly, and acknowledging uncertainty about conclusions could become the basis for mobilization by opponents.[15] Contingent findings and limits on the inferences that can be drawn from research also sharply distinguish researchers from policy advocates. As Henig notes, "Building a convincing case about causality is perhaps the most vexing and perplexing challenge researchers face."[16] In contrast, advocates and their policymaker supporters are more willing to assert confident claims about causality in arguing for a particular option. It will be more appealing to potential supporters if advocates can argue that enacting the policy will assuredly lead to the desired outcomes.

When policy advocates use research as part of a persuasive strategy, they often link it to a frame or narrative that is both supportive of their position and places it in a broader ideological or partisan context. So, for example, charter school supporters portray it as a strategy for enabling market-based choice, and those promoting standards-based reforms depict such policies as strengthening US global competitiveness. In relying on these broader ideological frames, policy advocates have to be selective in the research and other evidence (often stories) that they use, and in how they interpret and communicate them.

However, there are conditions when it is in a policy advocate's interest to use research responsibly for instrumental purposes. As Kevin Esterling argues in his study of policy expertise, "in contemporary lobbying, interest groups are deeply and profoundly influenced by expert policy concepts and ideas, not out of some philosophic love of knowledge but instead out of a desire to pursue their interests effectively on complex policy questions."[17] If a policy advocate is promoting a policy that is both complicated and requires support from diverse groups, a research-based solution will often be the optimal solution, and as such can appeal to a wider cross section of groups than non-research-based policies.[18] Once an advocacy IO determines that drawing on research evidence is in its interest, that evidence may become the basis for a broad-based coalition of groups, and together they may work to improve the quality of the causal beliefs underlying the policy alternative.

Policy advocate IOs, including the teacher unions and organizations representing state policymakers, were involved in the Common Core. For education groups, the CCSS did not initially tap into any major ideological or partisan cleavages. Rather, the Common Core was like a time-out from the political differences that typically divide education interest groups. As the leader of an organization representing local school districts noted in describing collaboration around the CCSS:

> It's almost like neutral ground. It is common territory that we all have to get right; in the group interest as well as the interest of shared constituents. There is less tension than in other situations where we work together. For instance, we can work with AFT without having to battle over collective bargaining issues.

What was most important for the teacher unions was that the professional judgment of their members was reflected in the standards:

> The decision for NEA to get involved in supporting CCSS was not difficult: it was clear that this was going to happen, and we felt we could push it in the right direction ... Most importantly, we wanted to press the need to involve teachers in the standards-writing process from the beginning.
>
> —*NEA staffer*

> We told NGA and CCSSO that we would support the CCSS if they responded to teachers' comments. We were very impressed with their response; we could see that whole comments from teachers had been incorporated into the revised standards.
>
> —*AFT staffer*

Because the policy entrepreneurs promoting the CCSS understood that the support of rank-and-file teachers was essential to its effectiveness, little persuasion by their advocates was needed to ensure that teacher voices were heard and taken seriously.

The role of policy advocates in the Common Core was critical during the short period during which individual states decided whether or not to adopt the standards. One of the most important tasks for CCSS groups was to build support among the leaders of their state affiliates and counterparts. One national organization executive described it in this way:

> The advocacy groups were in constant touch, particularly through the adoption phase. The adoption phase was run like a campaign. The groups would discuss how they would defend against attacks—who should be the messenger, who should lay low because if they didn't it might hurt the effort.

Both the NEA and the AFT worked with their state affiliates to prepare them for participation in the adoption process, assuring them that teachers' perspectives were reflected in the development process. Information was the primary resource the national organizations offered to potential state allies, and although it was customized to the interests and politics of individual states, messages in support of the CCSS were consistent across states and groups. That consistency was due to the ongoing communication and coordination among the groups and to shared polling data that helped identify language likely to be effective in gaining support.[19]

In contrast, another group of organizations became active in opposing the Common Core during its initial implementation once it had been adopted in several states. Some of these, such as the national Republican Party, fall within the definition of policy advocates in that they represent the economic and ideological interests of a clearly defined and relatively stable membership. Another set of opponents, such as Tea Party groups and state-specific opponents such as Hoosiers Against Common Core, are similar to policy advocates in that they use research sporadically when its interpretation appears to support their case, and ignore or downplay findings whose implications weaken their preferred positions. In one respect, however, these organizations are similar to the hybrids discussed in the next section in that they tend not to have a formal membership base like that of labor unions or political parties. Rather, they seek to attract ideological adherents who often support the group's position on a more universal, philosophical issue such as the appropriate role of government, and then extend that support on an ad hoc basis to the group's position on particular policies. In the case of the Common Core, a major frame used by opponents has been that it represents unwarranted federal intrusion and a threat to state autonomy. A representative of a Washington-based conservative group concisely summarized the argument:

> We're convinced that the CCSS is moving toward a single national standard imposed by the federal government . . . the standards movement is an unconstitutional attempt to centralize power in the federal government.

This discussion is not meant as a blanket condemnation of how policy advocates approach the use of research, because some groups use it responsibly as part of their persuasive strategies. Rather, the point is that these organizations lack a strong incentive to base their positions on research findings or to use results according to the norms of scientific inquiry if following these norms will not serve the interests of their members.

Hybrids

In contrast to policy advocates with their focus on members' interests, hybrid organizations pursue a policy agenda that is often consistent with a broader ideological perspective (e.g., market reforms or greater equalization of educational resources). We use the term *hybrid* because these groups are similar to translators and disseminators in that they produce and disseminate research and other evidence as a primary means to promote their goals, but they use research strategically like policy advocates. Included in this category are partisan think tanks such as the American Enterprise Institute (AEI) and the Center for American Progress (CAP), mission-oriented organizations such as All4Ed and the Education Trust, and policy-oriented foundations such as Gates, Ford, and Broad.[20]

Hybrids are not membership organizations, and they lack a well-defined audience, so one goal of their evidence use is to build a constituency that agrees with and supports their policy agenda.[21] That constituency can be quite diverse, and it may include other IOs, policy targets across governmental levels, potential funders, and research producers. As we have seen with governors Hunt and Wise, policy entrepreneurs often come from the leadership of hybrids. Because their long-term credibility is critical to hybrids for building and maintaining a constituency, they are likely to pay greater attention to the scientific canons governing the use of research. For some hybrids, there is a further, strong incentive to follow scientific norms: a number of hybrids, especially the partisan think tanks, produce their own research. Although that research is in the service of an organization's policy agenda, it still must withstand critical scrutiny from other research producers based at least partly on the quality of the analysis.

Among the hybrids supporting the Common Core were CAP, the Education Trust, the Thomas B. Fordham Institute, the Campaign for High School Equity, and the National Council of La Raza (now known as UnidosUS). Their reasons for supporting the CCSS varied depending on how the standards fit into their existing policy agenda. For example, Fordham had evaluated the quality and rigor of state standards periodically since 1997, and had found them to have gone from "bad to bad." It also viewed the variation in state accountability standards (essentially assessment cut scores used in establishing student proficiency levels) as a major problem. As an executive of the organization noted:

> We found that whether a school needs improvement or not depends on what state it's in, and you could change your status just by moving across the state line. It's ridiculous for a big modern country.

At the same time, partly because of its generally conservative philosophy and partly because of the failure of the George H. W. Bush administration to establish voluntary national standards, Fordham concluded that "the state standards aren't working and federal standards are politically impossible." Consequently, it saw the CCSS as a means of attaining one of its major goals with rigorous national standards that are voluntary and have the potential to be national without being federal:

> I think that a big modern country needs common standards for its schools. The federal government can't do this; the states can't do this, shouldn't be made to do this. So the Common Core is worth encouraging states to want to use.

Like Fordham, the civil rights hybrids are concerned about state variation, especially its effects on students of color. For them, the CCSS is part of a larger policy strategy for equalizing educational opportunity:

> This broad view, which focuses on the implications of inconsistent standards for communities of color, has been more influential than any particular source or type of evidence.

Much like the teacher unions, the civil rights groups have also pressed for inclusion in the CCSS implementation process to ensure that their constituents are treated fairly and receive needed resources:

> The greatest challenge going forward is the same one that we have been sensitive to all along—ensuring that communities of color are included in the decision-making process. At the implementation stage, it is all the more important that representatives of civil rights organizations and local community-based organizations are not an afterthought but fully included.

A number of large foundations have increasingly become among the most consequential hybrid organizations in education policy. In her study of the role of foundations in promoting education reform, Sarah Reckhow found that three changes in the nature of philanthropy have allowed them to play a more public role with greater influence on policy: major foundations are giving away more money, individual philanthropists and the institutions they lead have become more openly involved in policy advocacy, and major foundations have become more targeted in their grant-making strategies.[22] As a result, a number of large foundations are now well positioned to promote their policy ideas. Yet, like other hybrids, foundations do not claim to speak on behalf of a membership base. Rather, through their grant-making, they can help to build networks of organizations to promote new political coalitions and to build a constituency for their particular policy agenda.[23] Reckhow describes the agenda of the education foundations most noted for their policy entrepreneurship, such as Gates, Broad, and Walton, as that of the "Boardroom Progressives" focused on accountability and market strategies.[24] These foundations support some research production, including evaluations of their funded programs. Although foundations' concern for the credibility of their recommendations focuses attention on the quality of research, much of the evidence used in related policy deliberations is inevitably framed and communicated by the IO organizations that the foundations fund. Thus the foundations' strategic choice of grantees and their research topics is essential in shaping the supply of evidence that reaches policymakers.[25]

The role of the Gates Foundation in advancing the Common Core aptly illustrates how entrepreneurial foundations have functioned in promoting their policy agenda. The CCSS is consistent with its focus on educational accountability and creating conditions for more effective teaching.[26] Gates' primary role was to use its grant money strategically to build a diverse network in support of the Common Core. As one of its program officers explained:

> The foundation's goal is for 80 percent of students to be college ready, and that's an ambitious agenda. And, that agenda really has three pillars to it. First, a commitment to effective teaching—helping improve instruction in classrooms across the country. There's a recognition that standards alone aren't that helpful unless they're linked to transformations in classroom practice. So that focus on effective teaching is there, and second, what we call the foundation's commitment to college-ready work. Now that's a line of work which is designed to help foster and support effective teaching in classrooms. And third, there's where the foundation has invested in transitional tools for teachers to use to support the implementation of Common Core standards. So we've invested in a set of tools for mathematics and a set of tools to support literacy instruction.[27]

The program officer also noted that the foundation was "very convinced that the Common Core needed to originate from the states themselves," and that Gates wanted to support efforts across the spectrum of organizations to increase the likelihood that people would become aware of and support the Common Core.

Three organizational beneficiaries of Gates funding described its role:

> Gates funding really is a factor. Foundations like Ford got people to collaborate and funded joint ventures. But I can't remember anything this multifaceted, this national.

Gates is the elephant in the room: Gates funding the development of curricula; Gates trying to influence the assessment consortia.

—■-■-■—

Gates helped, funding most of the people involved in the standards ... [they] went around and consciously looked at the Washington policy scene, and placed grants—we got a million dollars, others got a million dollars. I think they consciously went about leveraging the points of opinion.

Between 2008 and mid-2013, the Gates Foundation spent slightly over $200 million in support of activities advancing the CCSS and the concept of college and career ready standards. About half of the funds ($98 million) were allocated to national organizations, with much of it supporting activities related to building support and informing policymakers and their constituents about the Common Core. The remainder was largely targeted on developing CCSS-aligned instructional materials, implementing those materials in local districts, providing professional development, and conducting research and development related to the Common Core—$37.5 million to fifteen private providers, $19.6 million to five state education agencies and thirteen state-level nongovernmental organizations (NGOs), $31.5 million to twenty local districts and nine local NGOs, and $17.9 million to ten research institutions.[28] In addition, foundations such as Hewlett, GE, and others have supported activities related to implementing the Common Core. The scope of these activities and the extent to which information was customized and targeted would not have been possible without the sustained support from foundations that viewed the Common Core as part of a major education reform strategy.[29]

The foundations, especially Gates, were also primary motivators in the groups' efforts to stay in contact, share resources, and in some cases, collaborate on joint projects. An organization executive described that process:

The foundation money certainly made a difference to the work on CCSS—crafting the standards, the writing and reviewing—it was crucial for NGA and CCSSO. What difference did it make for coordination? Well, there have been times for all of us when we've wanted to pull our hair out rather than going to another meeting or getting on another conference call. It sometimes felt oppressive, but we needed the time. It was a good way into the process before people began to trust each other . . . The fact that we had to keep coming together with all those people gave us sufficient time to develop trust, and that will be essential for the implementation phase.

CONCLUSIONS

Focusing on the participants in the policy process provides several insights into uses of evidence. Table 3.1 summarizes our distinctions among the different groups in their use of evidence.

In chapter 2, we showed that the emphasis on different types of evidence and how they are combined depends on how that evidence is being used to construct a policy argument. For example, experience with past and current policy may be a more valid source of evidence than basic research in assessing the feasibility of a particular policy option or for learning from the successes and shortcomings of past initiatives. In this chapter, we have focused on the diverse actors in the policymaking process. The context of the policy process provides a common environment, and the actors resemble each other in their quest to frame a convincing argument for their preferred policy alternative. But the differences among the actors condition how they use research and other types of evidence: each type of actor brings a distinct background and salient characteristics; they play distinct institutional roles; and, despite competing over the same policy issue, they have different policy goals and are oriented toward distinct audiences. For instance, university faculty and policy research institutes are commonly criticized for producing findings that confront theory more directly than they address pressing policy problems. But this is not a mistake; it follows from their primary identity as participants in a deliberation bounded by scientific values. Research producers are keenly aware of policy problems, in fact they are often the most creative at conceiving of alternatives. However, because they orient their investigations toward transparently evaluating competing hypotheses, their findings lack the partisan bite of advocates or the direct applicability of translators and disseminators.

For policy entrepreneurs, advocates, and hybrids, the overwhelming incentive in selecting among evidence is the desire to advance their preferred policies. Table 3 makes it clear that these categories lie along a single dimension. Kingdon's definition of policy entrepreneurs captures part of the

TABLE 3.1   Characteristics of evidence producers and users

	SALIENT CHARACTERISTICS	PURPOSE OF EVIDENCE USE
Research Producers	Scholars/researchers ■ Universities ■ Policy research institutes	■ Original knowledge, problem-solving ■ Identify new problems and potential solutions ■ Policy implementation and evaluation
Policy Entrepreneurs	■ Commitment to particular policy ideas/options ■ Political capital resources (time, money) ■ Understand what types of evidence are most convincing to policymakers ■ Understand timing—when to use evidence ■ Reputation/ accomplishments (good ideas, feasibility, coordination, and social skills) ■ Identity of actor varies (e.g., research producers, affiliated with hybrids or advocacy organizations)	■ Promote recognition of problem as defined by entrepreneur ■ Promote preferred policy alternative
Translators and Disseminators	■ Business model is research-based advice for practice ■ Reliable source of valid and generalizable evidence ■ Fits into local context ■ Often under contract to states and local districts	■ Tailor application of research findings to local context ■ Identify high-quality research ■ Understand the limits of the research (validity, generalizability) ■ Combine research with other types of evidence ■ Use professional judgment/ experience of practitioners
Advocates	■ Primarily membership organizations that represent group interests/ preferences (material, ideological) ■ Active at all three levels of the federal system	■ Promote members' interests ■ Frame narrative to point toward a definition of the problem and/ or a particular category of solution alternatives

INCENTIVES FOR EVIDENCE PRODUCTION/USE	EVIDENCE TARGETS	ADHERENCE TO CANONS OF SCIENTIFIC INQUIRY
■ Production: Status in scientific community, material rewards—future funding, grants, fellowships ■ Use: Recognition/reputation as problem-solver, commitment to research-based policy	■ Scientific community ■ Agenda setters, such as elite media, public intellectuals, policy-makers	High Primary orientation toward validity and generalizability, enforced by peer review
■ Enactment of preferred policy option ■ Public recognition as problem-solver	■ Policymakers ■ Staff ■ Agenda setters/ influentials—business, media, public intellectuals	High/ medium Concern for reputation/ credibility versus effective policy argument, given brief window of opportunity
■ Strengthen quality of education practice, based on making explicit the connection between evidence and acknowledged problems in local context, building on reputation for past technical assistance. ■ Adoption of recommended technical assistance (e.g., PD curriculum); practitioners testify that "it works"	■ Policymakers only when designing implementation/ evaluation ■ Practitioners rather than policymakers (teachers, administrators)	High Concern for reputation, future credibility; competition
■ Whatever works; use research strategically (selective or exaggerated claims, often linked to ideological frame) ■ Effectiveness requires valid information, especially with a complicated problem; ■ Constrained in attracting supporters (who may be skeptical of overpromising)	■ Policymakers ■ Agenda setters, often via public opinion	Low Oriented toward short-term success

(continued)

TABLE 3.1 Characteristics of evidence producers and users (*continued*)

	SALIENT CHARACTERISTICS	PURPOSE OF EVIDENCE USE
Hybrids	▪ Research a primary tool (similar to translators and disseminators) ▪ Research used strategically (similar to advocates) ▪ Broader ideological perspective	▪ Build a constituency for agenda and preferred policies

difference among these intermediary actors: it focuses rightly on their activities to promote their preferred position. But many advocates are also willing to "invest their resources . . . to promote a position."[30] Our investigation shows the importance of accounting for not only the advocates speaking to promote the preferred alternative, but also the willingness of a wide audience to attentively engage with the argument. Policy entrepreneurs such as Hunt and Wise are distinguished by their advocacy, to be sure, but also by their claim to the attention of an audience beyond their partisan constituency. Key to this distinction is their reputations for education policy accomplishments in difficult political circumstances, but also their willingness to let the evidence, rather than ideology, dictate the definition of the problem and the best solution.[31]

Finally, many intermediary organizations that belong to the category of translators and disseminators have built reputations on the basis of effective technical assistance across different educational contexts. Reputation is a valuable but fragile advantage. It lends credibility to the IO's advice in a new situation, but to preserve and strengthen its reputation, the organization's advice must visibly help to solve the problem toward which it is directed.

INCENTIVES FOR EVIDENCE PRODUCTION/USE	EVIDENCE TARGETS	ADHERENCE TO CANONS OF SCIENTIFIC INQUIRY
▪ Promote preferred policy alternatives	▪ Potential constituencies ▪ Other IOs, policymakers at all governmental levels ▪ Research producers ▪ Foundations (both targeted as potential funders, and also acting as hybrids themselves)	Medium/high Long-term credibility critical for building and maintaining a constituency. May also be research producers, so adherence to scientific canons underlies legitimacy of research findings.

Thus a rational concern for credibility and reputation motivates the use of the most valid and generalizable evidence the IO can obtain.

As we will see in the next chapter, strategic decisions about what types of evidence to use and how to balance the trade-offs among them can vary over stages of the policy process.

4

The "How"—Evidence Use Across Stages of the Policy Process

POLICYMAKING IS RARELY LINEAR—moving from problem definition to design, agenda setting, enactment, and finally, implementation. Rather, policy options may exist before a problem is defined, and during implementation, policies may cycle back for new enactments or fall off the agenda altogether. Nevertheless, despite nonlinearity and limited predictability about direction and duration, most policies move through well-defined stages, and past research suggests that evidence use varies across phases of the policy cycle. In this chapter, we focus on four distinct stages: 1) problem definition and promotion of a solution, 2) policy design, 3) policy enactment, and 4) initial implementation. We illustrate how patterns of evidence use shift across phases by examining the history of the Common Core.[1] Because the adoption and implementation of the Common Core has occurred at the state level, the next chapter analyzes evidence use in the four case study states—California, Indiana, Massachusetts, and Tennessee.

PROBLEM DEFINITION AND PROMOTION OF A SOLUTION

In his seminal work on agenda setting, John Kingdon details the interplay between disparate facts and their interpretation in the process of defining a given situation as a policy problem.[2] Indicator data or a body of research may, for instance, identify a problem—highway deaths are rising, childhood immunization rates are declining, program costs are increasing—or research might indicate that a current policy is not producing its intended effects. Typically, most members of a policy network will accept such research-based information as valid. At the same time, "there is a perceptual interpretative element" in defining policy problems.[3] That element is manifested in what data are highlighted and how they are interpreted, and in what factors are identified as causing the problem.

As Deborah Stone notes, problem definition is "the strategic representation of situations."[4] It is strategic and interpretative for several reasons. First, whether a given situation constitutes a policy problem depends on how participants perceive the discrepancy between the problem and some ideal state or social goal. What that goal is and the distance between its attainment and the status quo depend on their value preferences. Second, part of problem definition is identifying causes, and "to identify a cause in the polis is to place burden on one set of people instead of another."[5] How the cause is defined has direct implications for who will bear the costs of a policy and who will benefit from it. Therefore, those likely to be affected by a policy have a strong incentive to influence the selection and framing of relevant evidence. Finally, how a problem is defined shapes the policy solution proposed. So policy entrepreneurs promoting a particular policy option will select evidence that allows them to define a problem in such a way that their policy proposal becomes the preferred solution.

The nature of problem definition, then, suggests that although research results and indicator data play a role, other types of evidence may be equally important. These include appeals to values such as equality, liberty, and economic security. Metaphors may also be used to evoke strong political and cultural symbols (such as bureaucratic red tape or invasion of privacy).[6] Policy entrepreneurs also often try to put a human face on a problem through the use of anecdotes and other narrative devices.

The likelihood that a range of evidence will be used at this stage of the policy process increases for major policies that embody significant ideas. As we discussed in chapter 2, policy ideas are a special case of combining types of evidence, and they are particularly important when policy entrepreneurs are attempting to alter well-established policy monopolies. These dominant ideas have several advantages that allow their supporters to resist changes even when a policy is no longer producing its intended effects or is being challenged by competing ideas that embody alternative policy solutions. They are a) supported by powerful policy ideas that are connected to core political values, b) combine empirical information and emotive appeals, c) can be easily understood, and d) are communicated directly and simply through image and rhetoric. Over time, these conceptions of a policy problem and its appropriate solution become integrated into the operating assumptions of institutions, ranging from legislatures to individual schools. As such, they are reflected in how these agencies approach their organizational responsibilities and how they define new problems as they arise. Policy entrepreneurs can disrupt a policy monopoly and effect major change, but to do so they need to redefine the dominant policy image using ideas that challenge it and capture the imagination of the media, policymakers, and the public. Entrepreneurs provide new understandings of policy problems and new ways of conceptualizing solutions.[7]

A clear connection between problem definition and solution identification is critical if policy entrepreneurs are to be successful, and it requires an adroit use of evidence. Although the two tasks are related, they are also distinct. As Christina Wolbrecht and Michael Hartney wrote, "A policy problem defined one way may permit multiple, diverse solutions, and a particular policy solution might be applied to more than one policy problem or problem definition."[8] For this reason, policy entrepreneurs and their supporters need to combine and use evidence strategically in mounting an argument that is not only persuasive in convincing policy audiences a problem is serious and requires attention, but also that their preferred solution is the best option in addressing the problem.

In sum, the policy analysis literature suggests that during the problem definition and solution identification stage, research-based evidence is likely to be combined with evidence that appeals to elected officials' and their constituents' core values and evokes positive emotional responses. Normative evidence is especially important when the option being advocated embodies a significant idea and requires a major policy change. However, even in these cases, some evidence is necessary that demonstrates there is a reasonable likelihood the proposed policy option will result in the expected outcome.[9] That evidence may be selectively framed and interpreted, but it needs to be derived from systematically collected and analyzed data generally viewed as reliable and valid.

Common Standards: Defining the Problem and Promoting the Solution
The Common Core policy entrepreneurs identified their audience as the
national policy community—governors, chief state school officers, other state
officials, members of Congress, civil rights groups, foundations that might
support the effort, and the media. Their definition of the problem was strategically crafted to point to common K–12 standards across multiple states as
the solution. Together with the organizations they lead, governors Hunt and
Wise drew together findings from several lines of research to shape a clear
image of the policy challenge:

- The achievement of US students is low compared with the nation's
  global economic competitors.
- The US has an unacceptable achievement gap among students depending on their race and ethnicity, social class, and place of residence.
- US students leave high school inadequately prepared to succeed in
  college and employment.
- Countries with high achieving students have rigorous and coherent
  national standards.
- US standards vary considerably across states and are "a mile wide and
  an inch deep."
- Academic content standards common to multiple states are the solution
  to these problems.

Together with the proviso that the Common Core is an initiative led by
states for states, these arguments continued to form the essence of the Common Core rationale.

Although the competitiveness of the US in the global economy was central to the narrative, research showing dramatic variation among states came
to play an increasingly prominent role in the problem definition phase. An
NRC report sharpened the issues and brought two important lines of research
to the attention of the policy community.[10] One was research by Andrew Porter and his colleagues, a fine-grained analysis of thirty-one state standards in
three subjects, comparing state standards to each other and measuring their
alignment with the NCTM mathematics standards and the science standards
developed by the NRC. Focusing on topic coverage and the level of cognitive
demand, the researchers found little evidence to support the assumption that

a de facto national curriculum existed as a result of states' use of national documents such as the NCTM standards or the widespread adoption of similar textbooks. In fact, overlap in topic coverage across grade levels within the same state was greater than the alignment across states at the same grade level.[11] The conclusions that policy entrepreneurs drew from Porter's work were that there existed considerable state-to-state variability and substantial redundancy in current state standards. As one executive of an education interest group noted:

> [Porter's research] was part of the mix; I remember reading his report and his presenting it at a meeting. That was part of the backdrop. Politically, once things started to move, I'm not sure that work got cited in detail, but it comprised the intellectual backdrop that showed people that the fifty state standards were just not working—people may not have been able to cite the studies, but their impact came together so that the political people got a single message from the research, and they acted on that message.

This evidence of variability in content standards gained additional force as further research analyzed state-by-state variation in assessments and performance standards.[12] Mapping state proficiency standards in mathematics and reading for grades 4 and 8 onto the appropriate NAEP scale, researchers found that state differences in the percentage of students scoring at the proficient level on state assessments did not represent real differences in achievement as measured by NAEP, but reflected where a state set its proficiency levels. Most state cut points, moreover, fell below the equivalent of the NAEP proficient standard, and some even fell below the NAEP basic standard. A telling example, presented at the NRC workshop, was that a North Carolina student performing at the same level on the NAEP reading assessment as one in South Carolina would be deemed proficient in North Carolina, but performing at a basic level in South Carolina, with the possibility of having to attend a remedial class, because South Carolina's proficiency standard (cut score) was higher.[13] For advocacy groups supporting national standards, this discrepancy between student performance on state assessments and NAEP was powerful information to use in efforts to persuade state officials, because it contributed to a picture of states with significantly different, and typically low, expectations of students.

For governors and other state policymakers who wished to raise standards but faced potential opposition if students did not initially perform well on the higher ones, the idea of common standards provided political cover. Initial low student achievement on the more rigorous standards would be a shared political and educational challenge across multiple states. The data on differences between student scores on NAEP and those on state assessments had also come to the attention of members of Congress. According to a former Senate staffer:

> The first of those studies came out in 2007; I think the data from the NCES study intensified the focus on standards and heightened the concern with consistency from state to state and between state cut points and NAEP scores. At that time, the main concern was with these issues about the level of performance described as "proficient" and about the comparison to external benchmarks like NAEP rather than the content of the standards. There was a lot of interest in the gap—which could be eighty-five points on math—between a state cut point and NAEP. Several senators took up the question of standards, including Senator [Jeff] Bingaman [D-NM], who was preparing legislation, along with [Dick] Durbin [D-IL] and [Ted] Kennedy [D-MA], who were also very interested in rethinking NCLB.
>
> We began talking with the Chiefs [CCSSO] and NGA—mostly with the Chiefs—looking toward legislation that might move with the 2007 reauthorization of ESEA [the Elementary and Secondary Education Act]. There were clear political signals that legislation for national standards would be introduced if the Chiefs didn't move—I'm not sure that legislation was introduced, but we had drafted legislation with Senator Bingaman's office. Now that legislation died in 2007, but it did have the effect of moving the states toward common standards, and the Obama administration was able to pick up on that.

The case for common standards was crystallized in a report published by NGA, CCSSO, and Achieve.[14] Authored by an International Benchmarking Advisory Group, chaired by then-governor Janet Napolitano (Arizona), then-governor Sonny Perdue (Georgia), and Craig R. Barrett, the former chairman of the Intel Corporation board, the report drew heavily on research using data from the Programme for International Student Assessment (PISA) and

Trends in International Mathematics and Science Study (TIMSS).[15] The report focused on US students' low achievement as compared with international competitors, and documented the achievement gap separating US students from different socioeconomic backgrounds and the fact that the distribution of US students' scores puts the country among the most unequal in the world. It warned that "the United States is falling behind other countries in the resource that matters most in the new global economy: human capital."[16] The report recommended that states upgrade their standards "by adopting a common core of internationally benchmarked standards in mathematics and language arts for grades K–12 to ensure that students are equipped with the necessary knowledge and skills to be globally competitive."[17] The advisory group grounded its rationale for international benchmarking in William Schmidt's research on TIMSS, showing that standards in high performing countries are characterized by focus (fewer topics covered at greater depth), rigor, and coherence (an orderly progression of topics following the logic of the discipline and minimizing repetition).[18]

Evidence use during this phase of the CCSS process was quite consistent with what would be predicted by the policy research literature. The challenge for the entrepreneurs promoting national standards was to preserve the existing policy regime of standards and accountability while simultaneously seeking to dismantle one of the most deeply entrenched and strongest policy regimes in US education: the tradition of each state and its local districts deciding separately what students should be taught. In doing so, they had to define a set of problems to which their alternative policy idea was the solution. Research-based evidence was used to demonstrate that state-specific standards policies had resulted in considerable variability in curricular goals across states. Evidence of variability in content and performance standards across states, and differing levels of student achievement on standardized tests, was strong and generally accepted. There was, however, less agreement about the relationship between the two and the cause.[19]

The resulting need for interpretation allowed proponents to represent the situation strategically, attributing low achievement to states' variable and low-quality standards. Other researchers—especially those who study policy implementation—drew a different conclusion, emphasizing the lack of system capacity, especially supports for teachers and students.[20] They argued that the shortcomings documented in research findings are less the result of standards themselves than how policies have been implemented. Where the standards-based accountability ideal envisioned that curriculum and instructional materials, teacher training, and assessment would be closely coordinated, in practice the assessment portion had come to dominate and many schools lacked the capacity to bring all students to proficiency.[21]

These alternative inferences lead to different policy solutions, but all researchers could say with any certainty is that, at best, common standards might be a necessary but not sufficient condition for improved educational outcomes. The enabling conditions necessary for standards policies to work as envisioned are the various supports in which policymakers had underinvested in the past. Common Core advocates understood what researchers were telling them about enabling conditions. However, during this stage of the policy process, they chose to downplay them because they would complicate the agenda at a time when a policy window was opening but might not be open for long.[22] The Common Core's policy entrepreneurs also used research evidence strategically in how they framed its rationale, emphasizing global competitiveness because it carried great appeal among governors concerned about the economic health of their states—even though educators were less persuaded that this was a compelling reason for major curricular change. During this stage of the process, then, one particular set of inferences among the differing ones that could be drawn from research and indicator data was selected, and the inferences were framed in such a way as to persuade key policy audiences that common standards held the potential to rectify pressing educational and economic problems.

In one respect, the initial phase of the CCSS process differed from what happens typically when policy entrepreneurs define problems and promote solutions. The CCSS process did not rely heavily on the use of symbols and emotional appeals. Strongly held values, such as ensuring equality of educational opportunity and keeping the US globally competitive, were prominent in the discourse on national standards, and at one point, Governor Hunt likened the challenge to World War II.[23] However, perhaps because most of the appeals at this stage were to political elites and organizational leaders and not to the general public, data rather than symbols and stories were more prominent.

POLICY DESIGN

This stage of the policy process consists of technical tasks undertaken in a politicized context. A policy option has now moved to the decision agenda, and is being considered for formal enactment. At this point, legislative language is drafted, specifying such details as the funding mechanism and administrative arrangements. Legislative staff are primarily responsible for the work, and they draw on legal and fiscal expertise to ensure that the resulting language is consistent with existing policy and legislative authority. Related policies often serve as templates for how to structure the new policy. Staff may also draw on evaluations of past policies, and on research documenting the relationship between different types of intervention strategies and educational outcomes. Major sources of evidence at this stage are research, current and past policies, and the professional judgment of legislative and executive branch staff.[24]

The political context in which the details of a policy are developed has several implications for what additional evidence is used. First, those advancing the policy need to maintain support and blunt opposition. They also need to consider the interests and concerns of the agency staff and street-level bureaucrats who will be implementing the policy, and thus other evidence will come from these individuals and the groups that represent them. The evidence might be research findings and other data, if available, as well as professional judgment and personal experience. It can be presented formally in legislative hearings and also discussed in informal meetings with elected officials and their staffs. Often the most persuasive evidence will be local knowledge from an official's own constituents—for example, conversations with hometown educators about their classroom experience. A second political dimension involves timing. The opportunities for action on a policy proposal—the open policy window—may not be available for long.[25] Policy entrepreneurs, forced to move quickly before the window closes, may bring forward policy proposals that are not fully developed, and that miss or ignore evidence suggesting problems or unintended effects.

The evidence used at this stage, then, is less likely to include the type of normative and emotional arguments that are often central in the first stage. Evidence grounded in legal analysis, evaluation studies, and basic or applied research on the relationship between policy interventions and learning outcomes is likely to play a central role in drafting specific policy provisions. However, the political context means that less systematic sources of evidence are also considered, and that some research may be ignored.

Developing and Validating the CCSS

Because we drew on evidence use from the design phase of the CCSS as the primary illustrative example in chapter 2, we offer only a few conclusions here. The second stage of the CCSS process differed somewhat from the typical design phase of policymaking. The standards writers were not preparing legislation in the traditional sense, and states had only agreed to participate in a drafting process, not to adopt the new standards or even to put consideration of them on their decision agendas.[26] Nevertheless, to a considerable extent, standards development was akin to the policy design stage, and evidence use was similar. Political support had to be maintained, and the process had to move quickly to take advantage of an open policy window and opportunity for action. Grounding the standards as much as possible in research was an inspired political strategy that avoided not only past ideological controversies, but also the negotiations and horse trading that had led to bloated state standards in the past. At the same time, drawing on research ensured that the relationship between standards as a policy intervention and the desired goal of improved student learning was systematically considered during the development process, even if that relationship could not be completely and validly specified. As with policy design generally, development of the CCSS relied heavily on comparisons with current and past policies, evaluations of seemingly effective policies in other places, and on the professional judgment of those who would be responsible for implementing the policy.

POLICY ENACTMENT

The imperative at this stage is to build a minimal winning coalition in favor of the policy. So the evidence brought to bear is basically a reprise of what was used in the first stage to define the policy problem and promote a particular solution. However, because the policy has subsequently been developed from a general idea into a detailed legislative proposal, the evidence is likely to be more specific and to be targeted to address the questions and concerns of individual legislators, especially those who are still undecided about the policy.[27] At this point, legislators will continue to consult with relevant interest groups and constituents. But they will also look to colleagues who are experts in the policy domain (such as committee chairs) and to leaders of their partisan caucuses for cues about how to vote and for evidence to justify the vote.[28]

Political intelligence is a type of evidence, based largely on professional judgment, that is particularly useful during policy enactment. A policy's supporters and potential opponents are counting votes for its passage, and they need to identify which legislators are still undecided and what arguments or incentives are likely to convince them. In some cases, their support may depend on last-minute modifications to a bill (e.g., funding levels, funding formulas, or eligibility requirements), but sponsors need to avoid making changes at the expense of losing the votes of those who signed on to earlier versions of the legislation. Sponsors also draw on political intelligence in anticipating the arguments that potential opponents may make and how they might be refuted. Political intelligence comes from multiple sources: legislative leadership, staff, party officials, interest groups, the media, public opinion polls, and key local constituents. But political intelligence is also the product of political learning about how to use the institutional rules and norms of decision-making bodies to advantage, and is based on lessons gained from past legislative deliberations.

State Adoption of the Common Core State Standards

In most states, adoption of the CCSS to replace the state's existing standards required a vote by the state board of education (SBE) because of its authority over curriculum. Three factors explain the kinds of evidence that were used in anticipation of the SBE votes. First, the adoption stage was truncated. Even the Common Core's strongest supporters assumed that it would take three years or more for a majority of states to adopt the standards. They based that estimate on the extensive consultation and deliberation usually required when states adopt new content standards. However, the deadlines for the federal Race to the Top competition, which awarded up to seventy points (14 percent of the total) on applications from states that adopted common standards and assessments, meant the adoption process in most states was shortened to only a few months. Although the potential for federal funding prompted quick action by states, the Obama administration linked common standards to Race to the Top because its political intelligence indicated that the states were already supporting the Common Core. An Obama administration official noted:

> If we had not had confidence that there was a substantial coalition of states behind the standards process and that this was going along and likely to end up in a good place, we would not have put so much emphasis on this in Race to the Top. The fact that forty-four states were on board was very important . . . We were watching the process with a pretty high degree of confidence that it was coming together, and we were having conversations with states that were most involved, who (e.g., Roy Romer) were saying that we in the states can do this ourselves but we will need federal support. The CCSS are consistent with the administration's focus on international competitiveness. Also, having common standards allows a more consistent federal policy.

The process prior to state adoption often resembled a lobbying campaign targeted at individuals and groups who were likely to try to influence the SBE votes. Governors Hunt and Wise and the staffs of the Hunt Institute and All4Ed spent a year appearing at meetings of organizations such as the National Conference of State Legislatures and the Council of State Governments, and visiting individual states to persuade policymakers there.

CCSSO and NGA provided their constituents with a "messaging toolkit" that included answers to frequently asked questions, template letters to the editor, and a sample op-ed article that could be adapted depending on whether the author was a business leader, teacher, civil rights leader, or parent. The substance of these communication strategies highlighted central parts of the CCSS narrative: the focus on students' CCR preparation, US global competitiveness, the potential for commonality across states and local communities, the voluntary nature of state participation, and the inclusive state-led development process.[29]

The national educator, parent, education advocacy, and civil rights groups supporting the CCSS worked with their state affiliates and allies in providing information and other assistance. The policy entrepreneurs who had promoted the Common Core and the writers who had developed the standards made numerous appearances in states, briefing policymakers on the content and rationale for the CCSS. As a result, evidence during this phase was a version of the Common Core narrative that had been used in the first two stages, but now customized to various state audiences.

Federalism was a second factor shaping evidence use and requiring that it be tailored to particular states. Policymakers and the attentive public in states with especially rigorous standards had to be convinced that the CCSS were at least as rigorous as their current ones. So systematic, side-by-side analyses were prepared for a number of states, comparing the CCSS with state standards. In some instances, these were done by in-state agencies; in others, organizations such as Achieve and WestEd prepared the detailed comparisons showing topic and skill coverage arrayed by grade. To ensure commonality in the core of the standards across states, NGO and CCSSO required that states adopting the CCSS not change or delete standards. However, to accommodate some unique state preferences, they were allowed to add up to 15 percent additional standards to the CCSS math and ELA standards. In the preadoption phase, only three states—California, Massachusetts, and Montana—added standards.

Federalism was not only about ensuring that states could retain some measure of uniqueness even as they adopted common standards. It also meant that while states might accept the federal government as a supplemental funder of their standards and assessments, they would view its role quite differently if the federal government were seen to be driving the effort by incorporating the Common Core into the ESEA regulatory framework. Consequently, besides lobbying for state adoption, Common Core policy entrepreneurs had to ensure that the federal government maintained a respectful distance from the CCSS:

> We had one other role: to keep the federal legislators and policymakers informed, but out of it. The one time I thought this thing might sink was when newly elected president Obama had all the governors to the White House in conjunction with the national governors meeting, and he said something to the effect of "We might condition Title I dollars on this," and we immediately raised our concern and urged him not to be making those kinds of statements. And happily, he backed off.

A third factor was that except for a small group of CCSS opponents, there was little scrutiny of the research base during this stage. State policymakers and their staffs assumed that CCSSO and NGA had used the validation committee and other mechanisms to ensure that the CCSS had been adequately vetted and were grounded in relevant research. In addition, state education agency (SEA) staff, state teacher organizations, and other education-related groups knew that their colleagues had provided feedback, and that it was substantially reflected in the final standards. So trust in how the standards were developed, coupled with a fast-moving adoption process, meant that the research base was rarely a topic of discussion at the state level.

The adoption stage of the CCSS was generally consistent with what typically occurs during policy enactment, in that evidence was used primarily to mobilize decision-makers' support. However, instead of moving a policy proposal from a legislative committee to a floor vote, the CCSS were considered for adoption in more than forty states, each with slightly different information needs. Few state participants were concerned about the research supporting the CCSS. Rather, policymakers and groups whose members were likely to be affected by the CCSS wanted detailed comparisons between the Common Core and the state's status quo standards, and they sought persuasive arguments that the benefits would outweigh the substantial costs of such a major change.

IMPLEMENTATION

As policy is translated into practice, the main targets of evidence use shift from the officials who designed and enacted a policy to the practitioners who interpret its intent and embed activities consistent with that intent in the routines of schools and other agencies. Research-based evidence, largely drawn from studies of curriculum, school organization, and teaching and learning, is typically combined with educators' professional judgment and past experience about what works for their students, and with anecdotal evidence shared among fellow practitioners. Some implementation-related evidence can be communicated to educators by research producers such as universities that offer professional preparation and continuing education. Interest groups, such as the AFT, NEA, and their state and local affiliates, transmit information, synthesizing research studies and outlining their implications for the implementation of particular policies, while also providing venues where teachers can share their experience and collaborate on planning efforts.

State-level groups representing administrators and school boards provide similar types of information to their members. Local organizations representing parents, such as the PTA, La Raza, and the NAACP, typically focus their dissemination efforts on giving parents and other community members the informational tools to be knowledgeable participants in school activities and to ask questions of administrators and teachers about how policies are affecting their children. Third-party providers, in their role as translators and disseminators, often play a major role in the implementation of new policies. They typically work under contract to states and local districts adapting and introducing new curricular programs and engaging teachers and administrators in professional development.

Recent studies of research-practice linkages have focused on longer-term arrangements where research producers and consumers work collaboratively on projects aimed at improving educational practice and outcomes. The various terms describing this approach—*learning communities, research-practice partnerships, networked improvement communities*—all connote a shift in the central metaphor from consultation and one-way information dissemination to long-term partnerships.[30] To the extent that research-practice partnerships focus on implementation, like older forms of dissemination, they are informing what is essentially an administrative exercise—translating policies into street-level routines and seeking to understand sources of variation across local jurisdictions.

As a series of administrative actions focused on education practice, implementation varies substantially from policymaking. One difference stems from the time frame. The distinction between the two phases of the policy process in their time frames is not so much about length but pacing: one is episodic and the other more continuous. Although the history of a policy idea is usually a long one, the actual process of legislating and enacting is bounded and relatively brief. In this sense, policy enactment is often episodic—especially for major domestic policies—with proposals coming onto decision agendas, falling off or being rejected, and then reappearing in a different version years or even decades later. Earlier attempts to enact national standards and tests during the George H. W. Bush and Bill Clinton administrations, precursors to the Common Core are examples of an episodic policy falling off the agenda and reemerging twenty years later in a different guise. In contrast, policy implementation is a continuous process. It may be of short duration, taking a year or less. But for most policy change, particularly complex policies that involve fundamental alternations in the core mission and procedures of an agency, implementation takes much longer, with a time frame of several years or more. That time is spent putting in place the enacted policy, with variations resulting from how different implementers interpret it, not from changes in its formal provisions.

Differences between the time frames for enactment and implementation are reinforced by differences in the decision venues of each. Policy enactment is typically contained within one or two venues (e.g., the executive branch and Congress, or a state court and state legislature). Enactment or rejection results from decisions (e.g., committee and floor votes in a legislature) that are prescribed by a set of well-defined procedural rules and norms. The enactment process is by no means simple, and multiple veto points give the advantage to opponents of policy change—particularly in US politics where separation of powers systems at both national and state levels require the assent of legislative and executive branches.[31] Policymakers and their supporters have reasonable, although by no means complete, knowledge of how the process will unfold because of those institutional rules. Although the enactment stage is typified by relatively few decision venues, these venues vary in their visibility to outside observers and hence in the opportunities for monitoring by the media or the public. Depending on the policy, the process may be visible only to decision-makers and groups actively supporting or opposing it.[32] Even when a policy option is visible to the media and the public more generally, however, information about its costs and likely effects as well as political intelligence about prospects for its passage are typically concentrated in only a few sources that might include elected officials and their staff, interest groups, media, and academics.

The venues for implementation look quite different from those for enactment. The multiple levels of a federal system not only increase the number of venues but also foster more variation in the goals, processes, and vested interests involved at different governmental levels, geographic locations, and agencies. As it moves downward in the governmental system, a policy is no longer characterized by a limited number of up and down decisions made by a well-defined group of policymakers. Rather, implementers in different places and in an assortment of roles make many small decisions as they interpret and apply the policy and determine who is eligible for services and how those will be designed and delivered. Over time, these decisions by administrators and street-level bureaucrats aggregate and become embedded in agency policy and practice. Some of the effects of these many decisions are similar across venues, but some are quite localized depending on the commitment and capacity of the implementers. As a result of multiple implementing venues, each with its own unique participants and policy responses, implementation is more varied, more localized, and less predictable than enactment.

These institutional differences also mean that patterns of how research and other evidence are used also vary between policy and practice. Evidence use in policymaking typically follows well-defined milestones, marked by stages of the policy process. Most interactions between those providing evidence and their targets are episodic depending on the stage of the policy process. To the extent that sustained interactions occur, they typically happen prior to policy enactment, when research producers, policy entrepreneurs, IOs, and policymakers may collaborate, focusing on understanding longer-term problems with the hope that new policies can be designed and enacted in the future. The limited number of venues and the rules governing policy enactment also mean that the evidence communicated to decision-makers is available from a limited number of sources, most likely researchers and various IOs who testify before elected officials and work informally with staff.

In contrast, evidence use in education practice is a more continuous, but also more diffuse, process. Particularly in cases of research-practice partnerships or established relationships between third-party providers and local districts, various kinds of evidence are exchanged on an ongoing basis. However, the type, source, and quality of evidence are highly localized, varying across districts and schools. While the role of evidence in policymaking primarily depends on participants' political incentives or their will to transmit and use evidence, its use among practitioners often depends on local capacity to obtain appropriate research and other evidence and then to utilize it effectively. As we note in chapter 1, because of these significant differences, the model we outline only applies to the relationship between evidence and policy, and we assume that patterns of evidence use in education practice and the factors explaining them are different.

Nevertheless, we discuss implementation because there is another dimension to it in addition to being an integral part of education practice.

Implementation proceeds on two parallel trajectories: moving a policy from enactment into the ongoing routines of schools and classrooms, while also maintaining political support for the policy throughout a long and diffuse implementation process. Political sustainability and positive policy feedback are essential to the success of a policy. If political backing dissipates, the resources are unlikely to be available to support local implementation.

The essential challenge for advocates intent on sustaining a reform is keeping the enactment coalition united and mobilized during implementation. Implementation's longer time frame and multiple, diverse venues undermine the easy generation of supportive policy feedback. In addition, sustaining a new education policy is further complicated by the asymmetric flow of benefits and costs: promised benefits are often uncertain, diffuse, and far in the future (increased numbers of students prepared for postsecondary study, for example), whereas the costs are immediate and concentrated on a particular group such as classroom teachers. All these aspects of implementation have the effect of dissolving the glue that held the enacting coalition together and, at the same time, offering opposing interests new opportunities and the time to develop them.

Much of the evidence that a policy's supporters use to gauge its sustainability during implementation falls into the category of political intelligence—informal conversations with interest groups, other officials, and constituents; public opinion data; media accounts, including editorials; and social media traffic. However, not all the evidence that supporters (and opponents) draw on is informal or ad hoc. Studies of policy implementation and evaluation of the effects are also central to deciding not just on political tactics, but also on whether a policy requires substantive modifications to make it more effective. The research-based evidence useful to policymakers during implementation is at a more general level than what practitioners need. Policymakers require data that compares different types of local jurisdictions by broad categories such as resource levels and student characteristics, and identifies factors that explain any problems which may have arisen. In contrast, practitioners need deeper and more detailed analyses of what is working or not working in different types of classrooms within their own or similar districts. Studies that focus on policy information needs, as compared with those for practice, typically address different research questions with different units of analysis. However, these two purposes may be combined within the same study if these differing information requirements are understood and taken into consideration in the research design.

Implementing the Common Core from the National Level

Once the states had adopted the CCSS, its organizational supporters recognized that implementation would be a challenge, and that considerable attention and resources would be needed if the standards were to be translated successfully into classroom instruction. The president of a hybrid organization echoed the concerns of a number of her peers:

> My biggest worry is that way too many places are approaching implementation like they did the last time: workshops for teachers, where the typical teacher sits in the back of the room and goes "Yep, we can cross that off, they've covered that and that; haven't covered that yet." . . . The whole organization, the whole gestalt doesn't get absorbed. And I think if we leave as much of the load on individual classroom teachers to figure out, we're dead.

The national organizations that had promoted the Common Core understood that its implementation would depend primarily on the willingness and capacity of local educators and their communities along with some guidance from state education agencies. However, in the early stages, there were tasks that could best be accomplished at the national level. These included communicating how the CCSS should be interpreted, providing guidance to public and private providers of instructional materials, and encouraging cross-state collaborations.

Because the development of the Common Core had occurred quickly and with little public visibility, communicating its meaning to educators, parents, and the public was a critical first step. For educators, "there's the communication component—information, building buy-in, explaining how this is different from anything they may have done before." The availability of foundation funding meant that national organizations representing parents and local community groups had resources to design strategies for communicating the substance and intent of the CCSS:

> With a grant from Gates, we are putting together teams to work with community constituents, to develop systems for communicating from the top

down and the bottom up, with the goal of improving local understanding of CCSS, and involving community constituents in implementation.

—Vice president, hybrid organization

The greatest challenge we face as we move to implementation is introducing and explaining the standards to our parent members ... Our parents want to know what's in the standards, but they aren't going to read through them. We have worked with the standards writers, and by asking them questions we were able to get answers to the sort of questions our members have. We also learned who the right messengers were—not NGA, CCSSO, or other top-down groups, but parents and teachers. A military mom in Florida, or a mom in Mississippi, who could tell their stories and show the advantages of common state standards.

We have made a Common Core video, featuring our military mom and a teacher. Our chapters are showing the video and having conversations. In addition, we have developed parent guides, one for each grade, working with two of the standards writers. The drafting of these guides was meticulously wordsmithed, word by word—what is expected of students, what parents can do, questions and topics to help talk to your child's teacher. The guides are also available in Spanish.

—Advocacy group staff member

Concerned that publishers would release instructional materials alleged to be aligned with the Common Core but with no basis for evaluating that claim, Student Achievement Partners, a nonprofit established by several of the standards writers, issued a set of "publishers' criteria" designed to ensure that materials were consistent with the mathematics and ELA standards. These criteria were issued under the auspices of NGA, CCSSO, Achieve, the Council of the Great City Schools, and the National Association of State Boards of Education (NASBE). The evidence base is the standards themselves, and the criteria operationalize major concepts that constitute essential elements of the Common Core. So, for example, in outlining key criteria for selection of texts, choice of classroom tasks and questions, and student writing to sources and research, the ELA document stresses the components of text-dependent analysis, the appropriate balance among types of texts by grade levels, and materials that portray writing to sources as a central task. Similarly, the criteria for K–8 mathematics outline ten criteria to be applied in preparing and selecting materials and tools aligned to the standards. Each of these criteria operationalize central concepts such as coherent progressions in the standards, rigor and balance, and attention to mathematical reasoning.[33] Speaking as members of the Council of the Great City Schools, some of the largest local districts in the country pledged to purchase only materials that met the publishers' criteria.[34]

To aid in the production of instructional materials aligned with the Common Core, several foundations, with Gates as the primary funder, supported a number of translation and dissemination organizations. The combination of research, past experience, and professional judgment that these groups drew upon is discussed in chapter 3. They produced materials ranging from curriculum maps, where each included the relevant focus standard, sample activities, and lesson plans; formative assessments; structures for professional development; and instructional tools such as software for creating new curriculum modules and templates that could be customized for ELA instruction across different subject areas. These materials were produced with the active involvement of classroom teachers, and Gates also funded five SEAs and twenty local districts to assist in the design of the materials and to act as implementing sites for materials already developed.[35]

One of the rationales for the CCSS was that similar standards across multiple states would lead to economies of scale and interstate collaboration. As a way to foster that process, several national organizations representing state officials began convening their members to discuss Common Core implementation. One example was CCSSO's State Collaborative on Assessment and Student Standards (SCASS). It began in 2011, involved thirty-three states, and was based on a coaching model with six former chief state school officers or deputies working with the senior leadership of each participating SEA. Discussing his role in 2011, after the group had met twice, one of the coaches explained:

> The information these states need at this point is problem-solving information about implementation. The buckets we used include: instructional materials, with PD [professional development] organized around that; a communications bucket; a transition planning bucket, which we have

been dealing with early in the process; and an assessment bucket. States are in different places—some states are already looking at assessment. We coaches are not putting things into the buckets, the states are—but we as coaches are making sure that they pay attention to all the buckets, especially to transition and communication. The SCASS is trying to help states do system-changing within the state department as part of Common Core Standards, and that role is part of the coaching.

During the initial years of the Common Core implementation, the SCASS coaches would check in with the senior leadership of SEAs every few weeks, and CCSSO established an online collaboration site where states could pose questions and share documents.[36] Not surprisingly, when faced with the practical challenges of CCSS implementation, SEA staff relied primarily on professional judgment combined with their policy learning and that of their colleagues drawn from past experience implementing education reform.

From the perspective of research-based evidence, one aspect of the Common Core's implementation has been especially notable. Researchers mobilized quickly to begin studying the process by which the CCSS was being implemented at the state and local levels. In the four years between 2011 and 2015, twelve articles were published in three of the American Educational Research Association's highest impact journals on such topics as the alignment of textbooks with the Common Core, the language demands of the CCSS on English language learners, and the potential effect of text complexity on young readers.[37] The scope of the CCSS as a major policy initiative and the availability of foundation funding partly explain the speed with which research on the Common Core commenced. However, another significant development made such research possible. In focusing on the new standards, researchers were building on several decades of studies of standards and assessments, curriculum content and instructional strategies, policy implementation, and program evaluation. The findings from this body of research provided analysts with the theories, empirical insights, and analytical tools to examine a new generation of education reforms.

Three examples illustrate how Common Core research was able to build on past investments. Although these studies have implications for practice, our main purpose in focusing on them is to show how their findings can inform decisions that policymakers and national IOs make about facilitating state- and local-level implementation. The first study examines textbook alignment with the Common Core, one of the most serious challenges of moving the standards into classroom instruction. Using the Surveys of Enacted Curriculum (SEC), a content taxonomy that was developed over a decade to analyze mathematics content based on topic coverage and level of cognitive demand, Morgan Polikoff measured the alignment of seven fourth-grade mathematics texts with the CCSS. Although the majority of the standards are covered in the three texts claiming to be aligned with the Common Core, there are significant areas of misalignment. The textbooks systematically overemphasize procedures and memorization and underemphasize more conceptual skills as compared with their emphasis in the CCSS.[38] This study and similar ones confirmed CCSS supporters' concerns about the validity of publishers' claims, but it also suggested how content analyses to assess these claims might be conducted efficiently on behalf of state and local officials.

A second study tests two assumptions of the national organizations in implementing the Common Core: that SEAs would play a central role in providing curriculum and professional development resources to local districts, and that the standards would lead to collaboration among states and third-party providers. It uses social network analysis to examine the secondary ELA resources provided by fifty-one SEAs and 262 IOs during 2015–16. The results present an overview of the Common Core's early implementation from the state-level perspective. The researchers found that a quarter or more of the SEAs were linked to CCSSO, NGA, the Council of the Great City Schools, and NASBE. In addition to these national membership organizations, 25 percent of the SEAs included online links to third-party providers such as Student Achievement Partners and the Public Broadcasting Service (PBS). At least 10 percent of SEAs included a link to a resource provided by IOs such as ASCD, the National Writing Project, the NEA, and the Hunt Institute, and five states had five or more other SEAs linked to their online resources. However, for most of the IOs in the study sample, only one SEA provided a resource from that organization, and seven states were isolates unconnected to others in the network. The study also found that the majority of online resources SEAs provided were conceptual rather than practical in their content, consisting of professional development and curriculum guidelines rather than actual lesson or unit plans.[39] Although primarily descriptive, this study presents timely research-based evidence that has implications for both policy and practice.

Using a quasiexperimental design, a third study assessed the Literacy Design Collaborative (LDC), an IO funded by Gates. LDC built upon the concept of *mutual adaptation*, one of the major tenets derived from decades of past implementation research. With a template-based approach, LDC tools provide scaffolding to ensure alignment with the ELA standards, while also giving teachers the flexibility to design curricula that work for their own classrooms and schools. The study focuses on two sites: eighth-grade social studies and science teachers in districts across Kentucky, and sixth-grade advanced reading classes in a large Florida urban district. Data included twice-weekly teacher logs, an end-of-year teacher survey, a rubric-based analysis of the quality of the module artifacts, and student scores on the statewide assessments. Matched samples of control students were drawn from outside the treatment districts. The study found that overall in the two sites, the LDC was implemented with a reasonable level of fidelity, although implementation quality varied across teachers. Students and teachers in the study districts were engaged with Common Core content, and teachers viewed the usefulness of the LDC positively. Early (2012–13) student test results were modest and mixed, with moderate gains in only one of the sites, and lower ability students struggled to meet the CCSS-aligned demands.[40]

Because researchers—building on past work—were able to mobilize quickly, Common Core implementation studies were conducted in close to real time, and national-level implementors were provided with timely research-based evidence on the effectiveness of their strategies for translating the CCSS into classroom instruction. Consequently, although national supporters of the Common Core recognized that its implementation would most likely be more complex and challenging than states' earlier implementation of their own standards, they had the advantage of policy learning based on research and past experience.

In contrast, there was less guidance available for how to ensure the political sustainability of the Common Core. In the majority of states, its adoption had been quick and noncontroversial, with little media attention or public knowledge.[41] As a result, some analysts have argued that "Common Core advocates failed to anticipate the political backlash and to respond to it in a rapid or coordinated manner."[42] However, by September 2010—even before some states had adopted the CCSS—the major national organizations supporting the standards were participating in weekly conference calls (designated as "advocacy partner calls") to keep each other informed about their activities, and to plan responses to emerging opposition to the Common Core in individual states and on social media. Spreadsheets were prepared showing the planned activities of the twelve IOs regularly participating in the conference calls. In addition, information was gathered and shared about the CCSS-related activities of twenty-seven other national organizations that did not regularly participate in the conference calls, but were involved with constituents in supporting the standards. These included organizations representing higher education institutions, subject-matter associations, special-needs students, business leaders, state officials, and cross-state education networks (such as the Policy Innovators in Education (PIE) Network, representing state-level education advocacy organizations). They were engaged in a variety of activities to unpack the CCSS for their constituents through webinars, videos, policy briefs, workshops, and implementation pilots in several states. Questions were often raised in the conference calls about where best to place implementation materials for teachers, while at the same time, the partners expressed concern about the growing number of instructional materials that were unvetted but whose developers claimed they were aligned with the Common Core.

One major source of evidence that was shared was political intelligence about states where backlash was beginning to develop. Besides staying in contact with in-state supporters, the advocacy partners monitored traditional media sources and online dialogue. The consensus was that the overwhelming majority of media articles were neutral, with the remainder evenly balanced between ones that were primarily negative or positive in content. The continuing question for the groups during the first half of 2011 was whether they should respond to opposition messages when not many members of the public were aware of them. At the same time, they recognized that such messages could "catch fire, so we always want to take them seriously."

Two issues were continuing topics of discussion during the conference calls in 2011. One was growing backlash in several states, and awareness that the sources of opposition and the venues where it was being mobilized varied from state to state. In some, it was coming from Republican Party organizations, in others from groups loosely affiliated with the Tea Party. In some states, the initiative to move away from the Common Core was centered in the governor's office, in others, in the legislature or the state board.

Consequently, the advocacy partners understood that responses to the opposition needed to be customized to each state. However, the interstate informational networks that organizations such as CCSSO established allowed state officials supporting the standards to share strategies:

> There has been a core of states who have had these political issues. And there will be conversations among state delegations. So, for example, Alabama and New Hampshire both had huge pushbacks from the Tea Party, and sharing ideas between them was helpful—e.g., involving the military was a big one, identifying who the visible military leaders were in New Hampshire who could speak out in favor of the Common Core. So I think connecting states with each other is important.

The second concern related to the actions of the Obama administration. The CCSS policy entrepreneurs recognized that without the administration's award of $350 million to the Smarter Balanced Assessment Consortium (SBAC) and the Partnership for Assessment of Readiness for College and Careers (PARCC) for the development of assessments aligned with the Common Core, states—lacking resources to design new tests—would likely continue to use their current, unaligned assessments to meet NCLB requirements. Yet the advocates also realized that federal funding could fuel opposition claims. The conference call participants discussed whether they should be concerned about the Obama administration using the CCSS "shield" in the NCLB application waiver process. The participants questioned whether they should continue to distance themselves or let public recognition that the federal government supported the CCSS "die" without further intervention on their part. In a fall 2011 call, one participant argued that "President Obama is a toxic brand for many, so keeping the drum beat going about 'state-led' helps us. If we switched to say the federal government supports, it would open the door too far and help the opposition. There is danger in moving away from the state-led language." Other participants agreed, and the recurring message was that "you can't say state-run, state-led enough."

At the same time, they stressed another message: it's "good to emphasize that these standards are based on research and evidence, and built on what states have been doing previously." However, it was clear from their discussions that as IOs, the organizational representatives were much more

confident acting on political intelligence than basing their arguments in support of the CCSS on its claimed research base.[43]

The Common Core policy entrepreneurs recognized early on that standards shared by multiple states would pose serious challenges, and in the
analysis the Hunt Institute requested of the NRC committee in 2007, it asked
that researchers examine the financial, legal, and political feasibility of common standards. The political feasibility analysis drew on interviews with
policymakers in five states, a review of state processes for approving K–12
standards, the political history of state standards, and inferences drawn from
political science and policy analysis. It concluded:

> We now have two decades' experience with standards and related policies,
> so common standards advocates can benefit from a better understanding
> of the political pitfalls of this policy strategy and how to avoid them. At
> the same time, they will need to keep in mind that whatever form common
> standards may take, they are very likely to have a unique profile within
> each state. Because federalism is a powerful idea, buttressed by a variety of
> state and local institutions and the interests that support them, the com-
> mon standards movement is unlikely to change this defining characteristic
> of U.S. education policy.[44]

Although the analysis laid out the political opportunities and constraints
that common standards might encounter, the analysis was completed before
the standards were developed, so it could not take into consideration the
likely political impact of that process or the significant changes in the partisan makeup of state governments as a result of the 2010 election.

A few analysts recognized early in the Common Core's implementation
that the larger political environment could threaten its political sustainability
if either national or state-level interests created spillovers from politics and
policies outside education. So, for example, writing in 2011 before the Common Core had become a politically visible issue, a researcher scanned the
larger political environment and suggested that "public school curriculum
has long been a rallying point for cultural conservatives, and one could imagine this issue being joined to the Tea Party movement if taxes and health care
begin to lose their mobilizing force."[45] This prediction found support in some
venues. However, for state policies such as the CCSS, the national political

environment affects states and localities differently, depending on the extent to which groups choose to use national conditions as a basis for state-specific strategies.

Most studies of the Common Core, however, were not predictive, and instead sought explanations for the opposition only after it became widely visible in 2012. They confirmed the downsides of two significant trade-offs that Common Core advocates had acknowledged but had underestimated—namely, focusing primarily on political elites in advancing the standards and largely ignoring the public to avoid losing a window of political opportunity, and accepting federal support to speed up the design of CCSS-aligned assessments. In an examination of nineteen interest groups supporting the Common Core, Jonathan Supovitz and Patrick McGuinn found that only six of them included the public as a target audience for their messages even in late 2013 and early 2014, at the height of opposition to the CCSS. Interest group representatives also acknowledged that the quick adoption of the Common Core by states and several years of seeming low-key support had lulled the groups into not understanding the need for an aggressive, preemptive public campaign, and that unlike CCSS opponents, who used social media skillfully as a mobilization strategy, the supporters were still relying on more passive informational strategies.[46]

Several other studies identified the extent to which opposition to the standards focused not on the content of the Common Core, but on broader ideological issues such as the appropriate role of the federal government, and on related education policies that became attached to the CCSS, including the amount of required testing under NCLB, teacher evaluations, and data privacy. As the partisan composition of state governments changed, opposition to the Common Core became a test of Republican party loyalty, as reflected in the number of negative CCSS-related bills introduced in a number of state legislatures. Although bills critical of the Common Core were introduced in a majority of legislatures, only four states that had initially adopted the standards subsequently enacted legislation to abandon them.[47]

Another source of evidence for gauging the political sustainability of the Common Core was surveys of the public and teachers. Not surprisingly, given the low level of public outreach and limited media attention, 62 percent of the general public and 55 percent of public school parents reported in 2013 that they had never heard of the CCSS. One year later, after media coverage had become more prominent, 47 percent of a national sample of the public reported having heard "a great deal" or "a fair amount" about the CCSS, and those having heard nothing had declined to 19 percent.[48] During this same period when groups opposed to the Common Core were most active and visible, public support for the standards fell and became more polarized. For example, in the *Education Next* annual survey, 65 percent of the general public supported the standards in 2013, with that percentage falling to 53 percent in 2014, and significant differences in the level of opposition evident between Democrats (17 percent) and Republicans (37 percent) with intraparty differences among Republicans (57 percent support from "moderate" Republicans as compared with 38 percent among those describing themselves as "conservative").[49] However, even as the CCSS became more visible and respondents reported greater awareness of it, deeper survey probes suggested that their actual knowledge of it was shallow, and their perceptions did not match the Common Core's stated principles. In 2014, the *Education Next* survey asked the 43 percent of its respondents who reported having heard of the CCSS several true/false factual claims. Only 36 percent recognized "The federal government requires all states to use the Common Core" as a false statement; even fewer (15 percent) recognized as a false statement that the federal government would receive detailed data on student test performance in states using the Common Core.[50] *Education Next* also found, using a split sample, that when respondents were asked about support or opposition "to standards for reading and math that are the same across the states" without mentioning the Common Core label, support increased to 68 percent as compared with 53 percent when the CCSS label was included in the question.[51] This finding suggests that public support for the policy idea of standards shared across multiple states remained strong, but that public perceptions of the Common Core had shifted as controversy and opposition had grown.

Although research on the political sustainability of education reforms is less extensive and robust than studies of the administrative and educational aspects of implementation, it suggests two implications for how evidence can be used effectively. First, policy entrepreneurs and analysts need to consider systematically the potential downstream effects of decisions made during enactment that may pose trade-offs during implementation. This exercise requires a nuanced understanding of the current political and policy context, but also a retrospective examination of similar past policies and their policy feedback as a basis for hypothesizing about the likely course of a current policy.[52] Minimal opposition during the low visibility development process led advocates to underestimate the continuing power of related policies (e.g., assessment and accountability) to overwhelm perceptions about the instructional benefits of the Common Core once it became more visible to teachers and the public. The emphasis on "research and evidence" and on "state-led" reflected policy learning, but the CCSS policy entrepreneurs did not sufficiently weight either the negative backlash against NCLB or the longtime suspicion of federal government activism by a sizable segment of the public.

A second implication relates to reliance on political intelligence. It can be a reliable source of evidence for policymakers and IOs, but it typically provides discrete pieces of information from which it may be difficult to identify broader patterns or link to developing trends. As a result, actions based on such information are often reactive and disjointed, as evidenced by the Common Core supporters' responses to opponents' strategic assaults.

The CCSS experience suggests that policy entrepreneurs need to combine political intelligence with other types of evidence, including research grounded in political science and policy analysis, and that advocates should devise comprehensive, proactive outreach strategies. At the same time, the advocacy partners correctly recognized the necessity of state-specific responses, because even an overall national strategy requires adaptation to specific state contexts. Federalism, especially in education policy, means that political processes and the interests that influence them will vary across states, even when they are enacting and implementing similar policies.

CONCLUSION

Table 4.1 summarizes the "what" and "who" of evidence use over stages of the Common Core policy process, and it illustrates the more general relationship between the central political and instrumental objectives of each phase and how they shape choices about evidence use.

At each stage, decision-makers and IOs used research to inform their work. However, one or more elements integral to the main goal of each phase led them to combine research with other types of evidence. In the problem definition stage, advancing a particular policy solution requires that the problem be defined strategically so the policy entrepreneurs' preferred policy option is viewed by decision-makers as the best solution. Because data and research results can often be interpreted in multiple ways, the Common Core policy entrepreneurs and their supporters could emphasize an interpretation that framed the primary problem as one of weak and disparate content standards, rather than inadequate resources or inattention to the full range of necessary conditions to support improved student learning. To enhance the persuasive power of the research evidence, it was framed around the normative values of global economic competitiveness and education equity.

Ensuring that a policy proposal will work as intended provides a strong incentive for those charged with its design to draw heavily on valid and reliable research. The types of research most needed at this stage are empirical studies that assess the effectiveness of different education strategies in achieving a desired policy goal, such as more equitable student learning opportunities. In addition, results from policy analysis research are necessary to address issues related to the administrative, resource, and political feasibility of different policy design options. A significant element is research that can contribute to policy learning—understandings based on past policy successes and failures. For the Common Core, studies of teaching and learning and the organization of curriculum content were central. Current standards from states with rigorous ones and from countries with high achieving students augmented research-based evidence as a source of how standards operate in practice and as benchmarks to assess the rigor of the Common Core while it was being developed. Analyses of past attempts to develop national standards and ideological debates over the content of state standards led to policy learning, and to a resulting approach that emphasized research and evidence-based standards developed through a state-led initiative.

While the desire to persuade and the possibility of multiple interpretations motivate the melding of research with other evidence during the problem definition stage, the limitations of extant research require using additional evidence in the policy design phase. Two types were especially important for the CCSS. First, the professional judgment of teachers, employers, higher education faculty, and SEA personnel informed decisions about what standards should be included and how they should be organized. Second, where the learning trajectory research was weak or incomplete, inferences were drawn from theory and past empirical research.

TABLE 4.1   Common Core evidence use, by stages of the policy process

STAGE OF THE POLICY PROCESS	POLICY DECISION/ISSUES	DECISION-MAKERS
Defining the problem/ promoting standards as the solution	Memo committing to work together on common standards (48 states)	State governors (NGA) and state education leaders (CCSSO)
Policy design/ developing the standards	From College and Career Ready to draft Common Core Standards	▪ Standards writers ▪ Reviewers and validation committee ▪ State officials, especially re conditions for adoption
Policy enactment/ adoption	State-by-state adoption	State Boards of Education
Implementation	▪ Translate CCSS into curriculum for classroom instruction ▪ Maintain political support	▪ State and local officials ▪ School administrators and classroom teachers

Similar to the problem definition phase, persuasion is the dominant objective at the adoption stage, as policy entrepreneurs and their decision-maker allies seek to build a winning coalition for enactment. For the most part, the compilation of evidence used earlier in the policy process can be highlighted once again, and officials new to the deliberations will often defer to knowledgeable colleagues and trusted IO representatives on the assumption that they have adequately reviewed the evidence in recommending for

INTERMEDIARIES	HOW EVIDENCE WAS USED
■ Policy entrepreneurs, such as former governors Hunt and Wise ■ Education advocacy groups and hybrids (Achieve, Alliance, Fordham, among others)	■ Show wide variability in student outcomes (comparing US to other countries and comparing among states) ■ Interpret data to suggest weak content and low performance standards ■ Focus on data and research, but also appeal to values of global competitiveness and education equity
■ NGA and CCSSO ■ State and local education officials ■ Teacher unions and civil rights groups (advocacy organizations)	■ Develop CCR standards: survey faculty and employers ■ Define CCSS process: research- and evidence-based, state-directed ■ Draw on research: syntheses, expert panels, subject matter specialists ■ Compare with current policy: rigorous state and international standards ■ Use other evidence where research record was incomplete ■ Meld different types of evidence: professional judgment, theoretical and empirical inferences
■ NGA and CCSSO ■ Advocacy organizations, e.g., teacher unions, parent organizations, civil rights groups ■ Foundations	■ Detailed comparison to existing state standards ■ "Messaging tool kit" ■ Advocacy groups: articulate constituency concerns and build support in state ■ Foundations: fund CCSS initiatives and build networks ■ Context: truncated time frame, allowance for state-level variation ■ Relied on CCSSO and NGA, plus CCSS review and validation process; little detailed independent scrutiny of evidence
■ Third-party providers ■ Research producers ■ Advocacy organizations and hybrids	■ Design and vet curriculum materials and professional development resources ■ Identify and respond to sources of opposition

adoption. However, one new piece of evidence is often required, even for officials generally willing to accept the judgment of their more expert colleagues. That evidence focuses on how the policy under consideration will affect a policymaker's own constituents—Will benefits outweigh costs for them? Will they have adequate resources to do what the policy requires? How much change from status quo policies will be required of them? Is opposition likely to emerge? In the case of the Common Core, this latter information requirement explains the centrality of side-by-side analyses comparing a state's current standards with the CCSS. State board trust in SEA personnel, the standards writers, and IOs with connections to national groups, combined with the time pressures imposed by the Race to the Top application process, explain why most state officials accepted CCSSO-NGA assurances that the Common Core is grounded in research and evidence.

The dual objectives of the implementation phase—translating policy into street-level practice and sustaining it politically—dictate that research-based evidence be combined with the professional judgment of implementors and with political intelligence gathered from multiple perspectives. As we will see in the next chapter, the four case study states all were able to ground their initial CCSS implementation plans, at least to some extent, in research. However, the sources that Common Core supporters relied on for political intelligence varied considerably across states, as did their political skill in acting on them.

5

Adopting and Implementing the Common Core at the State Level

Four Comparative Cases

DESPITE TAKING DIVERGENT PATHS during the implementation of the Common Core, adoption of the standards in California, Indiana, Massachusetts, and Tennessee shared similar characteristics. The speed of the process was dictated by policymakers' desire in the four states to compete for Race to the Top funds. Although the state board of education (SBE) in each state was the ultimate adopting authority, other state institutions and groups were active participants in the process. Decision-makers largely accepted the CCSSO's and NGA's assurances, and those of the national groups supporting the Common Core, that it was research and evidence based. The new information needed in each state was an evidence-based argument that the Common Core was an improvement over the state's current standards. However, these commonalities during the adoption phase did not predict the course of the Common Core's implementation in each state.

Rather, much of the variation across states in their implementation of standards, including the financial resources and expertise devoted to the effort, can be traced back to differing levels of political support, and to policies that interact with the Common Core and define a state's broader education reform agenda. In the case of the four states we examined in detail, factors explaining whether the Common Core has been politically sustainable largely account for its status a decade later. We selected the four states to ensure variation in region, partisan makeup, and success in securing a Race to the Top grant. However, our sample is not representative, and became less so over time when Indiana and Tennessee decided to abandon the Common Core as their state standards—two of only five states to do so. Nevertheless, together these four states can tell us much about how political and policy contexts affect implementation, how those contexts can be manipulated to shape implementation outcomes, and how the relationship between research producers and state education officials affects the types of evidence available during implementation.[1]

CALIFORNIA

The course of the Common Core in California has been one of contrasts. Its adoption was highly politicized: the state commission charged with reviewing the standards only recommended their adoption at the last possible date in a dramatic cliff-hanger. Yet Common Core implementation in the state has encountered little political controversy, and the policy has enjoyed public support. California has a history of adopting education reforms and then abandoning or significantly altering them. However, its implementation of the CCSS has been stable. The standards are on their way to being institutionalized, continuing into the administration of a new governor, with California one of only a minority of states retaining the same Common Core–aligned assessment that it first administered. The California Department of Education (CDE) lacks sufficient capacity in its budget and staffing to assist local districts in the implementation process, but, partly compensating for this shortfall, the process has been well-informed because of the high capacity of research producers committed to studying implementation.

Adopting the Common Core

As in other states, the adoption process in California was truncated because of the short time between when the CCSS were completed and when Race to the Top applications were due.[2] In a compromise between Republican governor Arnold Schwarzenegger and the Democratic majority legislature, legislation establishing an Academic Content Standards Commission was enacted in January 2010. With twenty-one members—eleven appointed by the governor, five by the state's Senate Committee on Rules, and five by the

Speaker of the Assembly—the majority were to be classroom teachers. The commission's charge was to develop academic content standards in language arts and mathematics, with "at least 85 percent of these standards ... the common core academic standards developed by the consortium or interstate collaboration."[3] In essence, the commission was to review the CCSS and present to the SBE a recommendation for either adoption or rejection; the commission had the option of including up to 15 percent additional standards if it wished. Because of the delay in the public unveiling of the CCSS, appointment of the commission members was not completed until early June, with their recommendation due to the SBE no later than July 15. Consequently, the commission had only six days of meetings in which to review the standards.

The potential adoption of the CCSS presented the state with a political opportunity. But there were sensitivities around the mathematics standards that had to be addressed before the opportunity could be grasped. As one commission member explained:

> Without CCSS, California was going to be stuck with its old standards for a very long time. And those standards had pretty much reached the end of their useful life ... Gary Hart [former state senator and secretary of education] had tried to kick-start the state into revisions to the standards a couple years earlier and that just went nowhere. Because of the math wars, people were very afraid of the subject and afraid to get started again on the fight. They thought revisions would lead to the math wars again and we would be better off staying with the standards and not tinker with them.

However, two members of the commission had been instrumental in drafting the earlier standards, and they opposed the mathematics Common Core because they argued that, unlike the state's own standards, it did not require that all students should have the requisite skills to take algebra by the end of the seventh grade. This controversy had continued in California for over a decade, with the California Teachers Association (CTA) and the Association of California School Administrators suing the SBE for not adequately informing the public before mandating that, beginning in 2011, the Algebra I end-of-course exam was to be the sole test of record for measuring eighth graders' mathematical skills. The teachers on the commission reflected the position of the CTA in not wanting to approve standards requiring that all students, even unprepared ones, take algebra in the eighth grade. In contrast, Governor Schwarzenegger's office viewed standards linked to preparation for algebra in the eighth grade as critical:

> A particular point of controversy for us was algebra in eighth grade. The math standards in CCSS did not lead to algebra in the eighth grade. So for California, that would have been a step backwards. That was a particular issue that was problematic for the governor's office. Our general impression was that the ELA were okay. There were some modifications. There were some issues or things that needed to be tweaked. But generally, they were aligned with California's level of achievement that we were expecting. It was the math standards that were different—they were sequenced differently and they didn't have the series of steps needed to get to the potential for eighth grade algebra. We accepted that not every student is going to take eighth grade algebra, but we want it to be possible. We wanted the curriculum and standards to lead to, if it is possible, to eighth grade algebra. Students who were ready should be able to take the course.

Commission members who supported the CCSS took seriously the admonition from the governor's office, but they were also committed to adopting new state standards they viewed as necessary:

> The governor's office told us basically if we didn't have algebra standards for eighth grade, they would veto the whole thing and none of it would go forward. In order for California to qualify for Race to the Top funds, it had to go forward. I think a lot of people on the commission, including me, were interested in the standards because we needed new standards. We didn't care much about Race to the Top, but we really needed to update our standards. We had a real interest in CCSS going forward. I don't think Race to the Top qualitatively changed or impacted the adoption process. It just gave us a deadline that we had to meet.

Faced with the pressure from the governor's office and the strong opposition of Williamson Evers and Ze'ev Wurman, the two commissioners pressing for rejection of the mathematics standards, the other commissioners used the 15 percent rule to recommend that, consistent with the current California standards, the CCSS should also set the goal that eighth-grade students complete Algebra I, but they recommended that the standard also include a separate prealgebra track for students lacking the prerequisite skills for Algebra I.[4] The commission also shifted some CCSS mathematics standards from the eighth to the seventh grade and from the seventh to the sixth grade to strengthen students' preparation for Algebra I. The CTA leadership and some commission members expressed concern that allowing for both algebra and prealgebra courses in eighth grade would result in tracking low-income students and students of color. A county superintendent member of the commission, Charles Weis, acknowledged this possibility, but promised he would work to prevent tracking and argued that the Common Core would likely help prepare more students for algebra in the eighth grade.[5] Late in the evening of July 15, the members of the commission, with two dissenting votes from Evers and Wurman, approved the revised CCSS mathematics standards.[6]

Although the commission spent considerably more time discussing the ELA standards (four and a half days as compared with one and a half for mathematics), they were approved unanimously with a few additions under the 15 percent rule.[7] These include: "formal presentations" in the Speaking and Listening Standards, "penmanship" in the Language Standards, "career and consumer documents" in the Writing Standards, and "analysis of text features in informational text" in the Reading Standards for Informational Text. A number of commissioners were concerned about the impact of the ELA standards on English language learners (ELLs), particularly because 23 percent of California's K–12 students are classified as ELLs, and the ELA standards only indirectly address the implications of the CCSS for this group of students. The commission decided to adopt the short text in the introduction to the ELA standards that asserts "all students must have the opportunity to learn and meet the same high standards if they are to access the knowledge and skills necessary in their post–high school lives," on the assumption that the state would draft English language development standards aligned with the Common Core.[8]

Unlike in other states, the CDE was not involved in staffing the work of the commission.[9] Rather, Sue Stickel, a former CDE deputy superintendent and currently the deputy superintendent of the Sacramento County Office of Education, was asked by the governor's office to be the commission's staff director because of her long experience in drafting state standards and her reputation for working effectively in committees. Neither the governor nor the legislature had budgeted any funds. Consequently, the commission's work was supported by grants from the Hewlett and Broad Foundations. That funding allowed Stickel and her staff to provide the commission with a broad range of evidence. One of the most important was a three-inch-thick set of documents that compared each of the current California mathematics and ELA standards with the CCSS equivalent standard by grade level, noting the core strand covered and whether they were aligned. This side-by-side analysis (called a *crosswalk*) also noted any standards that were included in the CCSS, but not in the current California standards and vice versa.

In addition to this evidence, based on current policy, the lead developers of the CCSS briefed the commission and answered questions. Several members of the CCSS Validation Committee who supported the standards spoke with the commission by telephone, as did James Milgram and Sandra Stotsky, members of the validation committee who had voted not to validate the CCSS. The commission meetings were live-streamed, and fifty to seventy-five people attended each meeting in person, many representing major interest groups. Public comments were invited, and audience members caucused with commissioners during breaks.

The two commissioners opposed to the CCSS mathematics standards focused their evidence on the recommendations of the 2008 National Mathematics Advisory Panel that algebra in the eighth grade should be strongly promoted, on the increases in the proportion of California students taking algebra in eighth grade and testing proficient in the subject, and on what they viewed as deficiencies in how the CCSS approached topics such as proofs in geometry. They attributed their inability to obtain support for rejecting the standards to a "rushed, political process without much deliberation." Other commissioners, along with the governor's staff, attributed the lack of success to the argumentative style of the dissenters, citing "strategic errors," insisting on "powering over people," and "getting in their faces."[10]

Although the commissioners appreciated the evidence that had been compiled by the staff and consultants, they relied heavily on the professional judgment of the teacher members of the commission and the assurances provided by the CCSS developers that the standards were research and evidence based:

> The central question was, "Do these make sense to practitioners?" The other standard that could have been used was, "Are these research

based—e.g., should this content be taught at this time?" But my perspective was that I would listen to the teachers. For instance, we had teachers of first grade, third, junior high, and high school—the question for them is, "Does this continuum make sense?" Does it make sense that ELA would be taught in history and science classes? The general consensus was yes—"when I give a paper in English class, I expect the history teachers to use the same standards for writing." I hadn't thought about this before, but I think it's right that we looked to teachers' experience to evaluate the standards—a practitioner's perspective rather than a scholarly perspective.

------- ■ ■ ■ -------

By the time the CCSS were ready for the states to adopt, they had been worked on for quite a while by the development team and put out for different groups, states, and individuals for feedback. I thought they were very high quality. And the information we were given as a commission was also very high quality. I think the Sacramento County Office of Education outdid themselves giving us the information we needed to make a decision, such as the crosswalks and making sure we had access to all the standards we needed. We also got a lot of research and achievement data to back it up. So I thought it was very high quality. I wouldn't have wanted any more. It was almost more than we could handle.

On August 2, 2010, less than three weeks after the commission had completed its work, the SBE voted unanimously to adopt the CCSS mathematics and ELA standards, with California becoming the thirty-third state to adopt the Common Core. The state's major education interest groups, including the CTA, the state PTA, and the California Mathematics Council, all expressed strong support for the standards.[11] The legislation establishing the commission gave the SBE only the option of either accepting or rejecting the commission's recommendations.[12] Consequently, there was little detailed discussion of the Common Core's content or the evidence on which it was based. Several days prior to the vote, the board president, Ted Mitchell, published an op-ed article in the *San Francisco Chronicle* supporting the adoption of the Common Core. His arguments were essentially drawn from the messaging tool kit that the CCSS policy entrepreneurs had prepared, and mirrored the Common Core rationale they had promoted since its inception.[13]

Implementing the Common Core and Conditions for Its Sustainability

By the time the CCSS were to be implemented in California, the state had a new governor. Jerry Brown had already served two terms as governor in the 1970s, and he appointed as the SBE president Michael Kirst, who had also served as state board president during Brown's earlier terms. Kirst was a Stanford faculty member and a leading education policy analyst who had begun his career working in the Lyndon Johnson administration during the early implementation of the Elementary and Secondary Education Act. Both Brown and Kirst were strongly committed to the Common Core. They viewed it as "a way to shake up the system," and "to change almost everything." If implemented effectively, it would "impact almost all key state education policies in fundamental ways."[14]

Several aspects of California's Common Core implementation are notable. Perhaps most significant was Brown's and Kirst's recognition that because California is a large, diverse state, state government is severely limited in the level of guidance and support it can provide local districts. For Kirst, this realization came from more than four decades as a researcher and an active participant in state and federal policy development. For Brown, his policy learning was not just the product of his first time as governor, but also his eight years as mayor of Oakland.[15] As a result, several policies affecting the Common Core were designed to give local districts more resources and greater discretion.

The state's economy stabilized, and voters passed Proposition 30, a ballot initiative supported by Brown that raised the income tax rate on the wealthiest Californians, with much of the revenue allocated for education. Consequently, the 2013–14 budget included $1.25 billion ($200 per student) for building local districts' capacity to implement the CCSS. Districts could choose to use the funds to support one or more purposes: professional development, instructional materials, or technology for Common Core–aligned instruction and assessment. The Instructional Quality Commission (IQC), an advisory body to the SBE, issued frameworks to assist districts in developing curriculum and instructional approaches aligned with the CCSS and with new English Language Development (ELD) standards adopted by the state board in 2013. The IQC also reviewed ELA and mathematics instructional materials, and issued a list of approved ones. However, in a significant departure from past policy, it was only advisory rather than requiring that districts purchase from the approved list, thus further expanding local discretion.

In 2013, acting on Brown's strong advocacy, the legislature enacted a major change in state funding for K–12 education. The Local Control Funding Formula (LCFF) replaced the state's complex system of categorical grants with a per student base grant, supplemented by additional funding weights for ELLs, low-income students, and foster youth, as well as additional funding for districts with the highest concentrations of these students. At one level, the LCFF was another fundamental policy reform that districts were expected to implement simultaneously with the Common Core. However, besides serving as a mechanism for allocating additional funds to those students most in need of greater resources, it also represented a major devolution of authority to local districts. Freed from the strictures of categorical grants with their narrowly defined uses and detailed accounting requirements, districts have considerable discretion in how they spend LCFF funds. The primary accountability mechanism is the requirement for each district to develop a Local Control and Accountability Plan with broad public input and to specify how it plans to reach goals in eight priority areas, one of which is its plan for implementing the Common Core. The legislature and governor made it very clear that they expected the LCFF and the CCSS to be linked reforms.[16]

Brown and Kirst's recognition of limited state-level capacity was widely shared among local educators and state leaders. One state official labeled the problem as "the scanty infrastructure that exists in this state." A county superintendent described the gap in state capacity in terms of the shortcomings of the CDE:

> The CDE is not only resource-poor, but also poor in terms of who they have working there. The SDE simply does not have the best people working in the state, certainly not the best implementors in the state, and they can't recruit them . . . Now their salaries are frozen so they can't even get good people to start. They've asked me for names, and people have to take a $50,000 cut in salary—and move to Sacramento. There's no way. It's true that state departments' salaries have lagged locals before, but the gap is huge now. I feel for Tom [Torlakson, the elected superintendent of public

instruction], because I know he wants to make a difference—but he has to do it without resources and without the people.

The CDE staff tasked with supporting the Common Core implementation were aware of the limitations on what they could accomplish. As an initial step, and with assistance from county offices of education, subject-matter projects, and private vendors, the staff had designed fifteen professional learning modules on topics such as an overview of the Common Core, text complexity, writing across the curriculum, and mathematics progressions. They were made available free of charge to educators on the CDE's Digital Chalkboard. Each module was designed to be used by a group of teachers and to take several hours to complete. In addition, the CDE staff had established evaluation criteria for deciding what other materials would be posted on the website, and they immediately posted materials developed and endorsed by CCSSO-related groups such as Student Achievement Partners. However, the CDE staff were realistic about the limits on what they could accomplish for both political and capacity reasons:

> The thing that we always get criticized for is, are we doing too much or too little. At one point, we're not doing enough, and at another point, well, the state is giving too much direction. We are a local control state. That's an interesting experience because if you dictate something, then we're going to be paying for it . . . Nor do we have enough money in the state—or will we ever have enough money in the state—to train teachers classroom by classroom. You're going to have to build capacity within your district, and the only way that can happen is through your teacher leaders or your principals.[17]

Two other aspects of California's Common Core implementation are notable because they help compensate for the limited state-level capacity. The first are several collaborative networks established by local district leaders to support and learn from each other. Districts such as Long Beach, Fresno, and Garden Grove realized that to improve instructional opportunities, they could not count on the state but instead needed to look to each other for strategies to improve teaching and learning.[18] Several of these networks, such as the CORE districts and the California Collaborative on District Reform, predated the Common Core. By the time members of these networks were faced with

implementing the CCSS and LCFF, they not only had well-established relationships among themselves, but they had also secured foundation funding
and were engaged in active collaboration with research institutions.[19] These
and other locally based networks operate as alternatives to "scanty" state-
level infrastructures. With the advent of the Common Core, additional networks, such as the Consortium for the Implementation of the Common Core
State Standards and Math in Common, were established. These are funded
by foundation support and designed to facilitate coordination among districts and to provide implementation resources.

A second notable aspect of CCSS implementation in California that augments state capacity is the significant amount of policy research being produced on the process and its impacts. The Susan Moffitt et al. report is an
example, and is one of three papers focused on CCSS implementation prepared by Stanford and PACE as part of its Getting Down to Facts II series.[20]
Other PACE reports presented case studies of early CCSS implementation in
districts across the state, analyzed major challenges facing districts and how
they varied by a district's past history and capacity, and assessed the unique
implementation challenges facing districts that are part of the Rural Professional Learning Network.[21] Further contributing to learning from past policy,
the Collaborative produced a report that identified lessons from California's
experience in the 1990s with an innovative state assessment that faced political opposition and eventual termination.[22] These and other reports have provided state and local policymakers with research-based information on the
course of CCSS implementation, but they also drew on past studies to suggest potential solutions to the capacity shortfalls and other problems they
identified.

In its limited state capacity and unequal distribution of instructional supports across local districts, California is much like the other states in our
sample. Public knowledge about the Common Core and patterns of support
for it do not significantly differ from opinion at the national level.[23] Similarly,
while the research base is more extensive in California, and research-policy
linkages stronger, Massachusetts and Tennessee also have the advantage of
these resources.

What is most unique about California, however, is the Common Core's
political stability. Over the decade since its adoption, no serious opposition
has mobilized, and the CCSS standards and Smarter Balanced assessment

(SBAC) continue in much the same form as they began. The explanation for this political sustainability is state and local leadership that learned from past policy shortfalls, learned from research about how to translate policy effectively into classroom practice, and, through political intelligence and judgment, learned about what is necessary to maintain key support coalitions. The networks among local districts and the policies supporting the Common Core and LCFF are prime examples of this learning.

Another decision of the Brown administration set California apart from other states and ensured that a major interest group would continue to support the CCSS. At a time when the federal government offered states waivers from some of NCLB's accountability requirements if they would agree to use student assessment scores as one criterion in evaluating teachers, California refused. According to Michael Kirst, Governor Brown promised the CTA that the state would not initiate test-based teacher evaluations while it implemented the Common Core if the teacher union would support the administration on other policies.[24] As a result, the federal government did not grant California a waiver, and it was required to operate under what had become outmoded NCLB requirements.[25] The Brown administration then went a step further to smooth Common Core implementation and to act consistently with research-based testing standards. It temporarily suspended the state accountability system as California transitioned from its prior STAR assessment to Smarter Balanced. Because SBAC was still being field-tested in spring 2014, California decided not to use the results for NCLB and state accountability purposes. As a result, it prompted a stern warning from the Obama administration, which had the authority to withhold federal Title I funds from the state for noncompliance. However, state officials were willing to risk such penalties "to implement the Common Core quickly and thoroughly."[26] Although the federal government had sanctioned California in the past for noncompliance, in this instance, after a prolonged public airing of the issues, it backed down and did not withhold any funds.[27]

Conclusion
Research and the strong relationship between producers and state officials played a significant role in California's implementation of the Common Core. However, the evidence most central to the policy's political sustainability was the decades-long experience of its leaders and their political skill in melding

that experience into policy learning. They recognized that the Common Core represented a unique political opportunity not only to replace outmoded state standards, but also to use the CCSS as the centerpiece of a coherent initiative altering state education policy and its governance in ways that fundamentally rebalanced state and local authority. Perceiving the opportunity and implementing it required understanding evidence about the reform and knowledge about the institutions governing state education policy. But equally necessary to pursuing the opportunity to transform California education was an ability to gather reliable intelligence about sources of potential support and opposition, and expert judgment about what strategies would most likely build support and blunt opposition.

INDIANA

In contrast to California, Indiana's adoption of the Common Core was low-key and noncontroversial. However, its implementation was marked by significant political opposition, and in April 2014, Indiana became the first state to opt out of the CCSS. Each of these three stages was characterized by a different type of evidence. During the adoption phase, state decision-makers were presented with the evidence embodied in the national policy entrepreneurs' rationale for the Common Core; personal experience and political rhetoric dominated the phaseout of the CCSS; and educators' professional judgment played a major role in the design of the replacement standards.

Adopting the Common Core
Although the CCSS adoption process was not politicized, it occurred in a divisive policy environment that would later adversely affect the sustainability of the Common Core. The catalyst for adopting the Common Core was then-governor Mitch Daniels's and superintendent of public instruction (SPI) Tony Bennett's desire to compete for Race to the Top funds to support their education reform initiative. Although Indiana was not a finalist in the first round of Race to the Top applications, Bennett announced that the state would continue with adoption of the CCSS and implementing the Putting Students First agenda that included major changes in state laws on teacher evaluation, collective bargaining, school choice, and turnaround policies for low performing schools. The teacher evaluation provisions required that

local school districts implement new teacher evaluation policies that included measures of student achievement and growth, classroom observations, and other indicators of professional practice. The collective bargaining law limited bargaining to salaries, wages, and benefits, placing topics such as school calendar and teacher evaluation procedures outside the scope of bargaining. Other bills enacted at the same time expanded the number of charter school authorizers and created a state voucher program for low-income students. The four reform bills passed the Republican-dominated state legislature with virtually no Democratic support (one vote in the House and none in the Senate).[28] Although powerless to block them, the Indiana State Teachers Association (ISTA) opposed these policies along with the decreases in state funding for schools that had occurred under Governor Daniels.

Adoption of the Common Core in Indiana involved a two-step process. As in most states, the SBE has the authority to adopt state standards. However, in 1999, the state legislature established the Education Roundtable, whose charge included approving state standards and assessments and setting the passing score on the state assessment. The Roundtable then made recommendations to the SBE, which had only the option to accept or reject its recommendation. The Roundtable was cochaired by the governor and SPI. With its purpose of bringing real-world perspectives to education policy deliberations, the thirty members represented business, higher education, K–12 education, and various community groups, in addition to the chair and ranking member of the state legislative House and Senate Education Committees. In preparation for the Roundtable review, the Indiana Department of Education (IDOE) staff undertook several analyses. They used a tool developed by Achieve to assess how well the CCSS aligned with Indiana's current standards. They also performed the same exercise using the Surveys of Enacted Curriculum. In addition, the staff "reviewed the research base upon which the standards were formed. So looking at who were the researchers, who were consulted by the writers, also looking for the rationale and the studies that were cited." The staff then used these analyses in presenting summary briefings to the Roundtable. The IDOE and Roundtable staff recognized that it was particularly important that the evidence and arguments in favor of the CCSS be compelling because the state had just revised and adopted new mathematics standards in 2009:

I'm not sure that we handed them [the Roundtable] any research. They took it on faith that we did our due diligence and started to look into some other issues. In general, there's a fair amount of trust and expectation that we've done our homework, especially when we're asking them to back up and [reconsider] a decision that they had made. A lot of it was we're able to bring experts to the table, so if there were questions, it could get answered directly.

— ■ ■ ■ —

David Coleman did a presentation along with Matt Gandel from Achieve. They made the presentation to the Roundtable in the August meeting about the standards. It was extensive and there were many questions from the members of the Roundtable about the standards.

A legislator who was a member of the Roundtable agreed that the case for the Common Core had been persuasive:

At the Roundtable, we did receive research data that talked significantly about why we need to move to the Common Core and why it makes sense and also the rigor of it. At some point, our state has been recognized by Fordham and others for having great standards, but as I understand it, our standards are "a mile wide and an inch deep." So the Common Core is going to create more rigor within the standards and narrow it a bit as opposed to having it so broad. I would say the move toward the Common Core had significant impact on our state, since the decisions were made not just by legislators but by a number of people who are experts and were involved in the discussion.

I would say the evidence had a huge impact. For a long time, I've been very frustrated with why all fifty states have standards but there's no consistency in them. And the fact that NAEP is the only thing we really have to tell how we are doing compared to our neighboring states, and even that's not perfectly reflective. So all of that information was shared at the Roundtable and it had a significant impact in terms of why our superintendent was bringing the Common Core forward and why he was very supportive of it. I also think that's why there wasn't any opposition to the Common Core, as I recollected at the Roundtable.

The Education Roundtable recommended that the SBE adopt the Common Core standards, and in August 2010, the SBE unanimously voted to do so. The arguments and evidence presented to the SBE mirrored that presented to the Roundtable. A member of the SBE who described himself as politically conservative attributed the adoption to the governor's and the SPI's influence, as well as to knowledge of who developed the standards and the quality of the evidence presented:

> Without a strong superintendent, we couldn't have gotten the standards, especially in the state of Indiana . . . we tend to not want to be a part of any national movement . . . If the governor wasn't trusted and the superintendent wasn't trusted, those [opposition] groups might have had more of an opening. When you have strong leadership, the objectors' voices probably don't have the same credibility, but whether that's right or wrong is another issue.
>
> One of the things I heard was how the participation in the CCSS was set up so you know there are no outside groups trying to manipulate the curriculum or standards. That was important to me, I guess. I became confident in the standards after they explained the process of who was involved in writing the standards and I think I got some assurance that wouldn't be some political agenda for a group of people.

Even though these participants in the standards adoption were describing the process some eighteen months after it occurred, they still viewed the Common Core as beneficial for Indiana students, and believed that the Roundtable and SBE had made the right decision. Yet opposition to the CCSS was already emerging. Those who supported the Common Core as an improvement on Indiana's standards realized that linking its adoption to the Race to the Top application had serious downsides. A member of the SPI's executive staff noted:

> We felt confident that it was a good move for Indiana. I think, ironically, the longer and longer we dealt with it, the more and more we felt like it was a bit of a shotgun marriage because of the timing. I think, as the process went on, we continued to realize that these [the CCSS] were actually better. So it wasn't that we were just encouraged to do it, but it was the right thing for Indiana.

It would have been better if the specter of the Race to the Top wasn't hanging over it. I also wish we could have had a more robust conversation in as much that everyone could have felt that they were a part of the decision-making process. On the flip side, I'll say that Race to the Top was helpful that it got people off their rears and started working because of the timetable. So from the long-term perspective and watching it ... the fact that it was rushed, that kind of hurt the process because it was just chasing money. Then again, it would be disingenuous to say that Race to the Top didn't help mobilize the effort.

The lack of a "robust conversation" and the closed decision-making process meant that important groups were not aware of the evidence and arguments that members of the Roundtable weighed. The sense of having been excluded was felt especially by the ISTA leadership, who were encouraged by the NEA, their national organization, to support the Common Core:

> We actually had one particular meeting with a lady from the IDOE who said that teachers were really going to be the ones that will make or break the Common Core. She emphasized if we were going to go with the Common Core in Indiana, then teachers will really need to be on board. They wanted to have conversation and input ... but we actually never heard back from them after that. The only thing we actually heard about the Common Core during the process was when it would be presented to the state Education Roundtable or the state board, or when Dr. Bennett made a statement of some sort. But there were never any inclusion or conversations ... calling in teachers and saying "let's build a consensus and let's all go out and train folks and prepare folks to transition to the Common Core."

Not only were teachers not involved in the adoption process, but little effort was made by the governor, SPI, or IDOE staff to communicate to parents and the public the reasons for replacing Indiana's standards with the Common Core.

Implementing the Common Core and Political Opposition

Although the IDOE had adopted an implementation schedule for the transition from the Indiana standards to the CCSS to be completed by 2014–15, and had begun to develop curriculum maps to guide the process, support for the Common Core quickly eroded. In 2011, Hoosiers Against Common Core was founded by two mothers of Indianapolis students whose Catholic school had implemented the CCSS. They questioned the Common Core–aligned textbook that their children were using, finding it less challenging than the texts assigned to their older siblings prior to the CCSS adoption. Although Hoosiers Against Common Core would later adopt the political rhetoric of the Tea Party, the initial impetus was based on the personal experience of parents who questioned new curriculum in their children's schools. With support from Tea Party groups across the country, the organization was committed to "restore local control of education . . . quality standards . . . restore the rights of teachers to practice their craft . . . [and] reduce the power of standardized testing." Hoosiers Against Common Core is self-described as a "single issue" group of "parents concerned about the future of our children's education."[29] It held information sessions and rallies across the state, and was loosely affiliated with national anti-Common Core groups, such as the Pioneer Institute, and with state-level groups in Ohio, Utah, Iowa, and Missouri.

Allies in the state legislature invited well-known CCSS opponents, Sandra Stotsky and Williamson Evers, to testify that the Common Core is less rigorous than Indiana's own standards. Although the Indiana Chamber of Commerce supported the Common Core and had testified against bills to end it, the negative analysis from experts such as Stotsky raised concerns, particularly because she had assisted Indiana in drafting its earlier standards:

> When I testified on the bill [banning the CCSS], I told the committee we were opposed to the legislation and the reason why. But I also told them we are very concerned that the people whom we have relied on to evaluate our standards and who actually helped us with our standards to be where we are today, which is considered the best among the country, are now standing before us telling us we've got problems.

Consequently, the Chamber supported the establishment of a study committee to review the Common Core and compare it with Indiana's previous standards.[30]

In 2011, the opposition appeared to be largely coming from conservative groups and elected officials:

It's really a family fight. This is not the Democrats attacking Common Core State Standards . . . it's a faction of the Republican establishment fighting the Republicans who have adopted this.

However, that changed in the 2012 statewide election. Despite a significant campaign spending advantage, Tony Bennett, the incumbent SPI and a national education reform leader, was defeated by his Democratic opponent, veteran educator Glenda Ritz. Ritz's primary issue in the campaign was her opposition to ISTEP, the state assessment. Although she did not oppose the Common Core, she did advocate a more thorough review of it and perhaps a melding of it with the Indiana standards. Support for Ritz came from teachers opposed to Bennett's reform policies, but also from Tea Party adherents who opposed his support of the Common Core, viewing it as "Obamacore," another form of unwarranted federal intervention.[31]

Replacing the Common Core

Despite Ritz's victory, Indiana remained solidly Republican in its state leadership, with Mike Pence, a member of the Tea Party caucus while serving in Congress, elected to succeed Mitch Daniels, and both legislative chambers retaining strong Republican majorities. In May 2013, Governor Pence signed "pause legislation" that required the SBE to undertake a review of the CCSS, and to adopt College and Career Ready (CCR) standards no later than July 1, 2014. The process also required that information be collected about the costs involved in implementing the CCSS and the PARCC assessment. Ritz was charged with appointing academic standards committees in mathematics and ELA, and they were charged, in turn, with soliciting broad input from teachers, the public, and others knowledgeable about state standards and assessments. The SBE review involved a multiphase process. During the eleven-month review period, technical and advisory teams composed of educators, parents, community members, and representatives of higher education institutions reviewed the CCSS standards, then compared them with Indiana's 2006 ELA and 2009 mathematics standards to identify which standards would best meet the expectations for CCR. The teams then reached consensus on which standards should be retained, and looked to standards in other states to fill in gaps. Once the list was completed, it was posted for online public comments during February and March 2014. The evaluation teams then reconvened to incorporate the public comments and to align the progression of standards across grade levels. A final review was conducted by a CCR panel composed of representatives from higher education and private industry.

This review and revision of the state standards was considerably more transparent and publicly visible than the earlier adoption of the CCSS. The evidence base was essentially the professional judgment of educators and those who would ultimately evaluate the academic readiness of Indiana's K–12 graduates. In April, the Education Roundtable voted to recommend adoption of the new standards, with cochairs Pence and Ritz both voting for adoption; the SBE then acted on that recommendation and approved adoption of the replacement standards.

Two aspects of the 2014 Indiana Academic Standards (IAS) are notable. First, multiple reviews of the new standards by *Education Week*, Achieve, the Fordham Institute, and Hoosiers Against Common Core found little substantive difference between the Common Core and the IAS. The differences that do exist typically deal with the ordering of standards or how they are organized into different domains. For example, for sixth grade mathematics, the new standards are organized into four domains: 1) number sense and computation; 2) algebra and functions; 3) geometry and measurement; and 4) data analysis, statistics, and probability. This arrangement is slightly different from the CCSS, which organizes the standards into five domains: 1) ratios and proportional relationships, 2) the number system, 3) expressions and equations, 4) geometry, and 5) statistics and probability.[32] Using different criteria, Achieve and the Fordham Institute essentially reached a similar conclusion that the 2014 Indiana standards meet CCR expectations, and are rigorous in their content.[33] The Hoosiers Against Common Core report focused on the mathematics standards, and was prepared by Ze'ev Wurman, one of the dissenting votes in California's adoption of the Common Core. His side-by-side analysis concluded that "the majority of the standards have been imported, some word-for-word from the Common Core." He also reported that while the CCSS have 314 mathematics standards across grades K–8, the IAS have 455, thus leading the group to argue that 90 percent of the CCSS standards had been retained, with the remainder added from the state's earlier standards so as to appear responsive to teachers and parents.[34]

The similarities between the standards prompted two types of responses as they were being reviewed prior to adoption. Hoosiers Against Common Core organized a protest rally at the Roundtable's vote, and was strongly critical of the new standards during public hearings held throughout the state. In contrast, a number of teachers testified that the new standards would only confuse students and teachers, and create greater instability in classrooms. One mathematics specialist described the merged standards as a "confusing mess" for teachers, and noted that the 2009 Indiana mathematics standards had been thoroughly vetted while the IAS were rushed.[35]

A second characteristic of the switch to new standards is that it occurred during what the *New York Times* described as "one of the most public and combative political fights" to face the Pence administration.[36] Although Pence and Ritz had been allies in their vote to adopt new standards, they engaged in a power struggle over control of the SBE from the beginning of their terms of office. Although the governor had the authority to appoint SBE members, the independently elected SPI served as chair of the board. Through an executive order, Pence established a small separate agency, the Center for Education and Career Innovation (CECI) to serve as staff to the SBE, with its support taken from the IDOE agency budget. According to Pence and his staff, the CECI's mission was to break down "silos" and to align K–12, higher education, and workforce development strategies more effectively. However, Ritz viewed it as Pence orchestrating a "power grab" against the IDOE and her authority to direct the SBE's policy agenda. She unsuccessfully sued the SBE for violating the state's open meeting laws in requesting that a legislative agency take responsibility for the state's school accountability rankings rather than the IDOE. In addition, she walked out of an SBE meeting to prevent a vote.[37] Subsequent actions by the state legislature dissolved the Education Roundtable in 2015; removed the SPI as chair of the SBE; and, as of 2020, the SPI became a position appointed by the governor.[38]

The commitments Indiana had made to secure an NCLB waiver further complicated the implementation of the IAS and imposed additional burdens on local school districts. The state had an agreement with the federal government to have CCR standards in place and an assessment measuring student mastery of them by 2015. The replacement of the CCSS and the adoption of new standards left little time to prepare teachers. They basically had three months, while teachers had at least a year to prepare for the Common Core, and many had several years.[39] Throughout the summer of 2014, the IDOE held e-learning conferences to support teachers as they transitioned to the IAS, and it created a standards correlation document for mathematics and ELA that provided side-by-side comparisons of the pre–2010 state standards, the CCSS, and the 2014 IAS. The state agency also created an online "communities of practice" website to connect teachers and disseminate best practices. Overall, the IDOE's stated goal was to inform teachers and the public about the new standards, and "minimiz[e] standards transition fatigue" among teachers.[40]

Attempts to design and administer a state assessment aligned with the IAS and meeting state and federal accountability requirements led to serious substantive and logistical problems. Because a new assessment would not be ready until 2016, in 2015, students were administered a transitional test that was an amalgam of the old ISTEP items and ones that mirrored those on the forthcoming assessment. One media account summarized the problem: "The 2014-15 school year was unlike any other, as teachers and students tried to prepare for a test they've never seen based on new state standards they'd only begun to learn."[41] Problems with scoring led the state legislature to pass a "hold harmless" bill that prevented schools that year from receiving a ranking lower than what they had received the previous year. Between 2015 and 2019, the state used three different testing contractors: CTB/McGraw-Hill, Pearson, and AIR. Somewhat ironically, AIR relied on the Smarter Balanced Common Core–aligned item bank to build Indiana's assessment.

Conclusion

Indiana's adoption of the Common Core was largely an opportunistic attempt to secure a Race to the Top grant, but it was also consistent with Governor Daniels and SPI Bennett's education reform agenda. Nevertheless, the more politically consequential teacher evaluation and collective bargaining legislation, introduced by Bennett, eclipsed the CCSS in public attention. As in California, the evidence presented during the adoption process was essentially drawn from the national narrative supporting the Common Core, combined with a side-by-side analysis that compared it with Indiana's own standards. However, once Bennett was defeated in 2012, not only was research-based evidence incidental to standards policy, but the standards themselves were peripheral to competing partisan agendas that focused on expanding school choice through near-universal state vouchers and consolidating authority over state education policy within the governor's office. Consequently, there was no state official with sufficient incentive to maintain the political sustainability of either the Common Core or its successor standards.

MASSACHUSETTS

State officials in Massachusetts were in a unique position in considering whether to adopt the CCSS. For a number of years, Massachusetts students had been among the top performers on both NAEP and TIMSS, and in 2009, committees of educators were in the process of revising the state's mathematics and ELA standards.[42] Several different analyses comparing Massachusetts' current standards (referred to as Curriculum Frameworks) and the in-process revisions with the Common Core concluded that while on balance the CCSS were preferable on several dimensions, Massachusetts would continue to have excellent standards whether it retained its own or adopted the CCSS. Nevertheless, the state Board of Elementary and Secondary Education (BESE), voted to adopt the Common Core in August 2010. Further enhancing the state's position and its implementation of the CCSS was the award of a federal Race to the Top grant in October 2010. However, even with support from major state organizations and strengthened implementing capacity because of the Race to the Top grant, groups opposed to the Common Core came close to placing an initiative on the 2016 statewide ballot calling for Massachusetts to return to its own standards. Furthermore, the state ended up creating a hybrid assessment that combined PARCC items with its own state assessment, the Massachusetts Comprehensive Assessment System (MCAS). Still the Common Core continues as the state's mathematics and ELA curriculum frameworks, having gone through a routine revision in 2017. Throughout the decade-long process of adopting, implementing, and revising the CCSS in Massachusetts, sources of evidence have ranged from studies conducted by a variety of research producers to professional judgment and political rhetoric.

Adopting the Common Core

Massachusetts was among a number of states that had adopted a standards-based approach to education reform. The 1993 Massachusetts Education

Reform Act called for clear, measurable statewide standards and an assessment aligned with those standards. In 2007, the state education agency, the
Department of Elementary and Secondary Education (DESE), convened a
team of educators to revise the state's ELA curriculum framework, and in
2008, a similar team was convened to revise the mathematics framework.
At the same time, however, governor Deval Patrick and state education commissioner Mitchell Chester signed a memorandum of understanding with
CCSSO and NGA to participate in the development of the Common Core.
A DESE official involved in the process explained the reasoning behind this
dual approach:

> We were in the process of revising Massachusetts standards when the
> Common Core effort began. My strategy was, "Let's work on both at the
> same time concurrently, so that we can make both of them the best pos-
> sible." So in the end, if the Common Core is as good or better than the
> standards that we developed, then we can go there. If they're not, we have
> our own newly refined standards to fall back on.
>
> I saw it as an iterative process because we could learn from the Com-
> mon Core and they can learn from us as we went through all of that. It
> wasn't like we knew both documents would end up exactly the same, but it
> at least gave us the choice of two strong documents in the end, so that was
> the strategy I thought we would work on.

This same official noted that because of Massachusetts' highly regarded
standards and its students' test performance, the state could influence the
CCSS development:

> Given the fact that Massachusetts had good standards—had good assess-
> ment results on NAEP and other things, we have a lot of credibility. So
> people wanted to hear from us. I said, "Let's use that leverage—the fact
> that we have credibility—to build on and see the extent to which we could
> influence the Common Core." So that, in the end, because we believed it
> was a good thing for the country to identify common standards, that we
> could help the process. And if we wanted to go in that direction, there would
> have been a strong document in the end. We just believed in the goal but
> weren't wedded to adopt it no matter what.

The choice for Massachusetts, then, was between a revision of its own Curriculum Frameworks and the Common Core. Consequently, the analyses that were prepared compared the two sets of standards. A member of BESE described the evidence base and why it was particularly important to the board's decision:

> The department had done its own analysis of the Common Core as compared to the revised 2009 math and ELA standards. They had commissioned MBAE [Massachusetts Business Alliance for Education], who then commissioned WestEd to do an independent analysis, and we didn't know the results of that until two days before the board meeting. A third analysis was done by Achieve, so the board wanted to hear about all of those because we had to be able to stand tall to folks who like [that] Massachusetts had a national reputation for having the best standards and the best alignment between standards and our accountability system.

In addition to the side-by-side analysis prepared by the DESE staff, the department also convened review panels for both the ELA and mathematics standards. The eight-member ELA panel was composed of several English and reading teachers, district and charter school administrators, and two representatives from higher education, including the director of the Harvard College Writing Center. The panel voted seven to one in favor of the Common Core, but also recommended that parts of the Massachusetts standards be included in the adopted standards; among them were the Massachusetts PreK standards not included in the CCSS and the clear progression of standards from grade to grade that the panel found were either not readily distinguishable or nonexistent in the Common Core. In its report, the ELA review panel commended the Common Core for its focus on argumentation in the writing standards; the inclusion of history, social studies, and science to lend credence to the need for shared responsibility for developing students' literacy skills; the strategic combining of multiple print and digital sources; and the discussion of text complexity and models for measuring it. The dissenting member argued that the Massachusetts standards were more coherent and clearly organized, maintained a strong emphasis on literary study, and provided appendices more useful to teachers.[43]

The seven-member mathematics review panel included four university mathematicians and three district mathematics specialists. The members rated both the Common Core mathematics standards and the Massachusetts Curriculum Framework as "excellent," and concluded that they would be comfortable with the adoption of either as "both documents would support Massachusetts' quest for rigorous state standards in mathematics and the quest to prepare all students for college and career."[44] A member of the mathematics review panel described the process that resulted in its conclusions:

> I do [feel satisfied with the process]. I feel like the greatest challenge was the time frame, but we made it work. And I thought it was great to have the committee that we had together. There were a lot of strong people who really pushed and had to really convince others that they were right or not, get their point across. And I thought that was a great way to do it, to really look in detail at the standards and exactly what they said, and a lot of pushing and shoving, which was respectful pushing and shoving. But it was a real intellectual challenge and it was good. It was the way it should be.

An especially pivotal analysis of the Massachusetts frameworks and the Common Core was commissioned by MBAE and prepared by WestEd. The MBAE is an advocacy organization, established in 1988, to promote education reform through a standards-based strategy. The organization works in partnership with business groups such as the Massachusetts Business Roundtable and the Associated Industries of Massachusetts. It produced *Every Child a Winner*, the report that served as the framework for the 1993 Education Reform Act. Because of its longtime support for rigorous standards to prepare students for college and career, the Hunt Institute staff approached the MBAE to assist in persuading BESE to adopt the Common Core. However, the MBAE board indicated that it had not yet decided to support the CCSS. As one of its staff explained:

> Every analysis that was coming out was by somebody who'd already taken a position, and we, therefore, discounted it. We said, "You know, we have, as an organization, a strong history in bringing standards-based reform to Massachusetts. We have a stake in making sure that our standards don't get lowered." As so, while as business people we can understand the benefit of Common Core standards nationwide, we also don't want to take a

step back in Massachusetts. We don't have any ability to judge because everything that is coming out is biased by people who have made their conclusion before the final results [standards] came out.

As a result, MBAE raised funding primarily from the Gates Foundation to commission an in-depth analysis. WestEd created a crosswalk between the CCSS and Massachusetts standards on content skill and knowledge alignment, the depth of knowledge or cognitive complexity, and measurability.[45] The analysis found a high degree of alignment between the two sets of standards—96 percent full or partial alignment for the mathematics standards and 74 percent for the ELA standards—and the WestEd researchers concluded that "both sets have merits."[46] After a two-hour conference call with WestEd, the MBAE board and several of its partners concluded that they "couldn't go wrong either way," but the Alliance decided to speak in favor of the Common Core before BESE.

> Linda Noonan's [MBAE executive director] presentation to the board of education was very instrumental, I think. She herself has a lot of credibility because she is a straight shooter, and she believes in high standards. You have research studies, you have the groups, you have the comparative analysis, [but] some of the evidence is just, "Do you have credible individuals in the state?" Just because of their involvement for a long time in reform in the state were they on this? At the board of education meeting that day when the vote was taken, you had two or three former commissioners of education come in, and Linda Noonan.

A state board member agreed with the DESE official about the importance of the WestEd report, but also noted the influential role of the CCSS developers:

> Of the studies, I think the WestEd, given its independent nature, that was the most important of the analyses. Not that we didn't trust our own department or the national analysis, but WestEd specifically focused on Massachusetts. I [also] can't emphasize enough how important it was for our board to hear at least twice—and for me on many more occasions— from both Jason Zimba on math standards and Susan Pimentel on the literacy. Both individuals were exquisite—*exquisite*—in the rationale behind the changes, as opposed to just the changes. I can't say enough about Jason

and Susan, and I know they clearly influenced me, and I'm pretty positive they influenced the ten or however many board members were there.

The eight members of the BESE present on July 21, 2010, voted unanimously to adopt the CCSS. Despite the favorable vote, however, the decision to adopt the Common Core and to abandon MCAS and use PARCC as the state assessment was controversial. One of the strongest critics was the Pioneer Institute, whose executive director argued that the CCSS are less rigorous than Massachusetts's own standards. "Vocabulary-building in the common core is slower. And on the math side, they don't prepare eighth-grade students for algebra one, which is the gateway to higher math."[47] Charlie Baker, the 2010 Republican gubernatorial candidate and a former BESE member, delivered the only testimony before the state board in opposition to the Common Core, maintaining that "moving away from the state standards would be a mistake for students, schools, and this state. The state's status as a leader in K–12 education is one of the reasons why employers choose to locate here."[48] At the same time, as a representative of a national IO noted, Massachusetts's adoption of the Common Core strengthened the political status of the CCSS in other states:

> Our partners in Massachusetts worried that the CCSS might lead to lowering the level of standards they already had in place. But when others saw that Massachusetts could adopt the Common Core without watering down their standards, this gave lot of other people confidence that the idea would really work.

Massachusetts's special status as a top-performing state with rigorous standards, combined with its decision to coordinate the revision of its own frameworks with the development of the Common Core, meant that the pre-adoption process was a longer, more deliberate one than in the other three states in our case study. During this period, the chief developers of the CCSS mathematics and ELA standards came to Massachusetts to meet with the DESE staff who were leading the state revisions. According to Commissioner Chester, "the common core development was very much an iterative back-and-forth that involved Massachusetts very heavily."[49] Because the state revision process involved teams of educators who were kept informed about the underlying ideas and focus of the developing Common Core, subsequent comparisons of the two sets of standards were better understood by a broader group of educators. In addition, multiple sources of evidence were available: comparative analyses grounded in research and based on clearly defined criteria, the professional judgments of the education review panels and public comments on the standards, political judgments about the costs and benefits of shifting from current policy, and international benchmarking due to Massachusetts's participation in TIMSS.

Implementing the Common Core

The initial Common Core implementation process in Massachusetts focused on building awareness of the standards among educators.

> We used a variety of structures for that, including regional centers that were called our governor's revenue centers. We trained the trainers there so that they presented the same presentation across the state; so we have the same message across the state no matter where you live and no matter what region you're in, so that was our first step. That was our awareness step. We established educator-administrator networks monthly and provide[d] them with the most up-to-date information about the frameworks. So we have a series of structures in place to keep people updated.

Because a portion of the $215 million Race to the Top grant awarded to Massachusetts was designated to support Common Core implementation, the state had enhanced capacity for the task. The grant funded several major initiatives. One was a contract with the US Education Delivery Institute (EDI), a third-party provider with a focus on large-scale system change in public education. EDI applied strategies developed by its founder, Sir Michael Barber, based on his work for former British prime minister Tony Blair. As its name implies, the main idea behind EDI is "delivery," as defined in the implementation of top-down policy. An EDI manager explained:

> We create the delivery chain, the main purpose is to say how is this going to go from the state to the classroom? And you have to fill in all the people who are going to touch the work in-between the two. And then the next thing is how are you going to go, what are your intentions in working? Where is the feedback going to come from? And you set up those mechanisms to actually track that because every delivery unit leader is

responsible to the commissioner. Every two months they prepare a note saying, "This is how we're doing," and, "This is going well; this isn't going so well." Then the commissioner pushes them, saying, "You're doing a good job," or, "You're not doing such a good job." In Massachusetts, their commissioner said, "Your goals aren't ambitious enough. I really need you to go do more: this isn't good enough."

The director of the Massachusetts delivery team described her staff's work in this way:

> The program staff who are in charge of making sure that the standards get implemented have a whole bunch of strategies they're using to get the word out, and to make sure that people know what they are, what the differences are, know how to implement them, have the resources available . . . And so the program staff does that piece and our office's role is to check in with them, see how things are going. Are problems coming up that we need to shift course in our strategy? Are we reaching the teachers that we thought we would reach? You know, those kinds of troubleshooting and strengthening the process. And also getting specific goals for what we're trying to accomplish—what's the measurable outcome we should expect to see if we do all these things together?

In the states that it has worked with, EDI has applied analytical tools and strategies from management consulting to ensure that the delivery chain of implementation is clearly defined with the necessary resources available, and that the feedback loop from street-level bureaucrats back to agency staff and policymakers is functioning reliably. As a working model, delivery is an application of decades of implementation research and practice with an emphasis on connecting all the parts of a complicated system where the state may have limited knowledge of what is actually happening in schools and classrooms:

> Even people who have worked in the state education agency aren't aware. There's a lot going on in their own state that they don't know about, and that's why when we do the capacity review, districts tell us that they think the state doesn't know what's going on. They're very academic, very research-oriented, but they don't know what's happening on the ground . . . the folks at the end of the delivery chain, as we call it, know much

more than the people at the top of the chain. So the idea is to borrow what they're doing and make it work at the top. That way you make the whole chain stronger. Definitely for me, the bottom-up approach works; the problem is that it is not making its way up.

A second CCSS implementation initiative did not rely on external providers. It had several dimensions which focused on preparing teachers and building curriculum units aligned with the CCSS. Soon after the Race to the Top grant was awarded, districts receiving funds from it were required to submit implementation plans describing how they would make improvements in six areas, including increasing teacher and principal effectiveness, using data to improve instruction, increasing college and career readiness, and turning around the lowest performing schools. One project that districts were required to participate in to meet these goals was designed to align curriculum with the CCSS. To aid in that effort, DESE contracted with teachers from sixty local districts to develop model curriculum units spanning grades preK–12. A DESE official described the initiative:

> Our Race to the Top application said that we would develop one hundred sample or model units of instruction in four content areas: twenty-five in ELA, twenty-five in math, twenty-five in science, and twenty-five in social studies, using our state frameworks as the underpinning for those standards. That comes out to about two per grade, preK–12—between twenty-six and twenty-eight per content area when all is said and done.[50] We've enlisted teams of teachers, design teams, from across the state to work on creating these units of instruction and model units for use in Grant Wiggins and Jay McTighe's *Understanding by Design* and "backwards design" model as the centerpiece for that. We made a decision that we were not going to have vendors in this work. My goal is to build the capacity of educators in this state to do this work.[51]
>
> Part of the strategic piece of that decision is that we looked at the new framework, and we looked at where did we think it would be difficult for teachers to teach these new frameworks, where were there big shifts in the way you go about conveying this content to students, where teachers struggle—we know a lot of teachers . . . especially in elementary mathematics, that there are teachers that struggle with teaching a fraction. So we were determined to create a unit, specifically around the teaching of

fractions, that not only has the correct content in it, but the correct peda-
gogy as well in the instructional lesson design.

In addition, the state provided a number of resources to assist teachers
in preparing for Common Core instruction. For example, WGBH, the Boston
PBS affiliate, is also the hub for the network's LearningMedia, and its staff
worked with teams of teachers to identify digital resources linked to specific lesson plans. DESE staff also collaborated with Achieve and their state
agency counterparts in Rhode Island and New York to develop a rubric for
judging the quality of teacher-developed and commercial resources on how
well they align with the Common Core.

Through studies that DESE commissioned and ones conducted by various research producers, the implementation of the Common Core in Massachusetts was well analyzed. For example, in partnership with DESE, AIR
conducted a descriptive study that initially examined what local districts and
schools perceived as the necessary infrastructure to support implementation
of the curriculum frameworks. In subsequent phases, AIR focused on the
characteristics of high implementing classrooms, including teacher practices,
student activities and engagement, and the types of supports provided teachers. The researchers collected teacher surveys and classroom observational
and interview data from ten schools in five districts. They found that by 2013,
two years after implementation had begun, the majority of surveyed teachers had at least partially incorporated the frameworks in their classrooms,
but elementary teachers were more likely to report full implementation than
middle or high school teachers, with the latter groups feeling less supported
and needing more professional development.[52]

Since 2015, DESE, under a contract to Westat, has conducted a survey
of the universe of Massachusetts principals and superintendents, focusing on
alignment of instructional materials with the frameworks and on the sources
of the curriculum resources that schools are using. In the 2018 survey, fewer
than half of the responding administrators reported that their mathematics
and ELA curriculum is strongly aligned with the 2017 revised state frameworks.[53] One response by DESE has been the Curriculum Ratings by Teachers
(CURATE) initiative, which convenes panels of Massachusetts teachers to
review and rate evidence on the alignment and quality of curriculum materials.
The ratings are then published online to reduce local educators' information

costs in deciding which materials to use. DESE grounds its emphasis on curriculum in a substantial body of academic research showing the relationship between the quality of curricular materials and student learning outcomes. For example, this perspective is reflected in a DESE policy brief, prepared by two university researchers, that summarizes academic research on the adoption, implementation, and effects of curriculum materials.[54]

Not all the research on Common Core implementation in Massachusetts has been conducted under DESE's auspices. Several academic studies included Massachusetts as one of several sampled states analyzed to understand teacher responses to the CCSS and the curricular choices associated with the standards implementation.[55] A particularly notable project was undertaken by the Boston Teachers Union (BTU) with a grant from the national AFT Innovation Fund. Its purpose was to develop online instructional units aligned with the Common Core, and then to analyze their use in classrooms. As a codirector of the project, a middle school teacher, explained:

> Our work is very tightly aligned to the Common Core. Essentially what we try to do is we try to bring really excellent teachers together (I guess we say "highly effective teachers"), who are really good at planning instruction, and we have them work in teams to build full units of lessons. Not lesson plans, but actual full lessons. The creation of lessons happens around creating PowerPoint presentations. It's really a workshop-based lesson that is laid out on PowerPoint and it helps the teacher and class walk through what a good workshop lesson should look like. There's a warm-up, there's a period of direct instruction, a launch, an exploration, and then there is a summary (sometimes there are a few other components in there as well). Our goal here is to really create standards-based lessons that also act as real-time professional development, and allow teachers the opportunity to work with best practices–based strategies and research-based strategies so that they can up their game.

The sixty units that were developed are embedded with individual lessons containing a multimedia presentation, all classwork materials, homework assignments, and assessments. The teacher researchers then studied a sample of teachers: a control group that used its own lessons and an experimental group that was provided lessons aligned with the Common Core mathematics standards for grades 6–8. With a sample of 1,500 students and twenty-two teachers from four states, the BTU project used test scores to chart the effectiveness of full instructional units closely aligned with the CCSS standards, and found an average of 25 percent greater growth among students in the experimental group in pre- and postunit assessment scores.

Political Opposition and Its Aftermath

Although rhetoric claiming that the CCSS represents "federal overreach" was part of the opposition's arguments in Massachusetts, much of their case focused on disputing the evidence used to support Massachusetts's adoption of the Common Core. Reports issued by the Pioneer Institute and the Heartland Institute continued to argue that the CCSS were less rigorous than the state's previous standards, and that Massachusetts students were now less well-prepared for college and career.

Criticism of the state's decision to replace the MCAS with PARCC was also central to the opponents' case. Arguments in favor of the superiority of the MCAS gained further traction because of educators' and parents' unease about the transition from MCAS to PARCC, partly due to concerns about how PARCC would affect students' proficiency scores. Opposition to PARCC was not limited to politically conservative groups that had been critical of the Common Core initially. In 2010, the leadership of the Massachusetts Teachers Association (MTA) had supported the state's use of the PARCC assessment. However, in 2014, Barbara Madeloni, who had campaigned against high-stakes tests, was elected as the MTA's new president. Although she opposed high-stakes tests generally, her position further strengthened opposition to the largely unknown PARCC assessment.[56] To smooth the transition, BESE voted to delay statewide administration of PARCC beyond its scheduled first administration in spring 2015. For the school year 2014–15, local districts were given the option of administering either the new PARCC assessment or the MCAS, with about half the districts selecting each.[57]

During the same period, a grassroots group, End Common Core Massachusetts, began a drive to place an initiative on the 2016 statewide ballot to repeal the Common Core and reinstate Massachusetts's former standards as the state's curriculum frameworks.[58] In addition, the initiative mandated that state officials annually release all state assessment "questions, constructed responses, and essays for each grade and every subject." End Common Core gathered more than 76 thousand signatures, exceeding the number required to place it on the ballot. A poll, conducted by the University of Massachusetts Amherst in early 2016, found that 53 percent of those surveyed supported repeal, with 22 percent opposed and 25 percent undecided.[59]

Despite the seeming strength of the anti–Common Core movement, two decisions by different branches of state government curtailed its progress. First, in late 2015, BESE, on the recommendation of Commissioner Chester, approved by a vote of eight to three a "next generation MCAS" that would be a hybrid—an update of MCAS with elements of PARCC also included.[60] In a second decision, in June 2016, the state's Supreme Judicial Court ruled that the state attorney general had improperly certified the End Common Core ballot initiative, and as a result, it could not be placed on the November ballot. The basis of the court's ruling was that the section of the initiative mandating test item disclosure did not meet the requirement that petitions contain only subjects "which are related or which are mutually dependent" so that voters can decide on a unified statement of public policy. In the court's view, the mandate for test item disclosure was a separate subject, distinct from the repeal of the Common Core. The plaintiffs in the case were a group of parents and business leaders, including the chair of the MBAE board.[61]

As they had done throughout the adoption and implementation of the CCSS, Massachusetts officials relied heavily on an evidence-based approach to the 2017 revision of the mathematics and ELA frameworks. The assumption was that the revisions would build on the 2010 Common Core frameworks, and also draw on the earlier state standards where appropriate. Central to informing the revisions were the experience and professional judgment that Massachusetts educators had gained over the first six years of the framework's implementation. The revision process included multiple phases: an online survey with responses from several hundred educators who were asked about standards that they found unnecessary or inappropriate, standards that should be added, design features that were invaluable or unnecessary, and any technical errors or inaccuracies; standards review panels for mathematics and ELA that were asked to consider the public input and recommend revisions to the 2010 standards; and seven ELA and six mathematics content advisory groups to review and refine the proposed revisions. DESE contracted with Abt Associates to document the revisions process, and to assist the state board in considering and incorporating feedback from key stakeholders.[62] The resulting revisions clarified terms, increased coherence across grades, made some organizational changes such as shifting the grade level at which students are expected to master a standard, and in mathematics, provided more explicit guidance for high school course sequences. The 2017 revisions not only updated and clarified the 2010 frameworks, but they also signaled that the essence of the Common Core was now politically sustainable and had been institutionalized in Massachusetts.

Conclusion

Disputes about the validity of research-based evidence and professional judgment were more important in Massachusetts than the ideological rhetoric that dominated the CCSS repeal in Indiana. However, Massachusetts also differed in another significant way: the adoption process had essentially documented that although the CCSS had some advantages over the Massachusetts standards, they were both excellent and either could continue to form the basis for the state's standards-based reform strategy. Consequently, key officials had greater flexibility in how they approached the question of whether the Common Core was politically sustainable. As chair of the PARCC governing board, Commissioner Chester had a stake in that assessment's development. Nevertheless, he recognized that MCAS had served the state well, and that proposing a hybrid assessment would partly respond to the critics' demands and still allow Massachusetts to remain in the PARCC consortium. The hybrid assessment also allowed governor Charlie Baker, an opponent of CCSS adoption in 2010 and a strong supporter of MCAS, a way to distance himself from the 2016 ballot initiative while not angering his conservative constituents, and thus continue to be viewed as a political moderate in a state with largely left-of-center politics.[63]

TENNESSEE

As in Indiana, initial support for the Common Core in Tennessee was not politically sustainable once opponents mobilized and elected officials responded to their demands. The two states were also similar in that both chose to implement policies aimed at strengthening educator quality and accountability simultaneously with the CCSS. That strategy had the effect of severely diminishing teacher morale and their acceptance of the new standards. Although political rhetoric constituted a critical part of the evidence base that shaped the Common Core implementation in Tennessee, it resembled California and Massachusetts, with participants also drawing on research-based evidence and professional judgment.

Adopting the Common Core

For Tennessee, adoption of the Common Core was a natural progression of an education reform that had begun in 2007. Highly visible reports on the gap between Tennessee students' scores on the state assessment as compared with their NAEP scores prompted state officials to take action. Their motivation stemmed from both the actual test data and from embarrassment about how the state was being portrayed.

> One of our board members made a comment: "Tennessee does pretty good when it compares itself to itself." If you use Tennessee standards and Tennessee tests and Tennessee cut scores, we get 90 percent proficient and we look great. Everybody wants to be like Tennessee and have 90 percent of the kids proficient. But when you look at NAEP and we've got 25, 26, 28 percent proficient, we don't look so good. When you look at ACT and you've got 16 to 18 percent of the kids meeting those benchmarks that ACT sets, you don't look so good. So it became pretty obvious to us that we needed to look at raising our expectations; raising and improving our standards.
>
> —*Staff member, Tennessee State Board of Education*

We had been really challenged to increase rigor and relevance, and the governor was very upset because of the *Leaders and Laggards* report that came out of the US Chamber of Commerce that said Tennessee was a cream puff state, and basically, that our standards were weak and our proficiency levels were at D minus. With our standards being weak and our proficiency levels so weak, we're just misleading people.

So the governor said we're going to fix that. We began to work with the state board of education and set out on the Tennessee Diploma Project [TDP], and basically really got aggressive with Achieve and others to redo our standards, particularly math and reading language arts. We got into the process, got those standards revised, and then started to work on assessments against those standards, and then the Common Core talk began. We decided at that point in time that Tennessee would sign on to the Common Core very early on because we saw the alignment there. There was at that time—I'll use the word loosely—a guaranteed 85 percent match between the math standards and our standards. I wouldn't say 85 percent necessarily, but it's very close.

—Tennessee Department of Education (TDOE) official

Much of the preparatory analytical and political groundwork that other states had done during the CCSS adoption process, Tennessee had already completed as part of its implementation of the TDP. A TDOE manager enumerated the variety of evidence used in designing the TDP:

When I say "evidence," we used assessment scores; we used survey information that came from business roundtables. The governor actually went around the state and had these conversations, and they asked businesses and chambers of commerce to weigh in on their thoughts around what the expectations were for Tennessee students. We used achievement data from our [grades] 3 through 8 program; we use data from our inter-course program. Tennessee had an inter-course program that required students to actually pass three assessments before they received a high school diploma. So we used that data. We used ACT data; we tested every student in the state in the eleventh grade with the ACT or SAT assessments. We used Explore and Plan from eighth and tenth grade data. And then we also did a study for which we went back and concorded that work. And so we knew how our students were performing on the Explore and the Plan and ACT, and in many cases were able to go back and do a research study in which we matched students. As [a result,] we sort of found the place for our Tennessee Diploma Project standards, in terms of what student expectations matched what was taking place with our ACT assessments or College Board assessments.

Political support for the TDP and then the CCSS was widespread, including from the Tennessee Business Roundtable, the Tennessee Chamber of Commerce, the United Way, the Urban League, and the NAACP. For the Urban League in Tennessee, support for the Common Core was part of a larger national initiative:

Nationally, we [the Urban League] favor the adoption of Common Core standards and have organized ourselves programmatically around how—particularly in two states, Tennessee and Pennsylvania—how we help communities to understand the value of adopting Common Core standards. Of course, in favoring Common Core standards, we also have to be organized around advocacy and what's needed to support, particularly our community, which is largely the lower-performing end, with existing standards: What systems will do to support the transition from existing standards to Common Core; what resources will be put in place; how parents and families will be energized; how communities will be educated; how communities will be mobilized to lend academic support to students as we transition.

Education has always been a civil rights issue. And I think we recognize, particularly as we look at achievement gap data, that our communities are particularly vulnerable. And if we don't get organized around it [the CCSS], we're going to be left behind.

A leader of the state NAACP drew on her own experience in explaining why her organization supported the Common Core:

When I got on the school board, I was amazed to see that the level of rigor required by students wasn't the same that even I had in a segregated high school finishing in 1965. That amazed me because we had to have two foreign languages; we had to have all these sciences, at least the maths, all these things. You had to have Algebra I and Algebra II, and then you had to have a geometry, a trigonometry, a unified math, or something. It wasn't something real simple, that was required. So it amazed me. I said, "Wait a minute. Yeah, it's been forty years, but how in the world did we get from there to here? How in the world did a little segregated Black school in a poor county . . . ? If they knew what was right then, how have we gotten to where we are now?" I think I started saying again and again: It needs to be different. We need to make sure we've got the rigor we need. And when I talk to people that have lived one place and then transferred somewhere else . . . the difference in the schools made a difference.

Especially pivotal to the reform policy process was the State Collaborative on Reforming Education (SCORE), founded by former US Senate majority leader Bill Frist (R-TN) as a research and advocacy organization. Its mission is to ensure that all Tennessee students have equitable learning opportunities, especially as measured by test performance at or above grade level, and by college enrollment and degree attainment. As a SCORE staff member noted, work on the TDP spilled over to CCSS adoption:

> From the sales pitch to the state, it never seemed like a big jump ahead because we'd done the big jump with the Diploma Project. There was a lot of advocacy that was done around the Tennessee Diploma Project about why we have higher standards, why it's important to expect more in terms of what students are learning. So that communication has already happened around the Diploma Project.

To augment the TDP, Tennessee enacted the First to the Top Act in January 2010. The legislation was intended as comprehensive education reform policy that established an "Achievement School District" which allowed the state commissioner of education to intervene in failing schools; mandated a comprehensive evaluation system for teachers and principals based on multiple measures of effectiveness, including student achievement indicators; removed restrictions on the use of value-added data for promotion, retention, tenure, and compensation decisions; and authorized local school districts to adopt alternative salary schedules.[64] This legislation became the basis of Tennessee's Race to the Top application, and on March 29, 2010, the state received a $500 million grant—one of only two states to receive a Race to the Top award in the first round.[65] A former legislative leader described the reasons why the state's Race to the Top application enjoyed bipartisan support:

> The Race to the Top among some legislators, it meant different things. As an example, for a conservative member of the general assembly, it sent kind of a hackle sort of reaction of, "That's a federal program," and there was safety in the standards; there was safety in, "This proposal isn't really the goal. The plan that Tennessee has is the important thing, and if we happen to get wind in our sails for this opportunity, that's what we want to see happen." And that was actually a big part of it.
>
> Then on the other side, there were members who ... The potential for federal funding loosened some traditional resistance for, say, accountability through the teacher evaluation and First to the Top, which is probably

an important component of where we're going, and tying effectiveness and student achievement, in our efforts in Race to the Top.

On July 30, 2010, the SBE unanimously approved the CCSS as the state standards. The vote involved little discussion, and no dissenting opinions were expressed. A TDOE manager explained the primary reason:

The state board, I think, really appreciated the fact that we were able to take what we were currently doing and show the Common Core to them and its relationship to how we had built the Tennessee Diploma Project standards. It was kind [of] a really natural fit for them. And so, without much debate, there was approval.

Even with a gubernatorial election scheduled for 2010, Common Core supporters in Tennessee had reason to assume that the organizational and political support evident when the standards were adopted would continue. One reason was term-limited governor Phil Bredesen's foresight:

The governor was very much one of the people at the table. That was another thing with Race to the Top. So critically important was [that] the governor got every candidate, everybody in the primary to just sign on that they would continue this process and they believed in it. He had all these letters of support, so they really don't have a choice. I guess they do have a choice, but [Bill] Haslam [the incoming governor] was right there to start with. And of course, Senator [Jamie] Woodson at that time was the Speaker Pro Tem, but she'd also been the chair of the education commit- tee in the Senate, and she was one of our ringleaders in the whole process. She's very close to Governor Haslam, too, so those relationships are criti- cal to keeping that momentum, and we've had that. So hopefully, we just maintain it. I know Commissioner [Kevin] Huffman is committed to the whole process. He's a TFA-er [former Teach for America Corps member] himself, and they don't believe in the status quo. So it's good.

There was also evidence of public support for the state's education reform policies. A statewide poll that SCORE commissioned in July 2010 found that more than two-thirds of voters (69 percent) "strongly supported" the SBE's decision to raise standards in mathematics and reading. Even after respondents heard arguments for and against higher standards—including that student test scores could fall and costs to local school systems rise—71 percent expressed strong support. Support for other reforms was lower: 40 percent of voters supported the law mandating that half of a teacher's evaluation be based on student test scores, with 34 percent opposed to the law and 26 percent undecided. A majority (52 percent) supported the Achievement School District concept.[66] For close to two years after the adoption of the CCSS, the bipartisan political support that had been mobilized around the Race to the Top was sustained as Tennessee moved into the implementation phase.

Implementing the Common Core

As in Massachusetts, the Race to the Top grant provided Tennessee with additional resources that allowed it to put into place a comprehensive implementation plan and to draw on several third-party providers. Using $44 million from its Race to the Top grant, the state trained seventy thousand teachers, including thirty thousand in a single summer, in preparation for teaching the CCSS. The training sessions were led by seven hundred teacher coaches who were selected by the state based on their records of classroom effectiveness; they were each given two weeks of intensive training that focused on how the standards could be translated into classroom practice. According to *Education Week*, the Tennessee effort was the most comprehensive Common Core training in the country, both in the number of teachers trained and in the total cost.[67]

The state worked with the Institute for Learning at the University of Pittsburgh to design the content of the training, because the TDOE staff felt that the Pittsburgh researchers "had a good pulse on how the Common Core and PARCC linked together, and because they developed the PARCC prototype in ELA." TDOE also worked with Student Achievement Partners, drawing on preinstructional shifts in mathematics and ELA that SAP had developed. Sopris Learning was another third-party provider working with the state as part of its emphasis on K–3 reading foundational skills. Sopris designed the content of the teacher training in an iterative process with the TDOE staff, and then trained the lead teachers who would work with their colleagues.

Tennessee, more than most states, also recognized that preparation for teaching the Common Core had to extend beyond just practicing teachers to those in preprofessional training. Consequently, representatives of the higher education teacher training institutions in the state participated in the training for Common Core coaches, and began to think about what kinds of training would be needed for new teachers. As one of state's colleges of education deans explained:

> [The] Ayers Institute [at Lipscomb University] facilitated those conversations and determined that using Race to the Top funds through the Tennessee Higher Ed Commission and the state department [of education], that we really needed to create some very high quality resources that professors, faculty members, could actually use in their teacher preparation program to illustrate what Common Core looked like in a real classroom in Tennessee. So we created video resources after recruiting and working with five teachers from the state. We videotaped them using Common Core in their classrooms. It happened to be that half of those people who were on the video module were Common Core coaches themselves. So they were people who had been trained last summer and were implementing that in the fall. So we did trainings with all forty-four teacher prep institutions in Tennessee, plus the community colleges, plus six alternative teacher provider programs. Teach for America [and the] New Teacher Project we also invited to all of our five regional trainings.

As a result, 470 higher education faculty who prepare teachers in both arts and sciences departments and colleges of education were trained to understand what the CCSS looks like in classrooms, so they could incorporate that knowledge into the teacher preparation curriculum.

The Race to the Top grant required that the implementation and effects of the state's reform initiative be monitored and evaluated. Much of this research was conducted by the Tennessee Consortium on Research, Evaluation, and Development (TNCRED), a research center at Vanderbilt University that worked under contract to the TDOE.[68] TNCRED's research projects focused on six key reform efforts: teacher and principal evaluation systems; the Achievement School District and related issues of school turnaround; education compensation reform; workforce trends, including career pathways of educators and the distribution of high performing teachers and leaders; STEM professional development and network initiatives; and the quality, flexibility, and interconnectedness of Tennessee's educational data systems.

Of particular interest to the TDOE and TNCRED was the effect of teachers' Common Core training on their classroom activities:

> I think one of our biggest challenges is knowing what's happening at a statewide level and being able to monitor that. We've provided training to thousands of teachers, and that's great. But we need to get better about knowing how that is then translated back into the classroom. So we have a couple of things going on that I think help us get a snapshot; some of that is instructional practice. We truly believe that in order for a transition to the Common Core to actually make a difference for kids there has to be a change in instruction. At the state level it is very hard for us to measure instruction in individual classrooms. We are trying to do some of that through our different groups in talking about what's working and what's not working. Our lead teachers are a good example of that. Over the course of their service (they contract with us for a year), we adopted some surveys and curriculum type questions to ask them to measure over the course of a year to see if the way they're spending time in the classroom is changing. We also have statewide teacher evaluations. So we have been trying to think about what are the ways we can leverage that to give us more information about what is happening at the school level. At the classroom level, we think there are some indicators on our rubric for teacher evaluation that align really well with the Common Core and we would hope to see changes as teachers move to more conceptual understanding type of instruction.
>
> *—TDOE curriculum and instruction manager*

TNCRED also collaborated with SCORE, which collects data on its own in addition to analyzing state data as the basis for its annual reports. As one of its staff explained:

> SCORE's role is in monitoring the progress of implementation. So we spend a lot of time actually going through different trainings the state puts on. And we will conduct our own focus groups, one-on-one interviews with superintendents, principals, and teachers, and other people who have special roles in implementation like the Common Core coaches, people who serve on different leadership councils that the department has created, like the Common Core Leadership Council and the ELA leadership council.

In addition, the United Ways of Tennessee, with a grant from their parent organization, held sixty-one "listening sessions" in 2010 with over seven hundred individuals from rural, suburban, and urban communities throughout the state as the First to the Top reforms were initially implemented.[69]

Central to Tennessee's monitoring and evaluation efforts has been its Value-Added Assessment System (TVAAS), developed by the late William Sanders, a University of Tennessee statistician. The value-added method—which has become controversial as districts and states have applied it in high-stakes evaluations of teachers—measures the effects of a teacher, school, or district on student performance by tracking the progress of students against the progress they would be expected to make based on their previous performance. Tennessee's commitment to data-driven policy and practice extends beyond TVAAS to include a P20 longitudinal data system that links K–12 and higher education student data, and incorporates data from TDOE, higher education, the Tennessee Department of Labor and Workforce Development, and the Department of Children's Services.[70]

Although Tennessee emphasized research-based evidence in its Common Core implementation and evaluation plans, it also included a feedback mechanism based on professional judgment. The Common Core Leadership Council (CCLC) was a group of twenty-two school and district leaders from across the state. One of the members described its purpose and activities:

> The philosophy behind it was to leverage the expertise of practitioners around the state to contribute to the CCSS initiative . . . The whole idea was to brainstorm and come together and think about what makes the most sense. We spend a lot of time doing that. We also spend a lot of time writing, gaining a deeper understanding of the CCSS, interacting with the authors of the standards to have a really good understanding of the research behind the standards, to know what it really means to be college and career ready. Also, [we have] a lot of conversations looking at data in terms of where Tennessee lives nationally and globally in terms of our competition, and from that creating a sense of urgency. Out of all the brainstorming sessions we developed what we call the "three legs of the stool" [that] every district needs: assessment, transparency, and accountability. It is also curricular resources, instructional support, all of those things that a district would need, coupled with communication and leadership.

Political Opposition

Unlike in Indiana and Massachusetts, where most of the Common Core opponents were affiliated with grassroots groups established specifically to oppose the standards, opposition in Tennessee originated with national organizations or their state affiliates, typically ones with missions broader than only education. These included: the Tennessee Republican Party, the Tennessee chapter of the Koch brothers–funded Americans for Prosperity, the Tennessee Eagle Forum, and the Tennessee Freedom Coalition. A SCORE staff member described an opposition rally in April 2013 and the organization's response to it:

> Last Monday, there was an event in Williamson County and it was an anti–Common Core rally, and there were lots of national groups that had come in from DC who talk about how your state was forced to develop these standards, that we were coerced into doing it, nobody looked at the standards before, and that these standards hadn't been vetted. It's conservative, Tea Party–type groups that are very vocal against the standards. Even though they're in the minority, they are highly vocal, well coordinated, and funded, so they've been somewhat successful in terms of recruiting people—there were over seven hundred people who came to the event last week. And they talk to their legislators.
>
> Our communications and advocacy office has been on steroids trying to respond to this and trying to stay ahead of it a little bit. We just got a grant from Achieve to work on Common Core communications. So we've been putting op-eds in the paper, talking with reporters, putting them in touch with people they can talk to, answering questions they have. We have the Expect More, Achieve More Coalition and that's a group of over two hundred partners [including] school districts, businesses in Tennessee, [and] higher education—it's a broad-based group—and all of them support higher standards and specifically Common Core. So we've been doing a lot of work to extend membership in that coalition, get those people to talk with their networks and constituents about the new standards.[71]

However, opposition was not limited to conservative groups. In the 2014 TNCRED survey, only 39 percent of the teachers responding said that "teaching to the standards will improve student learning," a decrease from 60 percent in the 2013 survey; 56 percent of the teachers responding wanted to abandon the CCSS, while only 31 percent wished to continue it. The Vanderbilt researchers noted that several factors contributed to the teachers' opposition: a belief on the part of many that their training and the assistance they had received had been insufficient or ineffective, concerns about the impact of the Common Core on personnel evaluations, the difficulty of the new standards, and a too-abrupt transition for students, especially for those in the upper grades.[72]

A leader of the Tennessee Education Association (TEA), while praising the state's efforts to prepare teachers, argued that its other reform policies had lowered teacher morale and had spilled over into their attitudes toward the Common Core:

> Because of other political and policy changes in our state regarding public education, [teachers] are fearful—I know that morale is very low among teachers right now—and I'm fearful that the success of implementation [of the Common Core] will be impacted by teachers sort of feeling like this is another thing they are putting on top of us. Something else to add to our burden. Just a little bit of background, in the last two years legislative changes have ended collective bargaining for teachers in our state, they are currently changing the teacher retirement system (which will be a lesser benefit in the long run), and we're only in the second year of a brand new evaluation system under the Race to the Top grant. So teachers have been under a lot of stress with a lot [of] changes happening really fast. So our concern is to try and work them through the Common Core because this is something we believe in, and if it's done well then it will have a positive impact on student achievement. But it's a really difficult climate right now as far as helping teachers embrace it and be willing to really move forward with it. I think the state is doing a good job—I mean in all my years teaching in Tennessee I've never seen the kind of professional development and training opportunities offered by the state, so I can't speak negatively about that. But I am concerned about teachers' apprehension and anxiety around it and a lot of other issues that we're dealing with.

Legislators opposed to the CCSS allied with the TEA to delay implementation of the PARCC assessment. The Tennessee Comprehensive Assessment Program (TCAP), based on earlier standards and only partially aligned with the CCSS, was continued as the state assessment.

While still supporting the Common Core, Governor Haslam announced in October 2014 that the state would solicit public comments on the CCSS through a state-run website, and that two committees would work with the SBE and three other advisory committees to review the standards and recommend changes by the end of 2015.[73] During this period, the legislative leadership introduced several bills to replace the Common Core with new standards. Their arguments echoed those of state opposition groups and their national affiliates, emphasizing what they viewed as federal interference and a loss of local control.[74] In response, 114 of Tennessee's 141 local school superintendents signed a letter pleading with the legislature not to abandon the Common Core. They highlighted the millions of dollars that had been spent implementing it, and that Tennessee students had shown significant gains in test scores in recent years. In April 2015, the legislature passed a compromise bill that, instead of enacting a Common Core repeal bill, allowed the standards review process to proceed to its completion. The bill added another step of vetting by a panel appointed and approved by the legislature.[75] The legislation did not specify what changes to the standards should be made, but it did require that the state have new and improved standards by 2017–18, and that they should be developed by 2016, so teachers would have time to become accustomed to them.

Between November 2014 and April 2015, 2,262 participants (57 percent of them educators, 14 percent parents) provided online reviews of approximately two thousand mathematics and ELA standards. Reviewers had the choice of indicating whether a standard should be retained, removed, or replaced. Of the 131,424 reviews received, 56 percent registered support for keeping a specific standard. The state contracted with the Southern Regional Education Board (SREB) to prepare data reports and manage the review process.[76] A forty-two-member committee appointed by the SBE used the report prepared by SREB, comments from higher education institutions, and a public review of the committee's recommended changes to develop a revised set of standards that were submitted to the Standards Recommendation Committee.

In April 2016, after eighteen months of review and revision, the SBE voted unanimously to adopt the Tennessee Academic Standards (TAS) for mathematics and English language arts. The SBE executive director acknowledged that the Common Core continued to be the foundation of the TAS:

The Common Core standards were our starting point, but the revisions we have made are significant, and significant enough that we consider them new standards. The formatting is different. We've dropped standards, we've added standards, we've made changes to existing standards.[77]

Most of the revisions involved word changes to enhance clarity, changes in presentation to make them more user-friendly, and the movement of some standards to different grades and courses to make the progressions more logical.[78] Without the Race to the Top funds, TDOE had fewer resources to assist teachers in preparing to implement the TAS. So rather than the TDOE delivering training directly to teachers, it trained district-level teams that would then work with colleagues in their own districts.[79]

CONCLUSION

The pattern of evidence use during the Common Core adoption stage was remarkably similar across the four states. Time pressures and trust in the standards writers and their organizational sponsors meant that scrutiny of CCSS's evidence base was minimal, limited to cursory NAEP and state test score comparisons and examinations of international benchmarking standards. What was required in every state was some type of analysis that compared current standards with the CCSS to reassure decision-makers that the Common Core was an improvement.

During the implementation stage at the state level, research-based evidence was reflected in the design of curriculum modules and professional development resources, and in the administrative and survey data collected to monitor local efforts to translate the standards into classroom practice. In the Race to the Top states, each state education agency had the capacity either to generate and use such evidence on its own or to contract with research producers and third-party providers. Yet even in the Race to the Top states—both of which have SEAs with strong organizational cultures supporting research-based evidence—it was difficult for the state agency to know in a detailed or systematic way how the standards are being implemented in individual classrooms. All four states have primarily relied on self-reports from teachers, collected through periodic surveys and validated largely through informal methods.

The limited capacity of the California Department of Education was expanded by a range of local collaborative networks and by the commitment of PACE and other research institutions to examine the implementation and effects of the CCSS. Although it contracts with university-based research centers, the Indiana Department of Education lacks the strong, ongoing collaboration present in Tennessee. Yet in each state, there has been some press for research-based evidence, and where SEA capacity is limited, alternative institutional arrangements have been able to augment it.

In three of the states, opposition to the Common Core threatened its political sustainability. Grassroots and national groups primarily relied on the values-based political rhetoric of "federal overreach" and "loss of local control" to advance their cause. Their opposition to the Common Core was strengthened by spillovers from other reform policies that teachers viewed as unfairly targeting them. However, what has largely been missed in discussions of Common Core opposition is that once state officials agreed to replace the CCSS with revised state standards, political rhetoric largely ceased, and professional judgment became the dominant source of evidence. Unlike the standards and accountability disputes of the 1990s, opponents focused only incidentally on the content of the Common Core. So once a state agreed to take control of the standards revision process, most opponents backed off and allowed educators to assume responsibility. That process, relying on committees of educators, looked like earlier standards-setting exercises when each state had its own standards. The major difference was that now the revisions started with the Common Core, so its rigor and focus largely remained, minimizing the "clutter" of past state standards. The revision process became an opportunity for educators to bring their classroom experience to bear in making the standards more accessible and coherent from their perspective, and to provide a stronger sense of local ownership than was possible with the Common Core (because it had originated outside the state). Basing the revised state standards on educators' professional judgment also helped legitimate them to parents and the general public.

Comparing Common Core adoption and implementation across the four states also provides further insight into the forms that political sustainability and policy learning can take under different assumptions and state contexts. If political sustainability is defined as the preservation of the Common Core, it was not sustainable in Indiana and Tennessee. However, if sustainability is conceptualized more broadly as the continuation of the standards and accountability policy regime that the Common Core entrepreneurs were attempting to maintain, Indiana's and Tennessee's policies are still very much within that tradition. These differences in how sustainability is conceptualized suggest that in considering policymakers' incentives to use evidence in policy arguments, it is important to consider not only their immediate policy preferences, but also their broader, long-term goals. Disrupting a single policy may be an effective strategy for removing a short-term threat to a comprehensive reform agenda.

Implicit in the concept of policy learning is an assumption that officials will use evidence about their past experience to try a different approach to addressing a policy problem. When the evidence points to a policy falling short of its intended goals, an alternative is warranted. That was the case in California, where Brown and Kirst recognized that state government lacked the capacity to enforce centralized regulations, and that the categorical finance system was unfair and inefficient. Consequently, they turned to a fundamentally different strategy with the LCFF and more decentralized governance. However, in Indiana, Massachusetts, and Tennessee, policy learning from Common Core opposition led in a different direction. Rather than turning to a new approach, state officials chose to revert to an older strategy— homegrown standards and assessments developed by a committee of educators. It had worked well enough in the past, was familiar to educators and the interested public, and it was more transparent and visible than the Common Core adoption process had been. In all four states, policy learning occurred, but interpretation of the evidence led to different actions.

6

Evidence Use in the Children's Health Insurance Program

A Cross-Sector Case Study

THIS CHAPTER DETAILS the use of evidence in enacting and updating the Children's Health Insurance Program (CHIP). We chose this case because the program focuses on services for children, and hence the challenge of designing good policy brings up the same sort of research questions posed in K–12 education. A priori, we expected the commonality of evidence to anchor the case, while a number of characteristics would differentiate the use of evidence—CHIP was a national program, and hence the deliberation was centered in Congress; CHIP was an incremental expansion of a program dating to the 1960s, and hence we expected a replay of the predecessor program's politics. The story of CHIP turns out to be more revealing of the interplay between evidence use and the political context than our first enumeration of similarities and differences suggests. For one, since the Great Society, the distribution of political power had shifted toward the states, and the enactment process reflected this changed political context: CHIP differs significantly from the Medicaid pediatric program. Correspondingly, in later years, when CHIP was modified to improve implementation, virtually all the evidence came from the states and research on state-level programs. But CHIP's resemblance to the Common Core is not limited to the leading role of the states in its initiation and early implementation, for the ideological polarization of the national parties stimulated a sea change in the political context. In the case of CHIP, the rising conservative opposition had the effect of changing the criteria for judging the program a success; it provoked a new look at social science research on policies for youth and a thoroughgoing change in the use of evidence.

BACKGROUND ON CHIP/SCHIP

Note: The program was originally named the State Children's Health Insurance Program (SCHIP); the name was shortened to CHIP in the 2009 reauthorization, though some quoted sources refer to the program as CHIP before 2009. In this chapter, we use SCHIP to designate the program until 2009, CHIP after that date.

The origins of the Children's Health Insurance Program lie in one of largest policy accomplishments of President Lyndon Johnson's Great Society, the Medicaid program (enacted in 1965), which provides health insurance to low-income families. Although the category of eligible families was strictly limited, the pediatric component of Medicaid, compared to other components of the program, was generous in covering virtually the full list of needed health services for eligible children. Thirty years later, health care reformers intended CHIP to expand Medicaid's coverage to more low-income children. This provenance naturally suggests that the politics and policy designs of the two programs are similar; but the political context in the 1990s was quite different from the 1960s. Two elements have particular impact in altering the politics of the policy process, and hence the construction of advocacy arguments and the use of evidence: the rising power of the states in the federal system, and the growing ideological polarization of the two parties. The result was a political process and a program that departed radically from its predecessor, with corresponding changes in the advocates and their use of evidence.

Policy learning in a changed political context played a major role in shaping both the coalition-building strategies of advocates and the provisions of the legislation. The failure of two significant attempts to reform health care constituted the most salient events from which politicians needed to learn: President Clinton's ambitious health care reform proposal, and the Republican Party's initiative to convert Medicaid funding to a block grant. Advocates of reform took these failures to heart and crafted the SCHIP legislation so that its aim was less ambitious, narrowing the scope of the policy so that it built more transparently on an established program and focused on a defined, unusually sympathetic target population. The decision to incrementally expand the Medicaid program's pediatric services meant that the principle of government intervention did not need to be debated; the decision to restrict the policy change to improving access for children focused the deliberations on a sympathetic target population; and the decision to minimize interference with established employer-provided health insurance avoided a fight with powerful interests and decreased concerns over implementation. SCHIP's advocates were thus able to articulate a clear definition of the problem, which pointed to a solution that was modest and could be implemented without much change in current arrangements.

THE "WHO" AND THE "WHAT" OF EVIDENCE USE

The "Who"

In the case of SCHIP, the interaction of policy learning and political context both facilitated and complicated the use of evidence. Most obviously, because SCHIP proposed to expand a well-established component of Medicaid, research and data were available on the operation and impact of its predecessor program, and the inference from this record to predict the consequences of a change was unusually direct. Thus, reform advocates could mobilize reliable data to bound predictions about the prospective consequences of the new policy. But policy learning also advised pursuing a different coalition-building strategy from the one the Clinton administration pursued for the Health Security Act, in two respects. Advocates looked to Congress rather than the White House to take the lead, and they reached out to the states to build support for the reform. This had important implications for evidence use, because both choices had the effect of decentralizing the policy process, thus legitimating the use of a greater variety of evidence, especially evidence drawing on experience outside of Washington. The federalism component differentiated SCHIP from its predecessor: where Medicaid was administratively centered in Washington, the agenda for SCHIP envisioned a program in which the federal government offered financial incentives and delegated substantial discretion to the states. As the policy took shape, the role of the states in articulating their policy preferences and influencing the final provisions not only differed from the formulation of Medicaid in the 1960s, it deviated from typical national legislation.[1] In fact, the input of the states closely resembled their role in the formulation of the Common Core State Standards.

Table 6.1 shows the distribution of witnesses who appeared before congressional committees in all hearings (1997–2017) concerning the CHIP program.[2]

Representatives of federal agencies played a substantial role in SCHIP hearings. Following the decision to construct SCHIP as an incremental expansion, committees could call on research-based findings from quantitative evidence generated by almost three decades of the Medicaid program. The data collection, program monitoring, and regular reporting were mandated in the

TABLE 6.1   Witnesses and their organizational affiliations

WITNESS CATEGORY AND TYPE	NUMBER OF WITNESSES	PERCENT OF TOTAL WITNESSES
Federal	**13**	**9.6%**
Federal Administrative Agency	9	6.6
Federal Elected Official	4	2.9
Researchers	**42**	**30.9%**
University Researcher	9	6.6
Non-university Researcher	7	5.1
Federal Research Agency	26	19.1
Groups/Individuals	**38**	**27.9%**
Advocacy IO	12	8.8
Hybrid IO	15	11.0
Disseminator IO	3	2.2
Program Recipient	8	5.9
State	**40**	**29.4%**
State Administrative Agency	30	22.1
State Elected Official	10	7.4
Local	**3**	**2.2%**
Local Administrative Agency	1	0.7
Local Elected Official	2	1.5
Total	**136**	**100%**

legislation, and federal agencies were used to updating congressional committees on Medicaid. We have coded separately those witnesses whose affiliation was with an explicit research institution, including federal researchers tasked with evaluating the operation of their agencies' programs. Much of the data on the evolution of Medicaid's pediatric component originated with federal agencies, although it was analyzed by both federal research agencies and independent scholars, and researchers were well-represented in the hearings. Groups and organizations, ranging from advocates for expanding health care to trade associations representing employers and insurance companies, constituted just under thirty percent of the testimony; representatives of state governments made up a similar proportion.

The "What"

The testimony drew heavily on nationally representative statistical data to estimate the scope of the problem. For instance, Patrick Purcell, a researcher at the Congressional Research Service, used data from the Census Bureau and the National Center for Health Statistics to estimate the number of uninsured children (in an average month in 1994, 6.3 million employed heads of families were without health insurance, and three-quarters of these families included children), and to map the problem's correlates (these families were predominately young; the adults were employed by small firms in the retail sector and earned incomes that were lower than the national average).[3] Quantitative analysis was combined with other types of evidence to make a case that was based on policymakers' past experience, compelling anecdotes about children without insurance, and interest group arguments. Testimony showed that a surprising number of children lacked health insurance, that most of them were from working families whose incomes were above the Medicaid threshold but inadequate to pay the cost of premiums in the private insurance market, that the cost of health care deterred families from getting regular examinations or treatments, and that this resulted in avoidable illness and deaths.

State health department officials and even governors were active participants in the congressional hearings during 1997. The evidence base and many significant points of the policy agenda were held in common by national and state participants: counts of the number of uninsured low-income children based on state data comported with estimates from national statistics, state authorities supported the goal of expanding coverage, and they agreed in principle with concerns about *crowd-out*—making sure that the program did not induce families whose children were covered by job-related insurance to transfer to SCHIP.[4]

But state-level representatives devoted the bulk of their testimony to urging Congress to design SCHIP so that it allowed more discretion for states to adjust program mandates to local conditions. They advised against replicating Medicaid, complaining about the number of rules and about the legal entitlement to care, which was both inflexible and channeled problem cases into the federal judiciary rather than into the states. Their testimony relied on research-based analyses and statistics in part, but it was distinguished from that of national-level experts and academics by state officials' ability to call on two additional types of evidence: detailed descriptions of current policy as implemented in their states, and the use of professional judgment and practitioner experience with the Medicaid program to identify what worked (and didn't) and to reflect on changes that would improve their capacity to enroll more uninsured low-income children.[5] They underlined the importance of federal funding for state outreach efforts, but they insisted that allowing wide discretion for states would achieve the intentions of the legislation better than detailed national rules. They took inspiration from the testimony of the few states that had expanded their Medicaid programs to cover more children, reading their experience as not only identifying areas where SCHIP could improve on Medicaid's implementation, but underlining the importance of state-level discretion. For instance, Vermont governor Howard Dean described how his state had succeeded in cutting taxes and expanding Medicaid to cover every child under eighteen at 225 percent of poverty or below, through an intensive program of outreach.[6] State-level representatives proposed that SCHIP should allow states, as long as they were pursuing the goal of expanding health insurance coverage for low-income children, to take different approaches to increasing enrollment, assembling a package of benefits and premiums, and dealing with the potential for crowd-out. And Congress, in a marked deviation from convention, listened to and learned from the states: members of Congress invited states to testify much more frequently than in hearings on other health legislation, and the enacted legislation differed significantly from Medicaid—its services were not mandated as an entitlement, and its more flexible rules widened states' latitude for implementation. In sum, many of the most important specific provisions agreed with the ideas state representatives advocated.[7]

The hearings in 1999 and 2000 were slated as oversight of early implementation, with the primary purpose of disseminating information from states that had implemented the program early. These hearings gave state authorities the opportunity to tell how favorably SCHIP differed from Medicaid, and Senator William Roth (R-DE), chairman of the Senate Finance Committee, stressed Congress's commitment to gather information to improve the operation of the program.[8] There were more states whose programs were up and running, and more states were mounting formal policy evaluations, thus state authorities could ground their testimony in research-based evidence. For instance, Marilyn Ellwood described a report by Mathematica Policy Research that had evaluated implementation in several states, comparing Medicaid regulations to SCHIP. The report surveyed both administrators and staffers, and quoted one staffer: "I have given up trying to explain Medicaid eligibility to people. It is too complicated." Mathematica's report recommended: "Medicaid rules for the very poorest families should not be more complicated than the rules States use for higher income children under the CHIP program."[9] But states drew on the day-to-day experience of implementing the program when they shared insights into successful techniques or political strategies. Barbara Edwards of Ohio's Health Department, for example, drew her advice from practitioner experience: "[P]ay attention early to what really happens at the point of the eligibility application being submitted ... the interaction between the consumers and the public worker." Ohio's initial top-down procedure was scrapped when frontline workers who dealt directly with families realized that personal follow-up was needed if the application procedure and enrollment were to succeed.[10] At the same time, progressive reformers kept the normative goals that initially motivated SCHIP before the Congress, criticizing the limited and formulaic outreach as failing to measure up to the goal of making health care available to all children from poor families, and they called for more research to reveal and correct shortfalls. For instance, Congressman Fortney Stark (D-CA) took the Clinton administration to task for the Health Care Financing Administration's reliance on informal interviews rather than systematic research to improve enrollment in Medicaid and CHIP.[11]

Table 6.2 shows the "What" of evidence use in the deliberation over SCHIP, arraying the presentation of research-based evidence versus non-research-based evidence by affiliation of witnesses testifying at congressional hearings.[12]

As table 6.2 shows, most witnesses employ both RBE evidence (peer-reviewed research, policy analysis, evaluation studies, and statistical data) and non-RBE evidence (current policy, practitioner experience, stories, and normative or ideological appeals). Witnesses recognized that, to be effective, their testimony should address a process that is intrinsically a combination of

TABLE 6.2   Use of research-based (RBE) and non-research-based evidence, by affiliation of witnesses

WITNESS CATEGORY	NUMBER OF WITNESSES	RBE	NON-RBE	PERCENT USING ONLY NON-RBE
Federal	13	12	12	7.7%
Federal Administrative Agency	9	9	8	0.0
Federal Elected Official	4	3	4	25.0
Researcher	42	41	25	2.4%
University Researcher	9	8	8	11.1
Non-university Researcher	7	7	3	0.0
Federal Research Agency	26	26	14	0.0
Groups/Individuals	38	15	37	60.5%
Advocacy IO	12	5	12	58.3
Hybrid IO	15	10	14	33.3
Disseminator IO	3	0	3	100.0
Program Recipient	8	0	8	100.0
State	40	22	39	45.0%
State Administrative Agency	30	17	29	43.3
State Elected Official	10	5	10	50.0
Local	3	2	3	33.3%
Local Administrative Agency	1	1	1	0.0
Local Elected Official	2	1	2	50.0
Total	136	92	116	32.4%

"hard" scientific comparisons with "soft" reflections on current practices, as well as arguments for change that inevitably refer to ideological or normative beliefs that cannot be systematically verified.

The vocation and organizational affiliation of the witness clearly distinguished the use of evidence, as comparison of the data in the rightmost column, the proportion using only non-RBE evidence, shows. Researchers and witnesses from federal agencies relied heavily on research-based evidence; exclusive references to non-research-based evidence is under ten percent of their testimony. On the other hand, representatives of intermediary organizations and state governments rely solely on non-research-based evidence in about half of their testimony. Tables 6.3 and 6.4 give additional insight into the use of different kinds of evidence by witnesses distinguished by vocation and affiliation.

Table 6.3 shows that the content of the testimony delivered by researchers differs from the other categories of witnesses, in that researchers much more frequently presented basic or applied research and policy analysis. It is worth noting that these two are the most theory-rich types of evidence—basic or applied research entails designing observations so the results of the study will distinguish between causal mechanisms predicted by theory; policy analysis entails systematically comparing empirical findings to the policy theory. The image of researchers as presenting testimony that measures up to the canons of scientific method is also consistent with the difference in the frequency of statistical comparisons, where researchers and federal program administrators make much more use of quantitative evidence than representatives of intermediary groups and states. For instance, Jonathan Gruber, a professor at MIT, analyzed the quantitative record of Medicaid expansions, showing that successive increases in the number of children covered by the program lowered the infant mortality rate by 8.5 percent and the child mortality rate by 4.5 percent, averting more than five thousand deaths of children per year. Barbara DeBuono, of New York's Department of Health, cited "an extensive statewide evaluation" by the University of Rochester of the implementation of Medicaid's Pediatric Program, that found that the program "results in increases in all types of primary care visits and specialty care [and] reduces hospitalization by 4 percent."[13]

Table 6.4 complements Table 6.3, showing the use of non-research-based evidence in congressional testimony.

TABLE 6.3 Use of different types of research-based evidence, by affiliation of witnesses

WITNESS ROLE	NUMBER OF WITNESSES	BASIC/APPLIED RESEARCH (PERCENT)	POLICY ANALYSIS (PERCENT)	EVALUATION STUDIES (PERCENT)	STATISTICAL DATA (PERCENT)
Federal	13	15.4%	0%	15.4%	76.9%
Researcher	42	33.3%	50.0%	2.4%	73.8%
Groups/ Individuals	38	18.4%	5.3%	0%	34.2%
State	40	7.5%	2.5%	10.0%	50.0%
Local	3	0%	0%	0%	67.0%

TABLE 6.4 Use of different types of non-research-based evidence, by affiliation of witnesses

WITNESS ROLE	NUMBER OF WITNESSES	CURRENT POLICY (PERCENT)	PRACTITIONER JUDGMENT (PERCENT)	STORIES/ RHETORICAL DEVICES (PERCENT)	NORMATIVE/ IDEOLOGICAL ARGUMENTS (PERCENT)
Federal	13	76.9%	61.5%	15.4%	7.7%
Researcher	42	35.7%	28.6%	4.8%	2.4%
Groups/ Individuals	38	31.6%	44.7%	47.4%	26.3%
State	40	95.0%	50.0%	5.0%	2.5%
Local	3	66.7%	33.3%	33.3%	33.3%

The influence of affiliation and vocation are clear in table 6.4, as seen in the difference between intermediary organizations versus federal and state representatives. Both state and federal witnesses foreground current policy and invoke the judgment of practitioners, such as street-level bureaucrats, more frequently than other witnesses. These witnesses are virtually all program administrators, and their familiarity with day-to-day operations allows them to understand the importance of taking into account current policy and practice, both as a barrier to wholesale change and as a useful indicator of what works in the real world. For instance, current policy and practitioner experience was stressed by Kathleen Gifford of Indiana's Department of Family and Social Services: "We developed a snazzier card. We advertised. We simplified the enrollment form. We eliminated unnecessary verification requirements." And the frontline experience produced changes in how the program was framed by the state's political leaders: Governor Frank O'Bannon "continues to promote the enrollment of all eligible children in Hoosier Healthwise [and continues] to destigmatize the Medicaid Program and simplify the enrollment process . . . stat[ing] that we should shout from the rooftops . . . that the strong enrollments were good news despite the budget implications."[14]

The testimony of intermediary organizations and interest groups, on the other hand, is distinguished by their use of personal stories and other rhetorical devices. For instance, Dr. Judith Palfrey, a pediatrician representing Children's Hospital in Boston, the nation's largest pediatric medical center, told the committee that:

> [M]y colleagues and I see the frightening results of the lack of insurance. We see parents delay preventive care visits, put off surgeries, even refuse to have x-rays when their children have had an accident. I have had parents apologize to me for missing vaccinations when they have been laid off from their jobs . . . The consequences of missed routine preventive care [are] that the mother must call an ambulance. At the emergency room, the child receives the care that could easily have been administered at home if she had had a preventive visit . . . This is a problem not only for the family—children who are not immunized, for instance, for whooping cough or rubella, present a threat to small infants, pregnant women and the general public.[15]

Dr. Antoinette Eaton, a pediatrician representing the American Academy of Pediatrics and the National Association of Children's Hospitals, concluded her testimony by stating: "Providing appropriate health care coverage for children . . . is not only the right thing to do, it is the most cost-effective thing to do."[16]

THE INTERACTION OF POLITICAL CONTEXT AND THE USE OF EVIDENCE

Our discussion of the "What" and "Who" of evidence use considered the congressional hearings from 1997 to 2017 as a whole. This section describes how the arguments and evidence advanced for SCHIP varied over time in response to changes in the political context. Table 6.5 groups the data into

TABLE 6.5 Witnesses and evidence use during initial enactment (1997), early implementation (1998–2000), reauthorization (2006–2009), and late implementation (2014–2017)

	WITNESS TYPE	NUMBER OF TIMES PROVIDING TESTIMONY	RBE	NON-RBE
Era 1 1997	Federal	3 (15%)	2	3
	Researchers	6 (30%)	6	2
	Groups/Individuals	5 (25%)	4	5
	State	6 (30%)	4	6
	Local	0 (0%)	0	0
	Era 1 Total	**20**	**16**	**16**
Era 2 1998–2000	Federal	4 (19%)	4	4
	Researchers	4 (19%)	4	2
	Groups/Individuals	2 (9.5%)	2	2
	State	11 (52.4%)	6	10
	Local	0 (0%)	0	0
	Era 2 Total	**21**	**16**	**18**
Era 3 2006–2009	Federal	4 (5.3%)	4	4
	Researchers	22 (28.9%)	21	17
	Groups/Individuals	27 (35.5%)	7	27
	State	20 (26.3%)	10	20
	Local	3 (3.9%)	2	3
	Era 3 Total	**76**	**44**	**71**
Era 4 2014–2017	Federal	2 (10.5%)	2	1
	Researchers	10 (52.6%)	10	4
	Groups/Individuals	4 (21.1%)	2	3
	State	3 (15.8%)	2	3
	Local	0 (0%)	0	0
	Era 4 Total	**19**	**16**	**11**

four stages according to the breaks in the policy process: enactment, early implementation, reauthorization, and later implementation and reauthorization. This is the view from thirty thousand feet; it reveals the general configuration.

Evidence use in the two earlier stages followed a coherent path dictated by the program's goal of improving access to health insurance by low-income children. In the initial hearings, federal agencies provided the background, summarizing the history of SCHIP's predecessor program, the Medicaid pediatric component. The balance of the testimony is divided almost evenly among the main groups of stakeholders—state administrators, representatives of interest groups, and researchers—as the hearings canvassed alternative policy approaches to expanding the availability of health insurance for low-income children. If the first stage of hearings was about the design of the program, the second round brought information about its implementation: state-level authorities dominated the testimony, and the twin themes were the variety among the states in their implementation of the program, and networking about their shared interest in identifying and enrolling low-income children. The political context of the third and fourth stages was quite different, defined by the partisan polarization that has stalemated legislation and, during periods of divided government, soured relations between the White House and Congress. The increasing gap between the parties was apparent in deliberations over CHIP, and the next two sections describe the impact of the changed political context on framing and evidence use.

Reauthorization, 2006–2009: The Bush Vetoes and the Conservative Opposition

SCHIP was scheduled to be reauthorized in 2007, and observers were optimistic. The program was distinguished in two significant ways: it was unquestionably successful at accomplishing its material goals, and the ideational frame, especially the way recipients were treated, was quite different from other social programs. The state programs had accomplished a dramatic decline in the number of uninsured low-income children; moreover, in response to the concern about crowd-out, states had erected a number of administrative hurdles to shifting from job-based health insurance to SCHIP, including waiting periods, premiums and co-payments.[17] In addition, policy specialists recognized that SCHIP had escaped "the mentality that has historically ensnared welfare programs."[18] From the beginning, SCHIP's focus on identifying and enrolling all eligible children emphasized inclusion rather than suspiciousness; that difference had only grown over its first ten years, as states created new outreach campaigns and implemented welcoming enrollment and renewal procedures. Over time, the social values of care and equal opportunity became part of the "taken for granted" infrastructure of the program, situating SCHIP in a strong normative frame that envisioned the public interest being strengthened by government expenditures that demonstrated that the members of the community were willing to take responsibility for each other.[19]

Complementing the program's reputation, the political conditions looked favorable. The 2006 election had delivered majority control of both houses of Congress to the Democrats; the proposal to expand the program to cover more children had the backing of key Republicans and the support of a broad coalition of stakeholders in the health care field, as well as the endorsement of several governors.[20] This momentum led observers to predict that congressional review would not be politically conflictual; that legislative committees would approve the proposed increase in funding, using evidence about implementation to modify the program at the margins; and that the president would agree with the bipartisan majority.[21] In this scenario, evidence use would be based on more data and deeper analysis of familiar issues.

In preparing their case for reauthorization, advocates focused on two modifications of SCHIP: expansion of the program, and revision of the current rules on state allocations. The evidence for expanding the program was strong: nearly nine million children remained uninsured, and two-thirds were eligible for SCHIP or Medicaid; since 2000, the cost of health insurance on the private market had increased, and the percentage of firms offering health insurance had decreased; and as the states ramped up their programs, SCHIP spending increased beyond federal funding levels.[22] Experience also showed that SCHIP's partial reliance on state funds had the effect of worsening the impact of economic downturns, rather than cushioning recessions; this implied that shifting toward federal-level funding would make the program a more effective countercyclical instrument. The second problem was with the law's complicated provisions for redistributing funds; the current formula increased uncertainty among the states and required continual legislative modification.[23] Reauthorization, then, offered Congress the "opportunity . . .

to acknowledge the success of SCHIP" and facilitate states' expansion of the program.[24]

The evidence presented in congressional hearings praised the focus on children and documented the progress toward the program's goals of enrolling all low-income youth, drawing attention to SCHIP's normative frame, with advocates combining references to ethical purpose and material improvement. By the time SCHIP was up for reauthorization, congressional policymakers had access to a much larger body of research-based data. In addition to federal agencies tasked with oversight, all the states had practical experience with designing their programs, many of them had systematically tried out innovative strategies to identify and enroll low-income children, formal policy analyses and surveys of implementation had been conducted, and the growth of informal channels and professional networks had fostered communication and systematic comparison among state-level administrators.[25] Gaps in the coverage of the program were measured and subjected to sophisticated analysis, with an eye toward cost-effective ways to expand the program by disseminating schemes whose impact was verified by systematic, empirical comparison. For instance, Mark McLellan, describing an analysis for the federal Centers for Medicare and Medicaid Services (CMS), showed that the bulk of uninsured children are eligible for coverage under Medicaid or SCHIP. He concluded that coverage gaps were attributable to inadequate outreach to parents and variation in eligibility thresholds, and he reviewed how the most effective state strategies had emphasized outreach and education. In addition to quantitative data on state programs' expansion of coverage, witnesses from the states painted a picture of state programs as "learning organizations" that modified their outreach and enrollment practices in response to experience. Ann Clemency Kohler, of New Jersey's Department of Human Services, highlighted the value of state-by-state flexibility, explaining how her department had called on practitioner experience to simplify the application process and adjust benefit levels to the higher cost of living in the state.[26]

Statistical analysis was combined with other types of evidence to make a case that was based on policymakers' past experience and compelling anecdotes about children without insurance. Personal stories were invaluable for putting a human face on statistical and evaluative data. Unlike CCSS, CHIP has program recipients, and when they are called on to testify, their contribution is not broadly representative research, but anecdotes telling how the program worked for them or their community. This type of evidence took center stage when the committee traveled to regional locations to gather testimony from constituents about the value of SCHIP in the lives of local citizens. For instance, Melissa Anderson, self-employed and the mother of a son who was diagnosed with grand mal seizures, testified at a hearing in Montana that the SCHIP program had not only helped to pay for medications but had given her the peace of mind to return to work and make her business a success. In another hearing, Kathy Mingledorff took the committee back to when she became pregnant in college, dropped out to work, and lost eligibility under her parents' health insurance. She described how SCHIP allowed her to take care of her son and get back on her feet, working part-time and finishing her degree.[27]

Witnesses at the hearings on reauthorization also frequently invoked the normative values that framed the program. For instance, Republican governor Sonny Perdue of Georgia, representing the Southern Governors' Association, portrayed the central importance of SCHIP as equalizing access to health care for low-income children. He worried that funding cuts in Washington would curtail opportunity for families in his state. "Georgia engaged quickly . . . in fact . . . we got married with our Federal partners, and our fruitful union produced over 270,000 children . . . Now we are . . . talking about divorce, and we do not know what will happen to the health of those children."[28] Chris Gregoire, the Democratic governor of Washington, described covering children as a "moral imperative [that] brings with it very important societal benefits."[29] And Senator Orrin Hatch (R-UT), who had been working with the Democratic leadership to pass the bill, described supporting the program as "the moral thing to do."[30] Over the previous two years, to meet the increase in the population of uninsured children, states had expanded coverage to 250 percent of the federal poverty level; now, with the economy declining into recession, even moderate-income families were confronting heightened challenges to health care coverage, so twenty states raised the income threshold to 300 percent of FPL.[31]

The program's very momentum, however, gave rise to concern that it was growing beyond its mandate. The Bush White House, conservative interest groups, and their allies in Congress turned the celebration of growing enrollment on its head, criticizing the states for extending SCHIP coverage to middle-class families and to children of workers whose employers offered job-based coverage. These objections, over expansion and crowd-out, were familiar; from the earliest hearings even liberal Democrats had agreed that the program should be held accountable to these considerations, but as the program grew, these criticisms carried more bite.

President Bush sharpened the opposition's case when a new directive from the Centers for Medicare and Medicaid Services ordered state agencies to eliminate crowd-out and to stop including more children in the program by raising the income threshold.[32] The August 17, 2007 directive reversed CMS practice and halted SCHIP's growth at a time when economic conditions increased the need—with the recession deepening, fewer employers were offering health insurance and the price of commercial policies was rising, and the stagnation of working and middle-class wages meant that fewer families could afford to purchase health insurance.[33] The directive stated that CMS would not approve any moves to expand eligibility, unless states tightened up the barriers that inhibit families from moving to SCHIP from private insurance, and unless they could prove that 95 percent of the children below 200 percent FPL were already enrolled.[34] The policy change halted enrollment; CMS was sued by a number of states, and thirty governors publicly criticized the new policy. Both the House and Senate held hearings, including one that brought together five governors, of both parties, who decried the curtailment of coverage, and predicted that, even if the state modified its program to meet the directive's strictures, the new requirement of a twelve-month waiting period would deny coverage and care to eligible children.[35]

The initial phase of testimony had focused on long-standing concerns with identifying and enrolling eligible children, but this evidence did not address opponents' assertions that SCHIP was undermining the private insurance market. Conservatives argued that, as SCHIP was expanded by raising the income threshold for eligibility, parents of children newly eligible would drop (or might be encouraged by employers to drop) private insurance, and employers would stop offering insurance if a larger proportion of their workforce could qualify for SCHIP. There is little dispute that crowd-out increases as the income threshold for eligibility rises, but there were no authoritative estimates. The revivified argument over crowd-out focused evidence use: state administrators described the steps taken to reduce crowd-out, and the Congressional Budget Office (CBO) mounted an extensive review of the research literature and states' experience. Because good data were available and different analytical techniques converged on a narrow range of outcomes, the resolution of this empirical issue diminished the extent of disagreement between supporters and opponents. Peter Orszag of CBO and Chris Peterson of the Congressional Research Service gave the most authoritative estimate: as eligibility for SCHIP was expanded to children in higher income families, an increase of one hundred children in SCHIP would reduce the number in private coverage by thirty-three.[36] This narrowed the range of disagreement but did not resolve the concern with crowd-out, as several witnesses took up the implications for policy design and the underlying normative values. Nina Owcharenko, of the Heritage Foundation, interpreted the problem as not with SCHIP but with inadequate subsidies in the private insurance market: "policymakers should broaden their efforts to make private coverage more available [by] . . . offering a Federal tax credit [that] would give working families the ability to get and keep private health insurance."[37] Alan Weil, of the National Academy for State Health Policy, posed the trade-off starkly: whether providing health coverage to every low-income child justified enrolling a few whose families could get private insurance, versus whether minimizing crowd-out justified administrative barriers that left a significant number of children without health coverage.[38] The researchers at CBO had tried to come up with different policy instruments that would reduce crowd-out further, but concluded that the trade-off was now at a practical minimum—given the lower premiums and more inclusive benefits, it was rational for both employers and employees to move the children of low-income workers to SCHIP. The verdict of the CBO researchers was that the CMS directive's expectation that crowd-out could be reduced substantially was unrealistic:

> This means that for every three people enrolled in Medicaid or SCHIP . . . two would have been uninsured and one would have had other coverage in [the legislation's] absence . . . We don't see very many other policy options that would reduce the number of uninsured children by the same amount without creating more crowding. As one economist put it, it is like fishing for tuna, when you let down the tuna nets, you catch some dolphin too . . . [T]he policy question is, how much is acceptable?[39]

Armed with this testimony, the Senate and the House passed different versions of SCHIP reauthorization, both funding expansions of the program by increasing the federal cigarette tax. The conference committee product essentially matched the Senate bill, which authorized a smaller increase and garnered a substantial number of Republican votes, and it was passed 67 to 29 in the Senate and 265 to 159 in the House. President Bush vetoed the bill, and the attempt to override the veto fell short of the necessary two-thirds in the House.

Supporters were "befuddled by the White House approach." They thought the President had not appreciated the weight of evidence backing the bill, citing not only the dramatic decline in the number of uninsured children and the states' success at driving down crowd-out to its practical minimum, but also political intelligence which revealed very little support for Bush's idea to shift funding to tax expenditures. Democrats faulted the President for not seeking compromise, but the criticism from the senior leadership in the President's party was even more pointed. Charles Grassley (R-IA), the ranking member of the Senate Finance Committee, contradicted the President's vision of SCHIP: "[The White House's proposed reform] won't even cover kids on the program today, much less reach out to cover more kids." Orrin Hatch thought Bush's advisors "hadn't done [their homework]. And to do good health care bills, it takes years." Hatch concluded "that some have given the president bad advice on this matter . . . I know he's compassionate . . . but he's been sold a bill of goods."[40] Supporters on both sides of the aisle reached out to bargain with the White House, but "SCHIP advocates found it difficult to locate an official who could authoritatively negotiate with Congress on behalf of the administration."[41] Believing the modifications that restricted program eligibility had gone far toward answering conservative objections, supporters added limitations on family income and forbade coverage for adults and undocumented immigrants. Both houses passed the new bill. The President vetoed it again, making clear that his objections were ideological.[42]

These objections, although initially downplayed by the congressional majority, centered not on the negotiable details of funding or eligibility, but revealed deeply polarized ideological differences—over the limits of government intervention to remedy market-based inequalities, and over the autonomy of the states in a program funded by the federal government. President

Bush's objections, in effect, articulated a framing competition that had been brewing since the 1990s.[43] Supporters and opponents, in a word, perceived the program through very different ideational lenses. The conservatives' ideological critique transformed the use of evidence.

Instead of focusing on social values such as the collective responsibility to address poverty, the opponents centered their objections around individual values. For SCHIP's first ten years, debates emphasized the normative considerations of equality and inclusiveness, and the evidence showed success, as indicated by increasing enrollment and access to care. But conservatives saw SCHIP expansion as a step "down the path to government-run health care for every American"; they worried that the program would push the country toward "a single-payer health care system with rationing and price controls."[44] They took a much more skeptical view of government social welfare expenditures, insisting that the evidence of "success" would have to measure up to a different criterion. In this view, federal social welfare expenditures should be held up to the criterion of *economic investments*—they would not be justified unless the evidence showed that they contributed to the individual's becoming a more productive member of the economy.[45]

This was not inconsistent with the logic that had underlain CHIP from the beginning, a three-step causal mechanism in which increasing availability of health insurance was only the first step; low-income families need to use health care resources for regular checkups and serious illnesses, and better care should lead to improvements in health outcomes. Evidence about outcomes was not absent in earlier hearings, in fact the 1980s RAND health insurance experiment's demonstration that children who had health insurance received better quality care strongly influenced the passage of the original legislation.[46] But the link between access and health outcomes was taken for granted, as the legislative priority was on reducing the number of uninsured low-income children.

In short, the first two premises had been the focus of much testimony over the years, and evidence was strong that enrollment in CHIP did in fact result in more regular health care. But now opponents questioned what had been taken for granted, that the program would materially improve the lives of individuals and—pursuing the "investment" metaphor—that these outcomes would be lasting and would aggregate to raise the output of the economy as a whole. Responding to the critique, in the first instance, would require supporters to be much more explicit and systematic in correlating health outcomes to access. But correlations would not be enough to flesh out the concept of "investment." For this, supporters needed evidence of two sorts of outcomes: improved health impacts for children had to be lasting into adulthood, and the outcomes for individuals had to have favorable knock-on effects for the broader public. Goaded by President Bush's two vetoes, proponents realized that the case for expanding CHIP, regardless of the party of the incoming president, would have to give prominence to evidence about lasting outcomes—in health status and perhaps in other dimensions.[47] Congressional hearings generated two streams of evidence to meet conservative objections: findings from the growing body of peer-reviewed research on outcomes, and ordinary citizens' personal stories that illustrated the causal mechanism in the real world.

By the time SCHIP was up for reauthorization, Congress had monitoring reports on every state's program. Researchers used these data to yield a national picture, and several studies investigated implementation much more deeply in exemplary states. The research tracked the causal process from expansion of access to health insurance, to increased usage of health care resources, to outcomes ranging from the occurrence of illness and child mortality to school absenteeism and visits to the emergency room.[48] These separate studies were summarized and their validity evaluated in several wide-ranging reviews.[49] The consistent message of this research was that enrollment in SCHIP was correlated with more consistent use of regular health checkups and preventive care, fewer instances of foregone care, fewer illnesses and visits to the emergency room, better quality of care, and less absenteeism at school.

But did the favorable individual outcomes pay off for the whole society? A complementary but independent line of research on impacts was centered on developing the concept of "human capital policy" as investment. This research, most closely associated with James Heckman, took a different approach to evaluating public policies, and it focused on the question at the heart of the disagreement over the expansion of SCHIP, comparing the impacts of social and educational policies that targeted children versus policies that had their impact later in the life cycle. The analysis centered on the analogy between investment in human and physical capital, and the research was motivated by economic considerations, not by moral philosophy.[50]

The conclusion of the analysis amounted to a direct response to the conservatives' concern: Evaluating spending on social programs as investment showed that "the rate of return to a dollar of investment made while a person is young is higher than the rate of return to the same dollar made at a later age . . . [because] earlier investments are harvested over a longer horizon . . . [and they] raise the productivity of later investments . . . Human capital is synergistic."[51] The chairs of the congressional committees were especially proud of these findings and cited them often, and the research was quoted in testimony by state administrators and interest group representatives, in addition to researchers.[52] The testimony of Governor Deval Patrick of Massachusetts typified that of state-level representatives. He pointed out that the research showed that access to health care strengthened "many facets of child development—physical, cognitive, emotional—and . . . decrease[d] uncompensated care utilization," including emergency room visits.[53] Members of Congress shied away from the econometrics, but they were familiar with the "big idea" revealed by this research: public policies that remediated inequalities among children had much larger economic payoffs than intervention later in the life cycle.[54]

The other stream of evidence that impressed public officials was personal testimony. We have emphasized the distinction between RBE and non-RBE, arguing that RBE is more valid and representative. But of course humans learn from evidence that has a lesser pedigree, and politicians understand that personal stories are not only more memorable but often tell about impacts that aren't measured by quantitative research. Significantly enough, no individuals or families were called on to testify in the five hearings between 1997 and 2005; however, when delineating outcomes was at issue during the deliberation over reauthorization, one or more witnesses offered a personal story in each of the six hearings between 2006 and 2008.[55] For instance, in the February 1, 2007, hearings, the Senate Finance Committee heard from three members of the Bedford family. Job, the eldest child, has asthma, and he told how SCHIP, by providing reliable funding for the inhaler he carries with him at all times, had made him feel safe and expanded the activities he could participate in. The mother, Kim Lee, handles the family budget, and before SCHIP the family had bare-bones private insurance, which forced her to make "impossible health choices," for example, choosing which prescription for needed medicine to refill, or skipping the visit to the pediatrician in order to pay the insurance premium. SCHIP has relieved financial stress; by bringing "peace of mind" to health care decisions, it has "made the whole family healthier." The father, Craig, was determined to open his own business, but private insurance absorbed 36 percent of the family's gross income. SCHIP cut health care costs by 60 percent, enabling their family that "works hard and plays by the rules . . . to live the American dream."[56] At the March 1, 2007, hearing of the Subcommittee on Health of the House Committee on Energy and Commerce, Lolita McDavid, a pediatrician and the medical director of Rainbow Babies and Children's Hospital in Cleveland, described the experience of a little girl whose family was eligible for SCHIP—her asthma was diagnosed when she was seventeen months old, but it's now controlled by medications, she has regular checkups with a pulmonologist, and she is a competent, active first grader. Dr. McDavid contrasted this experience with the "emergency room visits, hospitalizations, and missed days of school (and work, for the parents)" that typifies families who don't have SCHIP coverage.[57]

To summarize, with CHIP's existing funding extended to March 2009, the hearings in 2008 were not directed toward winning over President Bush, but toward rounding out the case that would be presented to the next president, by assembling evidence that responded to the conservative concern about the economic return on investment in child health. Unfortunately, the 2008 election only increased the distance between the parties: the campaign heightened ideological fervor, and the newly elected Congress was more divided than ever.

Assured that the new President would sign the reauthorization, Democrats in Congress dropped the provisions meant to appeal to President Bush. The Children's Health Insurance Program Reauthorization Act (CHIPRA) not only expanded the program to cover more children who were eligible, but also required states to include dental benefits that met national standards, and enabled states to use federal funds to cover immigrant children and pregnant women. The vote on CHIPRA showed that the bipartisan coalition was seriously fragmented: three-quarters of House and Senate Republicans voted against it, including previously reliable backers Senators Hatch and Grassley. The larger debate during 2009–10 over reforming the health care system not only further worsened partisan polarization, but it brought to the surface divisions among Democrats and within the advocacy community over

CHIP. Progressives pointed out that the Affordable Care Act was envisioned as "near universal": once it was in place, a separate program to cover children would not be needed, and folding CHIP into an expanded Medicaid program would make coverage an entitlement, ending CHIP's intrinsic conservative structure as a block grant to the states.[58]

Even if ACA's implementation had been uncontested, working out the inconsistencies with CHIP would involve amending the Act.[59] But of course the political context was not what ACA supporters envisioned: ACA was unpopular, Republican-governed states resisted implementing it, the Supreme Court ruled in 2012 that Medicaid expansion would be optional for states, and the ACA's marketplace plans offered less coverage than state CHIP plans.[60] Events convinced even the most liberal Democrats that CHIP was not expendable, but deepening polarization over health care made it doubtful whether any agreement could be worked out with congressional Republicans.[61]

Reauthorization 2014–2015: Increasing Party Polarization

When Congress considered CHIP in 2014–15, it amounted to an opportunity for both sides, and committee chairs were aware of the way the presentation of evidence had the potential to frame the choice. Both the Senate and the House held hearings on CHIP at the end of 2014. In the Senate, Jay Rockefeller (D-WV) headed the Finance Committee's Health Care Subcommittee; his goal was to get the funding extension approved before he retired from Congress.[62] To accomplish that, it was necessary to firm up the case for CHIP and distance it from the continuing contention over ACA. The testimony drew on research-based evidence of the program's success at insuring low-income children and of lasting health impacts; but the witnesses also talked about nonquantitative evidence, reminding the committee of the program's unusual history of bipartisanship and describing the personal impacts of the funding cliff.[63] Bruce Lesley, of First Focus on Children, called on research that pointed to CHIP's achievements: cutting in half the proportion of uninsured children even as the share of adults lacking health insurance was rising; reducing disparities in access and health outcomes; and, in survey after survey, remaining popular with every demographic group. Then he invoked the legacy of bipartisanship: "the hallmark of CHIP has been the willingness of leaders on both sides of the aisle . . . to work together," emphasizing that bipartisan agreement was based on the particular characteristics of the program. "By definition, CHIP is child-focused . . . [based on] specific pediatric quality standards that address the unique development and health care needs of children . . . [I]t is a public/private partnership [that] gives States discretion . . . rather than having a one-size-fits-all Federal standard." The failure to fund CHIP would "spell disaster for more than eight million children." Dr. James Perrin, president of the American Academy of Pediatrics, complemented this testimony by elaborating on the health impacts for children, and Cathy Caldwell, director of Alabama's Bureau of Children's Health Insurance, depicted the effect on the state budget and its commitment to low-income families. Senator Rockefeller also called Douglas Holtz-Eakin, the conservative economist and former head of the Congressional Budget Office. His testimony clearly distinguished CHIP from the ACA, citing the narrow focus on children and the unusual flexibility for the states to structure their own programs. Although in the future a program such as CHIP may not be needed, he advised extending the funding for CHIP: "inaction looks very problematic . . . if nothing is done, States are going to be in significant budgetary trouble."[64]

The majority Republican House also held hearings in 2014, with Joseph Pitts (R-PA), the chair of the Energy and Commerce Committee's Subcommittee on Health, stating: "I believe we need to extend funding for this program in some fashion," and vowing that his approach would be "thoughtful and data-driven." He began by acknowledging that a majority of governors favored extending the program's funding, but then emphasized that he was concerned with crowd-out and the extension of the program by some states to enroll middle-class families.[65] Testimony came from four witnesses, all drawing exclusively on research-based evidence. Two were from the Congressional Research Service: Evelyne Baumrucker gave an overview of CHIP, noting the major changes enacted in 2009 and the significant variation across state programs, and Alison Mitchell summarized the impacts of ACA's "maintenance of effort" (MOE) provision for children, and the corresponding increment over Medicaid in the federal matching rate. Carolyn Yocom, director of health care for the Government Accountability Office, drew on GAO research to detail the impacts—on children and families as well as states' budgets—of curtailing financing for CHIP. Anne Schwartz, the executive director of the Medicaid and CHIP Payment and Access Commission (MACPAC, an expert panel set up to advise Congress, the secretary of Health and Human

Services, and state governments), told how the consensus of the commission was that CHIP financing be continued for two years, with the possibility that this transition period could be extended if there are still problems folding CHIP into ACA. The questions from the Republican members made it clear that they did not want to discontinue the program but that winning their support would hinge on substantial changes.

The attempt to extend CHIP in the lame duck session failed, and as the new Congress commenced, the gap between the parties had not diminished. It became much more pronounced in February when Senator Hatch and Representatives Pitts and Fred Upton (R-MI) put out a "discussion draft" making a two-year funding extension contingent on a set of amendments that Democrats and health reform groups described as "draconian."[66] The difference in the two parties' perceptions of CHIP, viewed through the separate lenses that emerged in the 2009 hearings, now portended a showdown.

That confrontation was avoided by a bargain reminiscent of the way Congress worked before the rise of polarization. The Medicare Sustainable Growth Rate (SGR) had governed the payments to physicians under Medicare since 1997, aiming to keep the increases below the rise of GDP.[67] But the formula did not consider other factors that increase the costs of medical care, and over time its application led doctors to stop taking Medicare patients. Since 2002, Congress had cancelled the cuts mandated by SGR. As the growth of health care costs slowed after 2010, the budgetary savings from applying the cuts diminished, and in 2015 the GOP leadership came out in favor of repeal. With the Republicans committed to SGR reform and the Democrats eager to pass CHIP without significant changes, the Medicare Access and CHIP Reauthorization Act (MACRA) was passed with overwhelming majorities. Although CHIP had escaped this danger, the extension was for only two years and the support for the program among the GOP rank and file was not strong.[68]

Funding for CHIP would run out on September 30, 2017, cutting the federal allocation from $20.4 billion in FY 2017 to $0 in FY 2018. The contradictory political currents made this a critical juncture. The partisan divide over CHIP that had begun in 2007 had only increased—Republicans in Congress had made repealing ACA the center of their fight with the Democrats, President Trump supported repeal and proposed further cuts in health care programs, and GOP control of both houses of Congress meant that Republican committee chairs would organize the hearings and the flow of evidence. On the other hand, the political advantages that had fostered bipartisanship were still prominent: CHIP targeted children, it left the structure of employer-sponsored insurance largely alone, it was relatively cheap, and it epitomized fiscal federalism by mandating a large role for the states. Adding to the constraints, time was short: for most of 2017, the Congress had been fixated on contentious efforts to repeal the ACA, and then the tax cut took priority over other issues. To build a winning coalition, supporters would have to use evidence to distinguish CHIP from the larger partisan conflict, at the same time addressing the relationship to the ACA.

Republicans in the House focused on how the ACA had moved CHIP further along the ideological divide between the parties, specifically by mandating that the states maintain enrollment thresholds and benefit levels through 2023, upping the incentive by increasing the federal match rate. Representative Michael Burgess (R-TX), chair of the Energy and Commerce Committee's Subcommittee on Health, described the reform as having "shifted the nature of shared responsibility . . . making the States more dependent on Federal dollars," and resolved to question each witness about this.[69] The panel of witnesses represented a local community health center, a state agency in charge of administering CHIP, and the head of the federal agency overseeing CHIP. Although the Republican members of the committee did not neglect ideological questions, the emphasis in the testimony was unambiguously on the impact of cutting CHIP. The testimony of Michael Holmes, the CEO of a community health center in Minnesota, touched on quantitative evidence of the number of families served, but he framed his presentation around the personal stories of individuals for whom federal funding had provided the first reliable access to health care. Jami Snyder, the director of Medicaid and CHIP programs for Texas, emphasized federalism and took an institutional focus, praising the way CHIP's flexibility allowed Texas to design a structure consistent "with the State's philosophy of ensuring accountability . . . and increasing personal responsibility for program participants." She painted the picture of a collaborative relationship between national and state authorities that had accumulated "a proven track record of success," and for which the state's "budgetary planning process had assumed continued funding." The failure of Congress to extend funding would present Texas with the "prospect of dismantling the CHIP program" without having anything to put in its place.

Cindy Mann, the former director of the Center for Medicaid and CHIP Services, gave an overview from a federal perspective. She emphasized both the program's success—"[It] brought the uninsurance rate for children below 5 percent [when] it was over 15 percent in 1997"—and its responsiveness to the states and Congress. The 2009 reauthorization, for instance, had "revamped the system for distributing dollars" to states, and CMS had quickly and successfully implemented the new formula. She pointed out that CMS research showed that ACA's MOE provision (and the enhanced federal matching rate) was necessary to ensure continued coverage for several million children.[70]

In the Senate, Finance Committee chair Orrin Hatch opened the hearings by posing two distinct directions for the legislation. The law needed significant modifications, as outlined in the version he and Representative Fred Upton had authored during negotiations two years earlier, and it was certainly within the committee's mandate to rewrite the law. On the other hand, the committee could focus more narrowly on the question of whether CHIP funding merited extension. Senator Ron Wyden (D-OR), the ranking minority member, used his opening statement to argue against the first alternative. But he skirted the substantive disagreement, leaning on procedural grounds: a rewrite would take time and careful deliberation, but the deadline of CHIP's expiration would not allow that. He then invoked the normative commitment that all the committee members shared—"putting kids first . . . because this program is a lifeline for almost nine million children." In elaborating on this shared value, Wyden did not draw on quantitative data showing the success of the program, but told a story that put a human face to the statistics. He described a "single mom who works multiple jobs, pays the bills, and handles all of what life throws at her by herself. The last thing that single mom needs is a government letter stamped 'notice of termination' explaining that her sick kids are on their own because CHIP funding has run out."[71] As in the House, the committee had assembled a panel of witnesses who looked at the program from separate vantage points. Leanna George, a mother of two children who need special medical care, talked about "how losing CHIP would impact my family"—her husband had been laid off and his insurance lapsed, but CHIP took care of the children's medical needs; if CHIP were not available, it would put "the services that [the children] need . . . pretty much out of our financial reach." Without CHIP, "working class families like mine . . . might have to ration medical care . . . CHIP provides families with financial security and moms like me with peace of mind." Linda Nablo, chief deputy director of Virginia's Department of Medical Assistance Services, detailed the importance to the states of continued funding for CHIP. Medicaid and CHIP "are the health insurance plan for almost one in three children" in Virginia; thanks to the allowance for state variation, CHIP "is now a mature program that is woven into the fabric of . . . all the States." Terminating funding on September 30 [2017] would have serious consequences, not only for children, families and providers, but also for state agencies like hers that had the responsibility for ensuring continuity of coverage. Nablo made another argument for stable, long-term funding, describing how removing uncertainty has facilitated states' investment and innovation, which in turn have bolstered the states' ability to fulfill the program's goals. Finally, Anne Schwartz, the executive director of MACPAC, the nonpartisan, expert advisory board, described how MACPAC had "reviewed available evidence about the quality and affordability of CHIP compared to other alternatives" and this had led to the consensus recommendation that "Federal funding for CHIP be extended for five years . . . [and also] the current CHIP maintenance of effort requirement and . . . the increase in the matching rate [be retained]." In addition, "looking to a future in which a more seamless system of children's coverage can be created . . . [MACPAC] recommends that demonstration grants be made available to States to develop and test new approaches . . . [in view of the fact] CHIP has provided a platform for State innovation."[72]

Shortly after these hearings, Senators Hatch and Wyden introduced the "Keep Kids' Insurance Dependable and Secure Act of 2017" (the House version, sponsored by Representative Burgess, was called the HEALTHY KIDS Act). The legislation raises CHIP's annual allotments slightly and authorizes funding through FY 2023, extends the ACA's maintenance of effort provision while allowing states to tighten up the enrollment threshold, and makes available grants to support innovative programs in the states. In response to Republicans' concern that the ACA was enriching spending on CHIP, the measure also phased out the enhanced CHIP match by FY 2021, restoring the financial partnership between the federal government and the states.[73] Hatch, as one of CHIP's original authors, stressed the legacy of bipartisanship. But in appealing to his Republican colleagues, he emphasized the new provisions (which explicitly responded to conservatives' concern about the growth of the federal role), and the evidence his committee had generated about the program's current operation (it maintained the focus on children, the states were active partners, and the private sector remained an important constraint). In spite of (or perhaps because of) its popularity, the CHIP extension was engulfed in the fights over the tax cut, repeal of the ACA, and the president's budgetary proposals. CHIP renewal was attached to the government shutdown, becoming "a bargaining chip, a noncontroversial measure that Republicans can use to force Democrats to vote for other provisions they might otherwise oppose." The bill was finally approved January 22, 2018, when a continuing resolution was signed by the President ending a three-day government shutdown.[74]

CONCLUSION

This conclusion summarizes the similarities and differences between CHIP and CCSS, making clear that the foundation for comparison is solid, but noting that the differences illuminate evidence use and partially account for the distinct political histories of the two programs. Our three central concepts—*policy learning, political entrepreneurs,* and *policy feedback*—provide insight into the history and political evolution of CHIP. Policy actors strive to improve their efforts by learning from policy failures, and both CCSS and CHIP followed attempts, by both parties, to enact ambitious, national reforms. After this experience, CHIP was circumscribed in several ways: it is a partial program not a universal reform, it builds on the success of the Medicaid program, it is targeted at children, and it works around established institutions (leaving in place employer-sponsored health insurance) and interests (requiring the program to minimize overlap with private insurance). The agenda setters were also mindful that the balance in the federal system had changed since the enactment of Medicare, and they carved out a larger role for the states. The efforts of policy entrepreneurs were necessary: Senators Orrin Hatch and Ted Kennedy devoted disproportionate time and effort to drafting the proposal and building the support coalition. And the specification of policy feedback is necessary to account for observed changes in evidence use and framing over the several occasions when Congress has reassessed the program. The evaluation Congress carries out when a program in reauthorized is meant not only to gauge the progress of the program but also to take account of shortfalls cited by critics; committee hearings are thus occasions for communicating policy feedback.[75]

Two other dimensions of similarity are the normative ideas that lend a coherent theme to the programs, and the politics of federalism. The central intention of the Children's Health Insurance Program was to cover all low-income children, and the normative theme of inclusiveness motivated significant enrollment innovations by state-level programs.[76] Similarly, one of the most important attractions of CCSS was that more uniform state educational standards would foster the equalization of opportunity to learn across disparities of income, minority status, and geographic location. At first glance, federalism does not seem to mark a similarity; after all, Congress was the primary locus of deliberation over CHIP, while the states were the focus of evidence use with the Common Core. But CHIP is unusual among national social welfare programs. Its enactment was distinguished by the extent to which Congress translated states' preferences into law; the federal role is limited to setting general rules and supplying funding, enabling wide state discretion in program design and implementation. CHIP is a block grant, rather than an entitlement, a significant departure from its predecessor, the Medicaid pediatric program, and most of the modifications since CHIP was enacted have responded to policy feedback from the states.[77] Similarly, the states are the major actors in the Common Core, an educational reform whose most salient characteristic is its intention to achieve the advantages of common standards as a result of voluntary participation by the states.

Most important, evidence use in the deliberations over both programs responded to the opportunities and constraints thrown up by the political context. Previous chapters (especially chapters 4 and 5) have traced the way evidence was used across stages of the CCSS policy process; especially notable are the state governor's actions either to frame the opposition to CCSS or to maintain the support coalition, and the extent and vehemence of grassroots opposition in the state. The present chapter has depicted the evolution of evidence use over CHIP's two decades, describing how framing and evidence use were conditioned by the political climate. The use of evidence was not a smooth, continuous process, because change in the political balance of forces was discontinuous. The story highlights two changes: the shift from federal agencies supplying most of the evidence in the enactment phase to state agencies and citizen witnesses providing the bulk of evidence as the state programs got up and running; and the shift from an emphasis on enrollment and use of health care services by low-income children to the analysis of evidence about health outcomes, in response to conservatives' critiques.

The comparative case analysis is founded on salient similarities, but we want to point out two aspects that distinguish CHIP from CCSS: the complexity of the causal process linking the reform to its intended consequences, and the maturity of the program when the conservative ideological opposition took root. These differences illuminate the distinctive role evidence played in the course of these programs. CHIP's causal process consists of three steps—providing insurance to pay for health care is the facilitating condition, the use of health services by the child translates that affordance into care, and the predicted improvement in health status indicates the effectiveness of the program. Each of these lends itself to precise conceptualization and quantitative measurement. In its first decade, CHIP focused on enrolling children, but after 2007, in response to questions about its impact, advocates specified this causal model and brought together peer-reviewed evidence validating each of the steps in the causal mechanism. This did not rebut conservatives' insistence that the expansion of CHIP amounted to governmental overreach, but the provision of evidence, by resolving some criticisms, narrowed the range of disagreement and allowed participants to distinguish empirical questions from ideological stances. The causal process for standards-based educational reform is more complex—before the more rigorous standards can have an impact on student performance, they need to be complemented by corresponding changes in curriculum, teacher preparation and professional development, and physical facilities.[78] Because the act of reforming standards occurs at the beginning of a multistage causal process, and because there are few sites where implementation has supplied all the supports needed, advocates for standards could never present an evidence-based argument that was comparable to CHIP's, tracing variation in student learning to the presence or absence of standards. Thus, opponents' claims conflated validated empirical evidence with uncertain empirical claims and with ideology, and the politics of the Common Core in some states were much more vehement and chaotic.

Mature programs—especially those such as CHIP that were enacted with overwhelming bipartisan support—have time to become entrenched, their reforms spawning institutional routines and interest group and public support. Because of this, they are more resilient in the face of the inevitable attacks by interests who were favored in the status quo ante.[79] The attacks on progressive reforms are more severe and more successful today, as the conservative opposition to governmental activism is larger and better organized than at any time in the post–World War II period, and liberal reformers are often caught off guard by the range and fierceness of this opposition.[80] This makes enacting changes of policy all the more difficult, and it makes reforms, once enacted, much more fragile. CHIP has come in for its share of partisan attacks, and its claim to bipartisanship has frayed, but its survival owes much to the infrastructure of support that its successful implementation has generated over time. The CCSS lacks this trait, of course, but it is notable that a majority of states still make use of the Common Core Standards even though the assessments have changed.

Creating Political Incentives for the Use of Evidence

SEVERAL ARTICLES THAT APPEARED in the *Los Angeles Times* as we began to write this chapter reminded us once again of the competing incentives that lead policymakers to turn to evidence other than research. One article describes a letter sent to the University of California by several advocacy groups threatening to sue the university if it does not eliminate the SAT and ACT as an admission requirement. The groups argued that the tests violate state civil rights laws by discriminating against students with disabilities, those from low income families, and underrepresented students of color.[1]

These shortcomings had already been recognized by the UC Board of Regents and the university administration. At a recent board meeting, UC President Janet Napolitano had pointed out that if UC were to drop the testing requirement, it would set a national precedent. So the university needed to get it right. A faculty task force, representing the Academic Senate responsible for setting admission requirements, had begun a review of the research on standardized testing as a basis for recommending whether or not to continue requiring such testing for UC admission. In a second article, the *LA Times* reporter described "an extraordinary and unscripted exchange" at the meeting that "revealed the enormous stakes, deep passions, and growing impatience surrounding the issue."[2] John Pérez, the chair of the Board of Regents and a former speaker of the State Assembly, asked the UC general counsel if the regents were required to wait for the faculty senate report before deciding the issue. Another regent argued that "we don't need any more studies." Other regents noted that "millions" of students would take the test and spend large sums on test preparation if the regents delayed action. Still others expressed concern that if UC drops the SAT requirement, it would still need another standardized test to assess student performance. The faculty chair of the Academic Senate maintained that any decision would need to be well grounded in research.[3]

The regents' discussion vividly illustrates that even at the nation's top-ranked public university, the role of research-based evidence in policymaking could be sidelined as decision-makers, faced with a serious problem, seek to avoid what Pérez called "analysis paralysis." Yet it is also clear that research could highlight alternatives to the current testing requirements. For example, a study by UC Davis faculty member Michal Kurlaender found that although high school grades are the best predictor of first-year college grades, scores on Smarter Balanced, the Common Core–aligned test, predict first-year grades at UC and the California State University (CSU) system as reliably as the SAT, but with less bias against low-income students and students of color. Smarter Balanced has the added advantage that all California public school students already take the test.[4]

We begin with this anecdote because stories are an integral component of evidence use in policymaking: their specificity often makes an argument compelling, and they can highlight broader themes beyond a single study. The regents' impatience as they awaited the results of the task force study also vividly illustrates the challenge that researchers face as they seek to inform the policy process. In this chapter, we address that challenge by summarizing five themes that emerge from our analysis of the Common Core and CHIP, and we outline three sets of recommendations for strengthening the use of evidence, with particular attention to creating political incentives in the policy process.

FIVE TAKEAWAYS

The first conclusion reiterates our initial reason for widening the scope of our inquiry beyond research-based evidence. **For several reasons, research will most likely be combined with other types of evidence in education policymaking.** Participants in the policy process may seek other evidence because research results are incomplete or inconsistent, thus providing little reliable information about possible remedies to a policy problem. Other evidence may be needed for instrumental purposes, such as professional judgment that can provide detailed and rich information about how a particular policy will work in schools and classrooms. While strong, rigorous research results may be persuasive, they may need to be augmented by anecdotes and concrete examples that provide specificity to quantitative data. Value-based arguments may convince policymakers that a particular option is consistent with their goals and views about how those goals can best be advanced. Research may also be insufficient because evidence in policymaking is typically used strategically in the intentional pursuit of a policy or political objective. Political intelligence about the preferences of potential supporters and opponents is critical to building winning enactment coalitions. Consequently, researchers committed to informing policy need to consider how their studies might be constructively integrated into a more diverse evidence portfolio.

A second takeaway outlines the **three major factors that explain the combination of types of evidence: the incentives of suppliers and users, the stage of the policy process, and federalism**. The discussion in chapter 3 outlines how incentives vary by role position. Although the incentives of researchers and policy entrepreneurs are quite well understood from past research, it is also important to assess the incentives of IOs, and how they vary by the different purposes of their evidence use. Those studying evidence use have increasingly recognized the central function that IOs play, but they have tended to lump them into a single general category. However, the varied purposes for which translators and disseminators, advocates, and hybrids use research shape their incentives and the extent to which they adhere to the canons of scientific inquiry. These incentives may include professional recognition for improving education practice, the promotion of economic or ideological group interests, or the enactment of specific policy agendas.

Although the policy process is rarely linear or predictable, it does encompass several distinct stages, with the objective of each influencing how different policy actors further their strategic use of evidence. For instance, policy entrepreneurs seek to define a problem in such a way that it points to their preferred policy option as the best solution, while the aim of researchers is often to generate a precise and comprehensive analysis of the problem so that policymakers have sufficient information in assessing and choosing from among multiple options. Policy enactment for entrepreneurs, advocates, and hybrids is largely about building a winning coalition for policies reflecting their preferred option or a broader agenda. At the same time, however, they need to ensure that the policy options they promote will work as intended.

Consequently, their use of evidence during the enactment stage may be primarily, but not entirely, strategic. Research results, professional judgment, and comparisons between current policy and its alternatives may be part of the evidence mix. Yet the constraint of needing to move quickly before a policy window closes can mean that supporters and their allies act on incomplete information or turn to less systematic sources, such as their personal experience. The main objective of the implementation stage is to translate policy into street-level practice, with research and professional judgment key sources for informing that process, and translation and dissemination IOs as prominent providers. However, accomplishing this purpose depends on whether a given policy is politically sustainable, an objective that typically relies on different types of evidence than the administrative dimension of implementation.

Federalism, a unique characteristic of the US education governance system, is a final factor explaining the ways that types of evidence are combined. The design of CHIP has allowed for the policy to take a different form in each state, and even the Common Core, a policy intended to be similar across multiple states, varies in how it has been translated into classroom curriculum and linked to state assessments. As a result, the types of evidence used have varied as information has been customized to the political context of the individual states. In the US, federalism embodies both a system of governance and a set of contested political values about the relative authority of different governmental levels. As such, it can shape evidence use independent of the policy actors involved or stage of the policy process.

A third conclusion is that **the use of research-based evidence should include policy analyses in addition to research on the functioning and effects of educational interventions**. Knowing the school and classroom conditions under which an intervention affects student learning provides critical knowledge. But it is incomplete if analyses of costs and their distribution, professional capacity requirements, sources of variation across local jurisdictions, and levels of political support and opposition are lacking. Similarly, although they are often less systematic than policy analyses and are based more on professional judgment, comparisons between current and proposed policies are also essential elements of evidence for policymaking. They are often a significant tool in understanding the different levels of policy mandates in a federal system because they can inform decision-makers about the scope of change a new policy will require.

The fourth takeaway suggests that a **more nuanced understanding of policy implementation must emphasize political sustainability**. As we argue in chapter 4 and illustrate with the state case studies in chapter 5, an understanding of the conditions for the political sustainability of a policy should be developed on a parallel track with studies of its translation from enacted policy to school and classroom practice. Education researchers now have a firm grasp of the administrative and professional practice dimensions of policy implementation, but they have largely ignored questions of political sustainability. This lack of attention has meant that policy may be slow to respond if opposition emerges, and on-the-ground implementers can be faced with policies that change abruptly or are even eliminated as officials negotiate new agreements with supporters and opponents. A better understanding of the conditions under which policies are sustainable is necessary to informing both policy and practice.

Developing such an understanding requires a combination of evidence. Policy analyses are needed to understand the downstream effects and trade-offs associated with decisions made during enactment. For example, what inferences can be drawn from an analysis of similar past policies and their policy feedback? Policymakers also need systematic assessments of the relative costs and benefits of different substantive and procedural alternatives. In the case of the Common Core, its proponents chose to focus on gaining support from political leaders and national organizations, and paid little attention to mobilizing the general public. Similarly, in the interest of moving quickly, they accepted federal funding for assessment development even though they had framed the Common Core as a state initiative. Those decisions were made based on political intelligence and the judgments of experienced politicians, with little input from education researchers and policy analysts. It is always easier to suggest better strategies with the benefit of hindsight. However, the Common Core case does suggest that in a number of states, implementation would have been less politically troublesome if national CCSS advocates had the benefit of complementing their experience-based evidence with more systematic, comparative analyses of variation in political context across states.

The final takeaway stems from the comparative analysis of the CCSS and CHIP cases, and suggests that the use of research-based evidence depends in part on the fit between **the complexity of the policy problem and the**

quality of the available evidence. As we indicate in chapter 6, the policy theory and causal process for CHIP is less complex and more straightforward than the one for CCSS. In the former, the assumption is that if youth have health insurance coverage, it will be used to access necessary medical services, and that care will result in better health outcomes than would occur without health insurance. In contrast, for the Common Core to produce its intended student learning outcomes, a host of other factors need to be operative—curriculum and instructional materials need to be aligned with the standards, educators need to have adequate resources and time to prepare instruction consistent with the standards, and learning supports for students need to be readily available. This complex causal process means that the effect of research evidence on the details of the policy is more contingent in the education case than in the health care case. Furthermore, CHIP has been in place for more than twenty years, as compared with only a decade for the Common Core. As a result, the research base is more voluminous and robust.

Not surprisingly, this comparison suggests that research-based evidence is more likely to be used for some policies than others, depending on the complexity of the assumed causal process underlying the policy theory. However, the quality of research evidence and the extent to which it needs to be combined with other evidence are also a product of the maturity of the policy. From a researcher's perspective, these differences mean that those working in education face a more challenging task because the results of their studies are often less certain, and encouraging use will require acknowledging limitations and seeking other kinds of evidence to buttress their findings.

THREE RECOMMENDATIONS

Discussions about creating incentives for the use of research and other types of evidence in policymaking have recently centered on improving the translation and transmission of research, especially through partnerships between researchers and IOs. Several strategies expand on this general recommendation: strengthening the fit between policymakers' information needs and the questions researchers examine; customizing research questions and the dissemination of results to different policy audiences at different levels of government and in different role positions; producing research in a timely manner that coincides with information needs during different stages in the policy cycle; being transparent about the reasons why research findings may be incomplete, inconsistent, or in contention; and understanding how research can be responsibly and effectively combined with other types of evidence. These are all sensible strategies that we have discussed in the preceding chapters, and they warrant continued consideration by those committed to increasing the use of research-based evidence in education policymaking.[5] Our perspective brings to the foreground the politics of the policy process, however, and this suggests three other recommendations aimed at creating incentives for evidence use.

First, we urge researchers to **consider policy ideas as part of their portfolios: they are among the most significant resources available to the policy community**. In melding research results with normative values, policy ideas can sometimes lead to completely new solutions to enduring problems. But often policy ideas are not new. Rather, they may borrow normative assumptions from other policy areas, as is the case with school choice policies. Or, if support for the underlying normative goals remains strong even if a policy is problematic, the integration of data and values may contribute to a reframing of an existing policy regime. In the case of the Common Core, supporters of standards-based reform recognized that research documenting NCLB's failure to meet its stated goals, and more generally the unintended consequences of state accountability policies, threatened to undermine the entire standards-based policy regime. Rather than attempting to challenge this negative evidence, supporters sought to preserve the existing policy monopoly. They did so by framing the CCSS as a strategy for addressing the shortcomings of existing standards and accountability policies, while still maintaining that the basic policy idea is sound. CHIP is also a restructuring of an existing policy idea for increasing access to health care for children from low-income families. In contrast to Medicaid, the states have greater discretion over CHIP's design, with eligibility requirements and provider arrangements customized to each state's needs and policy preferences. Although both these policies rest on a set of normative values about how education should be organized and health care delivered, their design and implementation have drawn heavily on decades of accumulated research.

Integrating research-based evidence with normative values imposes additional responsibilities on scholars. They are still bound to the standards of scientific inquiry, but they must also be transparent about the normative

assumptions framing their work, and about how those assumptions influence the interpretation of empirical results. Researchers additionally need to
provide evidence-based arguments for why their policy ideas are preferable
to alternatives.

A second recommendation is to **build incentives for evidence use into
a policy's initial design, through the rules and organizational structures
that it creates**. The primary intent of policy design is to create incentives
for targets to act in accordance with the policy's substantive goals, such as
increasing students' educational opportunities through more rigorous curriculum. However, purposes in addition to the primary goals can also be
built into a policy. One such goal is ensuring that decisions are grounded in
research evidence through requirements for how oversight will occur once
a policy is enacted and for the frequency and types of program evaluation.
Policymakers' decisions about the agency in which a policy is placed can
influence not only how effectively it is administered and its substantive goals
pursued, but also how evidence is valued and used. In agencies with a strong
evidence-based culture, the bureaucratic norms and incentives work in favor
of research being taken seriously. Building these types of incentives into a
policy's design locks in continued use of information throughout its history.

If legislators recognize that ongoing cross-sector collaboration between
researchers and policymakers can garner relevant information to reduce the
political costs of their decisions and foster policy learning, they will create
organizational structures and incentives to institutionalize these conditions.
These may include establishing analytical and evaluation units within the
agency. Such units will require staff with advanced research training, who
can participate in networks of researchers outside the agency and maintain
ongoing relationships with universities and other research institutions. At the
front end of the policy process, a major advantage of such arrangements is
access to data about the dimensions of policy problems and the availability
of feasibility analyses to aid in refining policy options under consideration.
At the back end, these institutional arrangements can facilitate policy implementation and program evaluation through both formal studies and monitoring systems that provide early warnings about potential problems requiring
adjustments to a policy.

Locking in the use of research-based evidence as a priority through
organizational rules and structures is especially critical in executive branch

agencies, where preferences across different presidential and gubernatorial administrations can shift dramatically. Not all of them will value research highly, and as recent cases have demonstrated, may even be openly hostile to research results at odds with their partisan preferences. Nevertheless, as we know from institutional research, the structural arrangements that are made by those enacting legislation are difficult to alter or discard once that coalition is no longer in the majority.[6] Funding for scientific bureaus within government agencies may be decreased and staffing capacity diminished.[7] However, that capacity can be rebuilt if the structures remain in place, and institutional rules favor their continuation. Such rules include requirements that all study results be made public, that annual reports be submitted to legislative bodies, and that agencies include scientific advisory bodies and independent offices such as an inspector general whose term is staggered with those of elected officials.

Finally, as noted in the National Research Council's report on using science in public policy, the **training of policy analysts should equip them to promote the use of research in policymaking venues.**[8] These professionals work in legislatures, public and private agencies, and intermediary organizations—sometimes producing the research that informs policy deliberations, but more often vetting, synthesizing, and applying extant research to questions posed by their policymaker principals. Their graduate education, often in schools of public policy, focuses on the competencies needed to assess policy-relevant knowledge. However, they also need to learn to identify and take advantage of the conditions that will encourage decision-makers to seek and use analytical evidence. As the NRC report suggests, building such skills requires a curriculum that acquaints students with how policies are framed in political argumentation, illuminates the institutional and cultural barriers to consideration of research knowledge that challenges status quo assumptions and policies, and gives the students strategies for combining research knowledge responsibly with other types of evidence. This long-term approach for strengthening evidence use in policy settings brings the process full circle back to those who produce, translate, and disseminate research by focusing their attention on the incentives and institutional contexts shaping policymakers' use of research and other evidence.

Appendix

THIS APPENDIX DESCRIBES the data sources and compilations of data that form the empirical base for this study: interviews and participant observation notes, documents, and profiles of state education policy processes and of third-party providers involved with the implementation of the Common Core. The goal of our research is to trace the dynamics of the use of evidence in the formulation, adoption, and early implementation of the Common Core, and we recognized that interviews with a wide range of actors at all levels of the policy system should be the primary source. But in preparation we needed to understand the policy system, select research sites whose observation would yield theoretically rich data, and identify participants whose actions had particular impact. We built on prior research on standards-based reform, personal knowledge from (McDonnell's) having served on the National Research Council committee examining the implications of state standards policies for common standards, consultation with Hunt Institute staff, and our document inventory. Below, we delineate the role positions of the national and state policymakers whom we interviewed, and we describe the conversations that we drew on for real-time participant observation of the process of maintaining support for the Common Core by its national proponents. We also summarize the document collection and the coding scheme by which we classified the use of evidence in the published record, and which we drew on for a preliminary picture of the policy process and the major actors. We also list the congressional hearings which are a primary source for our comparative case study of the Children's Health Insurance Program.

INTERVIEWS

We conducted interviews with leaders of the Common Core movement, interest groups supporting the CCSS, members of the work groups and committees charged with writing and validating the CCSS, national and state education policymakers, researchers, and groups critical of the CCSS. In addition to interviewing policymakers and researchers who played a direct part in drafting and validating the standards, we carefully monitored the CCSS process in national media and in the education media. We drew on the results of that monitoring to identify the organized interests involved in the process.[1] Our enumeration was quite inclusive, but when additional groups were mentioned in our interviews, or as new groups became involved with the Common Core (e.g., opponents, third-party providers), their documents were added to the database and, depending on their centrality to the process, one or more interviews were conducted.

We conducted 117 interviews between May 2011 and June 2013. Interviews were conducted at the national level and in California, Indiana, Massachusetts, and Tennessee. Twenty-two interviews were conducted over the telephone, and the remaining ninety-five were conducted in person. The average duration of the interviews was between forty-five and sixty minutes. All the interviews were recorded and transcribed. At the national level (N = 53), we interviewed leaders of the Common Core State Standards movement, interest groups supporting the Common Core, members of the work groups and committees charged with writing and validating the standards, White House and congressional staff, researchers, and groups critical of the Common Core. The interviews were semistructured, following an interview guide designed for each category of respondent. The topics covered included the politics and process of Common Core promotion, development, and adoption; why participants chose to use certain types of evidence; and what they see as major implementation challenges. We facilitated comparability by way of core questions that were shared across respondents, but the interview also included items keyed to each respondent's part in the process. The interview guides were grouped into three categories, depending on the role position of the respondent: a) policy entrepreneurs, with variants used for critics/skeptics, third-party providers, and state-level implementing agencies; b) targets, including constituency groups and policy audiences; and c) members of the writing and validation committee. These interview guides are archived at Dataverse. [2]

Participant Observer Notes

A second data source is participant observer notes from weekly conference calls among groups engaged in implementing the Common Core State Standards. The calls began in September 2010 and typically involved seven to fourteen "advocacy partners." They included organizations representing elected officials, teachers and administrators, higher education, parents, and nonprofit private providers. The participants discussed their individual and shared activities, political developments that advanced or threatened the Common Core, and upcoming information needs. Although the conference calls primarily discussed implementation strategies and political threats to the Common Core, they also attended to academic criticisms that claimed the standards had not adequately considered the full range of relevant research. The notes provide firsthand documentation of how a policy network, composed of groups that do not always agree on policy positions, operated in concert on this particular issue.

CASE STUDIES IN FOUR STATES

We examined the adoption and early implementation process in detail in four states (California, Indiana, Massachusetts, and Tennessee). After consulting with education policy researchers and our colleagues at the Hunt Institute, we selected these four states with an eye to balancing partisan policy history (state government controlled by Republicans or Democrats), incremental resources that could be used to put the new reform in place (Race to the Top winners and losers), and region, as shown in the following table.

TABLE A-1 Sample of states

	PARTISAN CONTROL	
Race to the Top winner	Democratic	Republican
Yes	Massachusetts	Tennessee
No	California	Indiana

With the guidance of the principal investigators, research assistants prepared a profile of the state's educational policy history, the process of adopting and implementing standards, and the current partisan policy lineup. In
the states, we interviewed state-level education policymakers and administrators, local teachers and principals, and groups supportive of and opposed
to the Common Core (N = 64).

THE DOCUMENT COLLECTION

The document collection informed our identification of interview respondents, gave us detailed information about the activities of participants during
the processes of agenda setting and formulation, and allowed us to compare
the documentary record to the responses from interview subjects. We set
out to collect every publicly available document that related to the Common
Core State Standards produced between 2006 and the end of 2011. Although
we cannot guarantee that we looked at everything, the archive of 1,656 documents comprises research reports, policy briefs, speeches, blog posts, press
releases, and congressional testimony, and includes media articles concerning
the Common Core published during the time period by the *New York Times*,
Washington Post, and *Education Week* (N = 492). Table A–2 lists the organizations whose documents were archived.

From this universe, we drew a sample of 524 documents, stratifying by
category of actor (policy entrepreneur, research producer, supportive organizations, opposing organizations) and by stage of the process (pre-2009,
2009–2010, post-2010). We then coded the selected documents manually
using categories that ranged from the general (how the document portrayed
CCSS in relation to other reforms, what components of CCSS the document
focused on), to more specific (does the document put forth a policy theory,
articulating a causal model for how standards-based reform would produce improvements in student performance), to the details of the evidence
presented in the document (for research-based evidence, original research
versus synthesis of multiple studies, research design, data source; for non-
research-based evidence, current law or policy, professional judgment based
on the experience of practitioners or political representatives, stories and
rhetorical devices, or ideology), and the intended use of the research (e.g.,
explanation, persuasion, or criticism).[3] Table A–3 lists example codes.

TABLE A-2 Organizations from which documents were collected

AASA: American Association of School Administrators

ACE: American Council on Education

Achieve

ACT Inc.

AERA: American Educational Research Association

AFT: American Federation of Teachers

ALEC: American Legislative Exchange Council

Alliance for Excellent Education

America's Choice

ASCD: Association for Supervision and Curriculum Development

Boston Globe

Brookings Institution

Business-Higher Education Forum

Campaign for High School Equity

Carnegie Corporation of New York

Cato Institute

CCSSI: Common Core State Standards Initiative

CCSSO: Council of Chief State School Officers

Center for American Progress

Center for the Study of Mathematics Curriculum

Center on Education Policy

Coalition for Student Achievement

College Board

Commercial Appeal (Memphis)

Common Core

Consortium for Policy Research in Education

Core Knowledge

Council of State Governments

Council of the Great City Schools

Education Commission of the States

Education Next

Education Trust

Education Week

Eduwonk

EPIC: Educational Policy Improvement Center

ETS

Fordham Institute

Gates Foundation

Harvard Graduate School of Education

Hunt Institute

Indiana Department of Education

Indianapolis Star

K12 Innovation

La Raza

Los Angeles Times

Massachusetts Department of Elementary and Secondary Education

MBAE: Massachusetts Business Alliance for Education

Michigan State University

Military Child Education Coalition

NASBE: National Association of State Boards of Education

National Association of State Directors of Career Technical Education Consortium

National Indian Education Association

National PTA

National Universal Design for Learning Task Force

NBPTS: National Board for Professional Teaching Standards

NCEA: National Center for Educational Achievement

NCPPHE: National Center for Public Policy and Higher Education

NCSL: National Conference of State Legislatures

NCTE: National Council of Teachers of English

NCTM: National Council of Teachers of Mathematics

NEA: National Education Association

NEPC: National Education Policy Center

New York Times

NGA: National Governors Association

NSBA: National School Boards Association

PARCC: Partnership for Assessment of Readiness for College and Careers

Partnership for 21st Century Skills

Pioneer Institute

REL Southwest

SETDA: State Educational Technology Directors Association

Shanker Institute

SHEEO: State Higher Education Executive Officers

SMARTER Balanced Assessment Consortium

SREB: Southern Regional Education Board

Stop National Standards

Student Achievement Partners

Time

Truthout

UC Berkeley Law School/Earl Warren Institute

US Army

US Congress: House Education and Labor Committee

US Congress: Senate HELP Committee

US Department of Education

Washington Post

WestEd

White House

TABLE A-3   Document collection—coding categories (abridged)

- Policy theory
- Type (of evidence)—research-based
  - Original research
  - Synthesis of multiple studies
  - Research design
  - Data source
- Type (of evidence)—non-research-based
  - Current law and policy
  - Personal/professional experience
    - Practitioner knowledge
    - Political experience
  - Stories/rhetorical devices
  - Normative/ideological statements

- Use
  - Description
    - Explanation
    - Guide to implementation
  - Argumentation
  - Criticism
    - Caution or caveat
    - Challenge claims of others

The document collection was a valuable resource in mapping the interactions at the agenda-setting stage of the policy process, in identifying salient actors, and in distinguishing between different groups' use of research and evidence. Tables A-4.1, A-4.2, and A-4.3 show the use of evidence by different categories of actors. These tables aggregate organizations (and individual actors) into 4 categories (policy entrepreneurs, documents coded = 62; researchers = 48; supportive organizations = 81; opposing organizations = 29). The tables include only the documents produced by the groups, and exclude media coverage. The entries in these tables show the proportion of documents (from organizations belonging to that type) that use that category of evidence. Because every occurrence of evidence use in a document is coded, entries do not sum to 100 percent.

TABLE A-4.1   Types of research-based evidence used by category of organization or individual entrepreneur

	POLICY THEORY	ORIGINAL RESEARCH	STATISTICAL DATA
Political Entrepreneurs	0.65	0.26	0.28
Researchers	0.46	0.35	0.42
Groups: Supporters	0.24	0.22	0.28
Groups: Opponents	0.41	0.21	0.35

Comparing the variation along the columns in this table shows systematic differences among the key actors in their use of research-based evidence. *Policy theory* captured whether the document articulated a conception of the causal mechanism linking the policy reform to a desirable outcome. This trait is most frequently noted in documents from policy entrepreneurs, a difference consistent with their goal of making the case to policymakers that reforming standards would raise students' performance. But researchers and groups opposing the Common Core, although at a lower frequency, also combined their advocacy with causal logic. Researchers are distinguished by publishing documents that disseminate the findings of original research and relying on quantitative evidence.

TABLE A-4.2 Types of non-research-based evidence used by category of organization or individual entrepreneurs

	CURRENT LAW AND POLICY	PRACTITIONER KNOWLEDGE	POLITICAL EXPERIENCE	STORIES AND RHETORICAL DEVICES	NORMATIVE OR IDEOLOGICAL APPEALS
Political Entrepreneurs	0.74	0.13	0.14	0.13	0.39
Researchers	0.52	0.42	0.06	0.10	0.17
Groups: Supporters	0.41	0.30	0.10	0.16	0.28
Groups: Opponents	0.59	0.21	0.17	0.24	0.32

This table shows some interesting differences—and also some similarities—in the use of non-research-based evidence by categories of actors. Policy entrepreneurs invoke current law and policy most frequently, but all the categories of actors refer to this aspect of the system—not surprising, given that current law and policy characterize the status quo which the reform is designed to improve. Distinguishing between *practitioner knowledge* and *political experience* reveals additional differences between categories of actors. Compared to other actors, researchers (followed by groups supportive of the Common Core), refer most frequently to what street-level bureaucrats know about the implementation in the classroom, and how that experiential knowledge equips them to translate research findings. As for references to political considerations, opponents invoke this consideration most frequently, followed by policy entrepreneurs. We regard this as showing that, compared to other actors, these groups are more oriented toward the challenge of building (or opposing) a political coalition to back the reform. None of the categories of policy actors made extensive use of stories, but the documents published by opponents use stories and other rhetorical devices more frequently. Policy entrepreneurs and opponents invoke normative or ideological themes in their documents, but this similarity masks an important difference. The documents of policy entrepreneurs were optimistic, referring to national aspirations such as raising the performance of US students in international comparisons, or increasing the opportunity to learn across racial or class boundaries; in contrast, the arguments of opponents invoked normative or ideological tropes to generate anger at the Common Core for "bureaucratic centralization" or "federal overreach."

TABLE A-4.3   Intentions or purposes of the document

	EXPLANATION	GUIDE TO IMPLEMEN- TATION	ARGUMENT/ ATTEMPT TO PERSUADE	CAVEAT	CHALLENGE STATEMENTS OF OTHERS
Political Entrepreneurs	0.72	0.50	0.79	0.31	0.11
Researchers	0.49	0.30	0.69	0.34	0.06
Groups: Supporters	0.39	0.19	0.64	0.21	0.04
Groups: Opponents	0.10	0.04	0.66	0.55	0.52

Deliberation and debate over a proposal to change policy or practice is intrinsic to the process, and this series of codes captures three components of policy debate. The first two columns include statements that describe or explain. *Explanation* refers to the details of the reform itself; *guide to implementation* is about putting the Common Core into practice. About three quarters of the documents from policy entrepreneurs contained explanatory material; this proportion declines successively for the other three categories of actors. The same gradient across categories of participants is visible in their attention to the implementation of the reform. The middle column shows that all four categories of actors used their published documents to argue for their preferred outcome. The two rightmost columns distinguish between critical comments in terms of their aggressiveness. *Caveat* strives to capture constructive criticisms, calls for revision rather than denunciations; *challenge* is meant to capture more uncompromising criticisms. Policy entrepreneurs, research producers, and supportive organizations all express their critical views predominantly in terms of caveats (the ratio of caveats to challenges ranges from 3:1 to 5:1). Critics/skeptics will have none of this: they challenge more frequently than the other categories of actors, and challenges represent a much greater proportion of their criticism.

These tabulations validate our conceptual distinctions among the categories of participants in the Common Core policy process. The document inventory is doubtless capable of responding to other questions, and we reserve the extensive analysis for future work.[4]

LIST OF CHIP-RELATED HEARINGS FROM 1997 TO 2019

- April 8, 1997: Children's Access to Health Coverage; House Committee on Ways and Means, Subcommittee on Health
- April 18, 1997: Improving the Health Status of Children; Senate Committee on Labor and Human Resources
- April 30, 1997: Increasing Children's Access to Healthcare; Senate Committee on Finance
- September 18, 1998: State Children's Health Insurance Program: A Progress Report; House Committee on Commerce, Subcommittee on Health and Environment
- April 29, 1999: Implementation of the State Children's Health Insurance Program; Senate Committee on Finance
- May 16, 2000: Health Coverage for Families Leaving Welfare; House Committee on Ways and Means, Subcommittee on Human Resources
- July 25, 2006: CHIP at 10: A Decade of Covering Children; Senate Committee on Finance, Subcommittee on Health Care
- November 16, 2006: CHIP Program from the States' Perspective; Senate Committee on Finance, Subcommittee on Health Care
- February 1, 2007: Future of CHIP: Improving the Health of America's Children; Senate Committee on Finance

- February 14, 2007 and March 1, 2007: Covering the Uninsured Through the Eyes of a Child; House Committee on Energy and Commerce, Subcommittee on Health
- April 4, 2007: CHIP in Action: A State's Perspective on CHIP; Senate Committee on Finance
- January 29, 2008: Covering Uninsured Kids: Missed Opportunities for Moving Forward; House Committee on Energy and Commerce, Subcommittee on Health
- February 26, 2008: Covering Uninsured Kids: Reversing Progress Already Made; House Committee on Energy and Commerce, Subcommittee on Health
- April 9, 2008: Covering Uninsured Children: The Impact of the August 17th CHIP Directive; Senate Committee on Finance, Subcommittee on Health Care
- May 15, 2008: H.R. 5998, the Protecting Children's Health Coverage Act of 2008; House Energy and Commerce Committee, Subcommittee on Health
- October 7, 2009: Medicaid's Effort to Reform Since the Preventable Death of Deamonte Driver: A Progress Report; House Committee on Oversight and Reform, Subcommittee on Domestic Policy
- September 16, 2014: The Children's Health Insurance Program: Protecting America's Children and Families; Senate Committee on Finance, Subcommittee on Health Care
- December 3, 2014: The Future of the Children's Health Insurance Program; House Committee on Energy and Commerce, Subcommittee on Health
- February 10, 2016: Examining Medicaid and CHIP's Federal Medical Assistance Percentage; Senate Committee on Finance
- July 13, 2016: Medicare Access and CHIP Reauthorization Act of 2015: Ensuring Successful Implementation of Physician Payment Reforms; Senate Committee on Finance
- March 17, 2016: Medicare Access and CHIP Reauthorization Act of 2015: Examining Implementation of Medicare Payment Reforms; House Committee on Energy and Commerce, Subcommittee on Health
- April 19, 2016: Medicare Access and CHIP Reauthorization Act of 2015: Examining Physician Efforts to Prepare for Medicare

Payment Reforms; House Committee on Energy and Commerce, Subcommittee on Health

- May 11, 2016: The Implementation of the Medicare Access and CHIP Reauthorization Act of 2015 (MACRA); House Committee on Ways and Means, Subcommittee on Health
- June 23, 2017: Examining the Extension of Safety Net Health Programs; House Committee on Energy and Commerce, Subcommittee on Health
- September 7, 2017: The Children's Health Insurance Program: The Path Forward; Senate Committee on Finance
- November 8, 2017: MACRA and Alternative Payment Models: Developing Options for Value-Based Care; House Committee on Energy and Commerce, Subcommittee on Health

Notes

CHAPTER 1

1. The requirement in ESSA is by no means exceptional; it carries forward the mandate to rely on research-based evidence in evaluating programs, especially in education and social policy, that typified authorization and appropriation in both the George W. Bush and Barack Obama administrations. On formal policy mandates regarding the use of research, see the Arnold Ventures Evidence-Based Policy initiative, https://www.arnoldventures.org/work/evidence-based-policy, or the UK Coalition for Evidence-Based Education, http://cebenetwork.org/blog/2014/06/26/problem-research-evidence-education. Haskins summarizes the growth of official mandates across a range of social policies. Ron Haskins and Greg Margolis, *Show Me the Evidence* (Washington, DC: Brookings Institution, 2014); and Ron Haskins and Jon Baron, *Building the Connection Between Policy and Evidence: The Obama Evidence-Based Initiatives* (Washington, DC: Brookings Institution, September 7, 2011), https://www.brookings.edu/research/building-the-connection-between-policy-and-evidence-the-obama-evidence-based-initiatives. The trend is especially prominent in education, where three major task force reports have called for changes to strengthen the influence of research on policy and practice: *Recommendations Regarding Research Priorities: An Advisory Report to the National Educational Research Policy and Priorities Board* (Washington, DC: National Academy of Education, 1999); M. Suzanne Donovan, Alexandra K. Wigdor, and Catherine E. Snow, eds., *Strategic Education Research Partnership* (Washington, DC: National Academies Press, 2003); and National Research Council, Committee on the Use of Social Science Knowledge in Public Policy, *Using Science as Evidence in Public Policy*, ed. Kenneth Prewitt, Thomas A. Schwandt, and Miron L. Straf (Washington, DC: National Academies Press, 2012), doi: 10.17226/13460. Cynthia E. Coburn and Joan E. Talbert, "Conceptions of Evidence Use in School Districts: Mapping the Terrain," *American Journal of Education* 112 (2006): 469–95, doi: 10.1086/505056; and Barbara D. Goodson, "Evidence at the Crossroads Pt. 5: Improving Implementation Research," 2015, http://wtgrantfoundation.org/evidence-at-the-crossroads-pt-5-improving-implementation-research. Hess's edited volume includes summaries from several perspectives: Frederick M. Hess, ed., *When Research Matters: How*

Scholarship Influences Education Policy (Cambridge, MA: Harvard Education Press, 2008).

2. The focus on the use of research in policymaking rather than practice pursues a long-standing tradition of research and theorizing in political science and policy studies, that of documenting intrinsic differences between policymaking and implementing. Similarly, our approach is distinguished from much recent literature on the use of research, which elides the difference between policy and practice. Some authors take practice as their predominant topic: Huw T.O. Davies, Sandra M. Nutley, and Peter C. Smith, *What Works? Evidence-Based Policy and Practice in Public Service* (London: Policy Press, 2000); Annette Boaz et al., eds., *What Works Now? Evidence-Informed Policy and Practice* (London: Policy Press, 2019); and Cynthia E. Coburn and Mary K. Stein, "Key Lessons About the Relationship Between Research and Practice," in *Research and Practice in Education: Building Alliances, Bridging the Divide*, ed. Cynthia E. Coburn and Mary K. Stein (Lanham, MD: Rowman & Littlefield, 2010), 201–26. Others, however, use the phrase "policy and practice" as shorthand even when their analysis closely observes and models solely or predominately the use of research by practitioners. For a review, see Vivian Tseng and Sandra Nutley, "Building the Infrastructure to Improve the Use and Usefulness of Research in Education," in *Using Research Evidence in Education: From Schoolhouse Door to Capitol Hill*, ed. Kara S. Finnigan and Alan J. Daly (New York: Springer, 2014), 163–75. Gamoran's review makes clear that the contingencies surrounding the use of research evidence in policy are not well understood: Adam Gamoran, "Evidence-Based Policy in the Real World: A Cautionary View," *Annals of the American Academy of Political and Social Science* 678 (2018), 180–91, doi: 10.1177/0002716218770138.

3. Giandomenico Majone, *Evidence, Argument, and Persuasion in the Policy Process* (New Haven, CT: Yale University Press, 1989); NRC, *Using Science as Evidence*.

4. Advocates cannot, however, choose evidence willy-nilly to serve their purposes; they are constrained by the competition over policy, in which opponents and neutral observers have an incentive to monitor the quality of policy argumentation and sanction weakly substantiated claims. Mucciaroni and Quirk, for instance, show that the use of evidence in congressional debate seldom measures up to the deliberative ideal, and yet legislators who assert verifiably false claims undercut the credibility of their argument. Gary Mucciaroni and Paul Quirk, *Deliberative Choices: Debating Public Policy in Congress* (Chicago: University of Chicago Press, 2006). A recent study that directly asked policymakers why they use research found that good evidence is valued not only because it contributes information but also serves social functions such as strengthening trust and enhancing the prospects for collaboration. Karen Bogenschneider, Elizabeth Day, and Emily Parrott, "Revisiting Theory on Research Use: Turning to Policymakers for Fresh Insights," *American Psychologist* 74, no. 7 (2019): 778–93, doi: 10.1037/amp0000460.

5. Peter J. May, "Policy Learning and Failure," *Journal of Public Policy* 12, no. 4 (October 1992): 331–54, doi: 10.1017/S0143814X00005602; Hugh Heclo, *Modern Social Politics in Britain and Sweden: From Relief to Income Maintenance* (New Haven, CT: Yale University Press, 1974); and Barbara Levitt and James G. March, "Organizational Learning," *Annual Review of Sociology* 14 (1988): 319–38, doi: 10.1146/annurev.so.14.080188.001535.

6. John Kingdon, *Agendas, Alternatives, and Public Policies,* updated 2nd ed. (New York: Longman, 2011); Frank R. Baumgartner and Bryan D. Jones, *Agendas and Instability in American Politics* (Chicago: University of Chicago Press, 1993); and Michael Mintrom, *Policy Entrepreneurs and School Choice* (Washington, DC: Georgetown University Press, 2000).

7. Paul Pierson, "When Effect Becomes Cause: Policy Feedback and Political Change," *World Politics* 45, no. 4 (1993): 595–628, doi: 10.2307/2950710; Eric Patashnik, *Reforms at Risk: What Happens After Major Policy Changes Are Enacted* (Princeton, NJ: Princeton University Press, 2008); Lorraine M. McDonnell, "Repositioning Politics in Education's Circle of Knowledge," *Educational Researcher* 38, no. 6 (August 2009): 417–27, doi: 10.3102/0013189X09342584; and Lorraine M. McDonnell, "Educational Accountability and Policy Feedback," *Educational Policy* 27, no. 2 (March 2013): 170–89, doi: 10.1177/0895904812465119.

8. Our approach differs in two respects from the approach that typifies most recent studies of the use of research evidence. The conventional approach focuses narrowly on the use of research. Alternatively, we conceptualize research as one among multiple types of evidence, and our theoretical framework employs the notion of "strategic use of evidence" to capture the incentives for a) using different kinds of evidence and b) combining types of evidence. These incentives stem from the role evidence is intended to play in contributing to a persuasive argument for a particular policy alternative, and from the organization's identity as a research producer or an advocate. Additionally the conventional approach is driven by questions and theories about the use of research in practice (especially the implementation of changes in practice), not policymaking. Thus, a vibrant literature has arisen to focus on Research-Practice Partnerships and Learning Communities. Cynthia E. Coburn and William R. Penuel, "Research-Practice Partnerships in Education: Outcomes, Dynamics, and Open Questions," *Educational Researcher* 45, no. 1 (January 2016): 48–54, doi: 10.3102/0013189X16631750; and Cynthia E. Coburn and Mary K. Stein, eds., *Research and Practice in Education: Building Alliances, Bridging the Divide* (Lanham, MD: Rowman & Littlefield, 2010). By focusing exclusively on practice, or implicitly assuming that the use of research is no different in policymaking, this literature begs the question of whether policymaking is different from implementing a change in practice, and runs counter to the political science and policy literatures, which distinguish between policy and implementation.

9. Alexander L. George and Andrew Bennett, *Case Studies and Theory Development in*

the Social Sciences (Cambridge, MA: MIT Press, 2005); John Gerring, "What Is a Case Study and What Is It Good For?," *American Political Science Review* 98, no. 2 (2004): 341–54, https://www.jstor.org/stable/4145316; and John Gerring, *Social Science Methodology: A Unified Framework* (New York: Cambridge University Press, 2011). These sources compare case study methodology to other observational techniques in terms of their potential for developing theory. Robert K. Yin, *Case Study Research: Design and Methods*, 4th ed. (Thousand Oaks, CA: Sage Publications, 2009) enumerates the qualities of good case studies. The criteria for case selection are insightfully reviewed in Henry E. Brady and David Collier, eds., *Rethinking Social Inquiry: Diverse Tools, Shared Standards*, 2nd ed. (Lanham, MD: Rowman & Littlefield, 2010); and Baumgartner and Jones, *Agendas and Instability*.

10. Gary King, Robert O. Keohane and Sidney Verba, *Designing Social Inquiry: Scientific Inference in Qualitative Research* (Princeton, NJ: Princeton University Press, 1994).

11. Three people were responsible for drafting the mathematics standards: Phil Daro, a former director of the New Standards project; William McCallum, a professor of mathematics at the University of Arizona; and Jason Zimba, a professor of mathematics and physics at Bennington College. Those responsible for drafting the ELA standards were David Coleman, the founder of Student Achievement Partners, and Sue Pimentel, the cofounder of Standards Work. Each set of standards writers was assisted by a large work team (fifty-one members in mathematics and fifty in ELA) that included educators, researchers, and others with expertise in curriculum and assessment design, cognitive development, and English language acquisition. This team was called upon to provide input and review drafts on an as-needed basis. In addition, there was a feedback group for each set of standards, consisting of members (twenty-one for mathematics and twelve for ELA) with expertise similar to that of the work group; they also reviewed drafts.

12. There is a voluminous and rich literature documenting the history of standards-based reforms from several different perspectives. Analyses which focus on how states' experiences with standards and accountability policies shaped NCLB include: Kevin Kosar, *Failing Grades: The Federal Politics of Education Standards* (Boulder, CO: Lynne Rienner, 2005); Paul Manna, *School's In: Federalism and the National Education Agenda* (Washington, DC: Georgetown University Press, 2006); Patrick J. McGuinn, *No Child Left Behind and the Transformation of Federal Education Policy, 1965–2005* (Lawrence: University Press of Kansas, 2006); and Jesse Rhodes, *An Education in Politics: The Origins and Evolution of No Child Left Behind* (Ithaca, NY: Cornell University Press, 2012). Others have examined the implementation of state standards: David K. Cohen and Heather C. Hill, *Learning Policy: When State Education Reform Works* (New Haven, CT: Yale University Press, 2001); Lorraine M. McDonnell, *Politics, Persuasion, and Educational Testing* (Cambridge, MA: Harvard University Press, 2004); David K. Cohen and Susan L. Moffitt, *The Ordeal of Equality: Did Federal Regulation Fix the Schools?* (Cambridge, MA: Harvard

University Press, 2009); and Kathryn A. McDermott, *High-Stakes Reform: The Politics of Educational Accountability* (Washington, DC: Georgetown University Press, 2011).

13. *Improving our Competitiveness: Common Core Education Standards, Hearing Before the Committee on Education and Labor,* US House of Representatives, 111th Cong., 1st sess., 28 (December 8, 2009) (prepared statement of Gene Wilhoit, executive director, Council of Chief State School Officers), https://www.govinfo.gov/content/pkg/CHRG-111hhrg53732/pdf/CHRG-111hhrg53732.pdf.

14. Because participants in the CCSS process who were interviewed were promised confidentiality, they are identified only by their role position.

15. Margaret E. Goertz, "Standards-Based Reform: Lessons from the Past, Directions for the Future" (paper presented at Clio at the Table: A Conference on the Uses of History to Inform and Improve Education Policy, Brown University, Providence, RI, June 2007), http://citeseerx.ist.psu.edu/viewdoc/download?doi=10.1.1.184.3306&rep=rep1&type=pdf; Cohen and Moffitt, *The Ordeal of Equality.*

16. McDonnell was chair of the NRC committee.

17. Although not primarily oriented toward the function of transmitting and translating research findings, research producers serve as the baseline in that their research and dissemination most closely adhere to the principles of scientific method. These organizations (e.g., universities, policy research institutions such as RAND or Brookings, and NRC committees) are primarily concerned with the production of high-quality research—discovering new facts or connections, theory building—thus the canons of scientific method exert constraints on the production of research and the framing of findings; their focus on dissemination, although important, is secondary.

CHAPTER 2

1. National Research Council, Committee on the Use of Social Science Knowledge in Public Policy, *Using Science as Evidence in Public Policy,* ed. Kenneth Prewitt, Thomas A. Schwandt, and Miron L. Straf (Washington, DC: National Academies Press, 2012), doi: 10.17226/13460; Abraham Kaplan, *The Conduct of Inquiry: Methodology for Behavioral Science* (San Francisco: Chandler, 1964).

2. The nature and quality of the Common Core evidence base is most salient in how it is reflected in the mathematics and ELA standards. Consequently, in this chapter, we draw most of the examples of evidence use in the CCSS process from what was considered in developing the actual standards and in ultimately shaping their content and structure. In subsequent chapters, we focus on evidence use during other phases: when the initiative was first proposed, adopted by states, and begun to be implemented.

3. The sample of works consulted in the final, public version of the CCR math standards lists seventy-one entries. Of these, thirty-three (47 percent) are either syntheses of peer-reviewed research; reports on single empirical studies; or statistical

compilations of demographic, survey, or test data. Seventeen (24 percent) are standards documents from twelve high performing countries or countries of interest, and five are from states viewed as having strong standards. The remainder of the entries primarily describe various approaches to math instruction or make recommendations about how mathematics education should be structured.

4. Sheila W. Valencia, P. David Pearson, and Karen K. Wixson, *Assessing and Tracking Progress in Reading Comprehension* (paper commissioned by the Center for K–12 Assessment and Performance Management, Educational Testing Service, Princeton, NJ, April 2011), http://www.ets.org/Media/Research/pdf/TCSA_Symposium_Final_Paper_Valencia_Pearson_Wixson.pdf; Cindy Long, "Here Come the Common Core Standards," *NEAToday* (blog), March 17, 2011, http://neatoday.org/2011/05/17/here-come-the-common-core-standards-2; *R&D Alert: Academic Literacy for Adolescents* (San Francisco, CA: WestEd, October 10, 2011); *Reading Between the Lines: What the ACT Reveals About College Readiness in Reading* (Iowa City, IA: ACT) 2006, https://eric.ed.gov/?id=ED490828; Randy Bomer and Beth Maloch, "Relating Policy to Research and Practice: The Common Core Standards," *Language Arts* 89, no. 1 (September 2011), https://secure.ncte.org/library/NCTEFiles/Resources/Journals/LA/0891-sep2011/LA0891Research.pdf; William H. Schmidt, Leland S. Cogan, and Curtis C. McKnight, "Equality of Educational Opportunity: Myth or Reality in U.S. Schooling?" *American Educator* 34, no. 4 (2011), https://www.aft.org/sites/default/files/periodicals/Schmidt_1.pdf; and American Institutes for Research, *Informing Grades 1–6 Mathematics Standards Development: What Can Be Learned from High-Performing Hong Kong, Korea, and Singapore* (Washington, DC: AIR, December 2009), https://www.air.org/sites/default/files/downloads/report/MathStandards_0.pdf.

5. David Conley and researchers at the Education Policy Improvement Center tested the final version of the CCSS against this criterion, surveying a sample of university faculty to assess their judgment whether the standards would lead to high school graduates who were college ready. Catherine Gewertz, "Academics Find Common Standards Fit for College: But Academics Maintain Some Skills are Missing," *Education Week*, August 25, 2011, https://www.edweek.org/ew/articles/2011/08/25/02collegeready_ep.h31.html; *Comparing the Common Core State Standards in Mathematics and NCTM's Curriculum Focal Points* (Washington, DC: Achieve, 2010), https://www.achieve.org/files/CCSSandFocalPoints.pdf; *Out of Many, One: Toward Rigorous Common Core Standards from the Ground Up* (Washington, DC: Achieve, 2008), https://www.achieve.org/files/OutofManyOne.pdf; *Ready or Not: Creating a High School Diploma That Counts* (Washington, DC: Achieve, 2004), https://www.achieve.org/files/ReadyorNot.pdf; Linda Darling-Hammond and Ray Pecheone, *Developing an Internationally Comparable Balanced Assessment System That Supports High-Quality Learning* (Princeton, NJ: ETS, March 8, 2010), https://www.ets.org/Media/Research/pdf/Darling-HammondPechoneSystemModel.pdf; *Affirming the*

Goal: Is College and Career Readiness an Internationally Competitive Standard? (Iowa City, IA: ACT, 2011), https://eric.ed.gov/?id=ED520009; and Beth Hart et al., *Common Core State Standards Alignment*, College Board Research Report no. 2011–8 (New York: College Board, 2011), http://secure-media.collegeboard.org/digitalServices/pdf/research/RR2011–8.pdf.

6. National Research Council, *Common Standards for K–12 Education? Considering the Evidence: Summary of a Workshop Series*, Committee on State Standards in Education (Washington, DC: National Academies Press, 2008), 61, doi: 10.17226/12462.

7. *Common Standards: The Time Is Now* (Washington, DC: All4Ed, 2009), https://all4ed.org/reports-factsheets/common-standards-the-time-is-now; Grover J. Whitehurst, *Don't Forget Curriculum* (Washington, DC: Brookings Institution, 2009), https://www.brookings.edu/research/dont-forget-curriculum; *2009 National Curriculum Survey Report* (Iowa City, IA: ACT, 2010), http://www.act.org/content/dam/act/unsecured/documents/NationalCurriculumSurvey2009.pdf; Stephen Sawchuk, "Common Standards Judged Better Than Most States," *Education Week*, July 21, 2010, https://www.edweek.org/ew/articles/2010/07/21/37fordham.h29.html; and Council of Chief State School Officers, *SEC Content Analysis of Standards* (Washington, DC: CCSSO, October 12, 2010), https://files.eric.ed.gov/fulltext/ED543314.pdf.

8. Learning trajectories or progressions are defined as "empirically supported hypotheses about the levels or waypoints of thinking, knowledge, and skill in using knowledge, that students are likely to go through as they learn mathematics and, one hopes, reach or exceed the common goals set for their learning. Trajectories include hypotheses both about the order and nature of the steps in the growth of students' mathematical understanding, and about the nature of the instructional experiences that might support them in moving step by step toward the goals of school mathematics." Phil Daro, Frederic A. Mosher, and Tom Corcoran, *Learning Trajectories in Mathematics: A Foundation for Standards, Curriculum, Assessment, and Instruction*, CPRE Research Report # RR-68 (Philadelphia: Consortium for Policy Research in Education, 2011), 12, doi: 10.12698/cpre.2011.rr68. Researchers acknowledge the probabilistic nature of learning progressions and that existing ones require additional empirical examination. Paola Sztajn et al., "Learning Trajectory Based Instruction: Toward a Theory of Teaching," *Educational Researcher* 41, no. 5 (June 2012), doi: 10.3102/0013189X12442801.

9. Douglas Clements, "What Do We Know About Content and Curriculum," in *Research in Mathematics Education: Where Do We Go from Here?* (conference proceedings, Michigan State University Institute for Research on Mathematics and Science Education, Washington, DC, 2011).

10. A teaching and learning researcher, involved in reviewing the Common Core, described the learning sequences in the math standards as a hypothesis:

    There's not enough research yet to support the learning progressions. Right now, they are a great big hypothesis space that will discipline the production of the assessments ... Mark Wilson [UC Berkeley] spent five years working on learning progressions that cover one quarter of the seventh-grade math curriculum. I asked Mark if he could work faster, and he said he couldn't. But the learning progressions are our best guess now for the money. They are based on a hypothesis, but we'll get masses of data even if the hypothesis is wrong.

11. "Progressions Documents for the Common Core Math Standards," Institute for Mathematics and Education website, University of Arizona, 2013, http://ime.math .arizona.edu/progressions.

12. P. David Pearson and Elfrieda H. Hiebert, "Understanding the Common Core State Standards," in *Teaching with the Common Core State Standards for English Language Arts, PreK–2*, ed. Lesley Mandel Morrow, Timothy Shanahan, and Karen K. Wixson (New York: Guilford Press, 2012).

13. "Appendix A: Research Supporting Key Elements of the Standards," in *Common Core State Standards for English Language Arts and Literacy in History/Social Studies, Science, and Technical Subjects* (Washington, DC: National Governors Association and Council of Chief State School Officers, 2010), 7, http://www.corestandards .org/assets/Appendix_A.pdf.

To ensure that research on the measurement of text complexity and its limitations would inform the ELA standards development, David Pearson, a major figure in reading research, joined with David Coleman, one of the standards writers, to organize a conference on text complexity. The participants focused on identifying what dimensions could be measured quantitatively and what aspects require qualitative analysis and professional judgment. One participant noted, "the standards writers took seriously the takeaways from the meeting, but they had a problem in acting on them because of the state of knowledge."

Part of the reason that measuring text complexity and deciding on a text's placement at the appropriate grade level requires considerable judgment is that students' comprehension difficulty is associated not only with the nature of the text, but also the nature of the task. A text may appear simple in terms of its length and language, but the task associated with it may be challenging (for example, a requirement to assess the claims made in a primary text such as a political speech against the broader historical text).

14. Vicki Phillips, "More Is Not Better," *Education Week*, September 30, 2009, https:// www.edweek.org/ew/articles/2009/09/30/05phillips_ep.h29.html; Catherine Gewertz, "Aligning Standards and Curriculum Begets Questions," *Education Week*, May 18, 2010, https://www.edweek.org/ew/articles/2010/05/19/32common-curric_ep.h29.html; Alyson Klein, "In Standards Push, Lawmakers Cheer States' Initiative," *Education Week*, May 13, 2009, https://www.edweek.org/ew/articles/ 2009/05/13/31standards-2.h28.html; Alyson Klein, "Critics Pan Obama Plan to Tie Title I to Standards," *Education Week*, February 26, 2010, https://www.edweek

.org/ew/articles/2010/02/26/23esea_ep-2.h29.html; and Alyson Klein, "Federal Role Touchy in Standards Push," *Education Week*, September 1, 2010, https://www .edweek.org/ew/articles/2010/09/01/02policy.h30.html.

15. According to a participant in the standards-writing process, "the AFT teachers spent two days reviewing the standards. When we went to meet with the review team at the AFT, the math teachers had actually cut up the standards and had deliberated about whether the learning progressions made sense. So, we started with the research, and they looked at the research and then reviewed the standards based on their experience. Some revisions we made were actually based on classroom teachers' experience."

16. Catherine Gewertz, "Union Details Teacher Influence on Common Standards," *Curriculum Matters* (blog), Education Week, April 16, 2010, https://blogs.edweek .org/edweek/curriculum/2010/04/union_details_teacher_influenc.html; "Core Standards," American Federation of Teachers website, April 15, 2010, https://www .aft.org/news/core-standards; "ELL Forum Stresses Alignment of State Standards," American Federation of Teachers website, October 21, 2010, https://www.aft.org/ news/ell-forum-stresses-alignment-state-standards; "NEA Comments on K–12 Common Core Standards Draft," news release, National Education Association, March 11, 2010; Christina A. Samuels, "Special Educators Look to Tie IEPs to Common Core," *Education Week*, December 27, 2010, https://www.edweek.org/ ew/articles/2010/12/27/15iep_ep.h30.html; Long, "Here Come the Common Core Standards"; *Making College and Career Readiness the Mission for High Schools* (Washington, DC: Achieve and the Education Trust, 2008), https://www.achieve.org/ files/MakingCollegeandCareerReadinesstheMissionforHighSchool.pdf; and Catherine Gewertz, "Both Value and Harm Seen in K–3 Common Standards," *Education Week*, April 7, 2010, https://www.edweek.org/ew/articles/2010/04/07/28common .h29.html.

17. The other standards development principles that served as criteria for the committee's validation of the CCSS were "evidence of the knowledge and skills that students need to be college and career ready; a proper level of clarity and specificity; [and] evidence that the standards are comparable with other leading countries' expectations." *Reaching Higher: The Common Core State Standards Validation Committee* (Washington, DC: National Governors Association and Council of Chief State School Officers, 2010), 1.

18. Another member of the validation committee described the professional judgment of his fellow members in this way: "You had a lot of people who carried this stuff in their heads and so their evidence base is their personal knowledge structure, and it's pretty imposing for some of these people. So, they don't necessarily have to go chapter and verse."

19. For example, a practitioner member of the validation committee outlined how trust in the standards writers factored into his judgment process: "For me, personally,

I had faith that they [the standards writers] had done their job and done it well. Plus knowing some of the groups that had been working on this—College Board, Achieve, and others—knowing those individuals . . . I know many of these people; I know their work, their level of rigor, and where they're going."

Similarly, a leader of a national interest group whose institutional members supported the Common Core noted: "I think that [the standards development process] was about as good as anyone had ever seen. I think there was a great deal of confidence in it. And a lot of us knew the main writers and we had confidence in them . . . the trust factor—not just personal trust, but trust in their intellectual integrity."

20. Giandomenico Majone, *Evidence, Argument, and Persuasion in the Policy Process* (New Haven, CT: Yale University Press, 1989); Jennifer L. Hochschild and Nathan Scovronick, *The American Dream and the Public Schools* (New York: Oxford University Press, 2003).

21. As we discuss in chapters 3, 4, and 5, the CCSS became more ideological during their implementation as opponents joined their criticisms of the Common Core to the larger ideological debate about the role of the federal government.

22. Schmidt, Coggan, and McKnight, "Equality of Educational Opportunity."

23. *Equal Education for All* (Washington, DC: PTA, March 1, 2010); *Raising the Bar: Implementing Common Core State Standards for Latino Student Success* (Washington, DC: National Council of La Raza, 2012), publications.unidosus.org/bitstream/handle/123456789/371/raisingthebar.pdf; *Strengthening America's Competitiveness Through Common Academic Standards, Hearing Before the Committee on Education and Labor*, US House of Representatives, 111th Cong., 1st sess. (April 29, 2009) (testimony of James B. Hunt Jr., former governor of North Carolina), https://www .govinfo.gov/content/pkg/CHRG-111hhrg48732/pdf/CHRG-111hhrg48732.pdf; "Tennessee Gov. Haslam Says 'Immoral' Education Gaps Must Be Closed," *Commercial Appeal* (Memphis, TN), August 11, 2011; *Benchmarking for Success: Ensuring U.S. Students Receive a World-Class Education* (Washington, DC: NGA, CCSSO, and Achieve, 2008), http://www.corestandards.org/assets/0812BENCHMARKING. pdf; "We Need National Reading Standards," *Boston Globe*, June 12, 2007; *The Instructional Demands of Standards-Based Reform* (Washington, DC: AFT, June 2009), https://www.aft.org/sites/default/files/instructionaldemands0609.pdf; and Jason Amos, "Nationalize the Schools (. . . A Little)!: Report Calls for National Standards, Increased Federal Role in Education," *Straight A's: Public Education Policy and Progress* 8, no. 6 (March 24, 2008), https://all4ed.org/articles/nationalize-the-schools-a-little-report-calls-for-national-standards-increased-federal-role-in-education.

24. Andrew J. Coulson, "The Case Against National School Standards," Cato Institute, August 14, 2009, https://www.cato.org/publications/commentary/case-against-national-school-standards; Paul L. Thomas, "Why Common Standards

Won't Work," *Education Week*, August 9, 2010, https://www.edweek.org/ew/articles/2010/08/11/37thomas.h29.html; Jim Stergios, "National Standards Will Define Local Curricula," Pioneer Institute, November 21, 2011, https://pioneerinstitute.org/education/national-standards-will-define-local-curricula; and Jim Stergios, "Questioning the Convergence on National Standards," Pioneer Institute, November 23, 2010, https://pioneerinstitute.org/education/questioning-the-convergence-on-national-standards. The argument that standards won't work because "all children are unique" was parried by the AFT: "One wonders what these same critics might do if their own child's teacher expressed no concern when their third grader had yet to demonstrate any interest or ability to read. Or if they found themselves parent to a tenth grader who could not produce a coherent written assignment." AFT, *Instructional Demands*.

25. Gary Mucciaroni and Paul Quirk, *Deliberative Choices: Debating Public Policy in Congress* (Chicago: University of Chicago Press, 2006), 156–57; Deborah A. Stone, *Policy Paradox and Political Reason*, 3rd ed. (New York: W.W. Norton, 2012), 158–59; William T. Gormley Jr., *Voices for Children: Rhetoric and Public Policy* (Washington, DC: Brookings Institution, 2012), 130–31.

26. *Strengthening America's Competitiveness Hearing* (testimony of James B. Hunt Jr.).

27. Tom Loveless, *How Well Are American Students Learning?* (Washington, DC: Brown Center on Education Policy, Brookings Institution, 2012); Grover Whitehurst, "Don't Forget Curriculum."

28. William H. Schmidt and Richard T. Houang, "Curricular Coherence and the Common Core State Standards for Mathematics," *Educational Researcher* 41, no. 8 (November 2012), 294–308, doi: 10.3102/0013189X12464517.

29. The respondent explained his criticism of the CCSS development process:

> I have not intended to and do not fault the developers of the Common Core for what they did. I think they did a good job, and I don't think there's a lot of evidence out there that they ignored that, had they not ignored, it would have produced a different product. But I do cast some aspersions with the degree to which the process—which was probably about as good as it could have been—was explained and sold as an evidence-driven process.
>
> I think the rhetoric about the standards being evidence based doesn't comport with the kind of evidence I would think would be ideal for developmental standards. Now, to be fair to everybody, that evidence doesn't exist. So what you have, I think, is not only well intentioned but I think generally well-executed effort to try to use the consensus process that is at the core of standards-setting to generate a new set of standards that a lot of states can sign on to. That's the way standards are generally built and nobody, to my knowledge, has ever looked empirically at whether particular standard content has a strong and exclusive prediction function on outcomes that are valued.

30. National Research Council, *Common Standards for K–12 Education?*

31. In March 2010, NGA and CCSSO released a draft of the CCSS for public com-
    ment. Approximately ten thousand individuals, about half of whom were teach-
    ers, responded to an online survey. The overwhelming majority of respondents
    supported the concept of common standards, and their comments focused on
    areas that required clearer language, more examples, and greater detail. How-
    ever, according to the summary issued by CCSSO and NGA, a significant num-
    ber perceived the CCSS to be federal standards and expressed opposition to them
    on principle. Another group, representing hundreds of respondents, pressed for
    health standards to be issued with the CCSS. One group questioned the CCSS on
    research grounds, arguing that they were developmentally inappropriate and at
    odds with the research on how children learn. They expressed concern that the
    standards, in starting with kindergarten students, placed too heavy an empha-
    sis on academic knowledge and skills in early grades and did not match the early
    learning standards for preK–3 that many states had adopted. *Reactions to the March
    2010 Draft Common Core State Standards: Highlights and Themes from the Public Feed-
    back* (Washington, DC: CCSSO and NGA, 2010), http://www.corestandards.org/
    assets/k-12-feedback-summary.pdf.
32. Jane J. Mansbridge, ed., *Beyond Self-Interest* (Chicago: University of Chicago Press,
    1990); Steven Kelman, *Making Public Policy: A Hopeful View of American Government*
    (New York: Basic Books, 1987); and Robert B. Reich, ed., *The Power of Public Ideas*
    (Cambridge, MA: Ballinger, 1988).
33. John Kingdon, *Agendas, Alternatives, and Public Policies*, updated 2nd ed. (New York:
    Longman, 2011); Majone, *Evidence, Argument, and Persuasion*.
34. John L. Campbell, "Ideas, Politics, and Public Policy," *Annual Review of Sociology* 28
    (2002): 21–38, doi: 10.1146/annurev.soc.28.110601.141111.
35. Daniel Beland, "Ideas and Social Policy: An Institutionalist Perspective," *Social Pol-
    icy and Administration* 39, no. 1 (2005): 1–18, doi: 10.1111/j.1467-9515.2005.00421.x.
36. John E. Chubb and Terry M. Moe, *Politics, Markets, and America's Schools* (Washing-
    ton, DC: Brookings Institution, 1990).
37. William H. Schmidt and Adam Maier, "Opportunity to Learn," in *Handbook of Edu-
    cation Policy Research*, ed. Gary Sykes, Barbara Schneider, and David N. Plank (New
    York: Routledge, 2009), 541–59; Lorraine M. McDonnell, "Opportunity to Learn
    as a Research Concept and a Policy Instrument," *Educational Evaluation and Policy
    Analysis* 17, no. 3 (September 1995): 305–22, doi: 10.3102/01623737017003305.
38. Campbell, "Ideas, Politics, and Public Policy."
39. Frank R. Baumgartner and Bryan D. Jones, *Agendas and Instability in American Poli-
    tics* (Chicago: University of Chicago Press, 1993).
40. Jennifer A. O'Day and Marshall A. Smith, "Systemic School Reform," in *Designing
    Coherent Education Policy: Improving the System*, ed. Susan H. Fuhrman (San Fran-
    cisco: Jossey-Bass, 1993); David K. Cohen and James P. Spillane, "Policy and Prac-
    tice: The Relations Between Governance and Instruction," *Review of Research in*

Education 18 (1992): 3–49, doi: 10.2307/1167296; David K. Cohen and Susan L. Moffitt, *The Ordeal of Equality: Did Federal Regulation Fix the Schools?* (Cambridge, MA: Harvard University Press, 2009); and Jal Mehta, *The Allure of Order* (New York: Oxford University Press, 2013).

CHAPTER 3

1. Our approach disaggregates the concept of intermediary organizations, detailing the properties that distinguish different types of IOs. The tradition in research on evidence use is to group all intermediary organizations into one category, emphasizing how their "bridging" function distinguishes them from producers and consumers of research. Nathan Caplan, "The Two-Communities Theory and Knowledge Utilization," *American Behavioral Scientist* 22, no. 3 (1979): 459–70, doi: 10.1177/000276427902200308; and Karen Bogenschneider and Thomas J. Corbett, *Evidence-Based Policymaking: Insights from Policy-Minded Researchers and Research-Minded Policymakers* (NY: Routledge, 2010). This conceptualization was productive in the early stages of research on evidence use: investigators were just beginning to document the function of IOs to identify new findings and then translate those findings from academic or theoretical jargon into useful knowledge for practitioners. The accumulation of empirical research, however, has shown that intermediaries perform a variety of functions, and that their incentives and organizational configurations differ. We draw on the policy literature to distinguish among IOs, depending on their organizational characteristics, the goals and incentives for evidence production and use, and the way their target audience shapes their use of research and other evidence.

2. Frank R. Baumgartner and Bryan D. Jones, *Agendas and Instability in American Politics* (Chicago: University of Chicago Press, 1993); John Kingdon, *Agendas, Alternatives, and Public Policies*, updated 2nd ed. (New York: Longman, 2011); Michael Mintrom, *Policy Entrepreneurs and School Choice* (Washington, DC: Georgetown University Press, 2000); and Adam Sheingate, "Political Entrepreneurship, Institutional Change, and American Development," *Studies in American Political Development* 17, no. 2 (2003): 185–203, doi: 10.1017/S0898588X03000129.

3. Kingdon, *Agendas*, 179.

4. Kingdon, *Agendas*.

5. Giandomenico Majone, *Evidence, Argument, and Persuasion in the Policy Process* (New Haven, CT: Yale University Press, 1989); Deborah A. Stone, *Policy Paradox and Political Reason*, 3rd ed. (New York: W.W. Norton, 2012).

6. Mintrom, *Policy Entrepreneurs*, 268.

7. Mintrom, 271.

8. Mintrom, 273.

9. National Research Council, Committee on the Use of Social Science Knowledge in Public Policy, *Using Science as Evidence in Public Policy*, ed. Kenneth Prewitt, Thomas

A. Schwandt, and Miron L. Straf (Washington, DC: National Academies Press, 2012), 7, doi: 10.17226/13460; William T. Gormley Jr., *Voices for Children: Rhetoric and Public Policy* (Washington, DC: Brookings Institution, 2012).

10. In their study of congressional deliberation, Mucciaroni and Quirk note "that legislators only need to understand information about effects, not the process that led to the effects. It is usually the processes that are complicated and that may require specialized knowledge." Gary Mucciaroni and Paul Quirk, *Deliberative Choices: Debating Public Policy in Congress* (Chicago: University of Chicago Press, 2006), 264, fn. 3.

11. Roy Romer is an education policy entrepreneur who served twelve years as governor of Colorado (1987–99) and six years as the superintendent of the Los Angeles Unified School District (2000–6). Although Governor Romer was not as deeply involved in promoting the CCSS, he participated in a number of meetings as the chair of Ed in 08, an information campaign funded by the Gates and Broad Foundations, intended to encourage the 2008 presidential candidates to include education in their campaign proposals.

12. Robert Rothman, *Something in Common: The Common Core Standards and the Next Chapter in American Education* (Cambridge, MA: Harvard Education Press, 2011).

13. One indicator of the Common Core entrepreneurs' lack of focus on the general public is its low visibility in the media while the standards were being developed. Based on a LexisNexis search of media articles mentioning the Common Core, McShane and Hess found that during its development (2009), fewer than 100 articles were published per month. The rate of coverage increased in March 2010 when the first Race to the Top winners were announced. However, it was not until August 2012 that the number of articles reached 1,000 per month, and for the next year the number continued to trend upward until it reached 3,300 per month. Michael Q. McShane and Frederick Hess, "Flying Under the Radar? Analyzing Common Core Media Coverage" (Washington, DC: American Enterprise Institute, March 2014), https://www.aei.org/research-products/report/flying-under-the-radar-analyzing-common-core-media-coverage.

14. R. Kent Weaver, *Ending Welfare as We Know It* (Washington, DC: Brookings Institution, 2000), 164.

15. Jeffrey R. Henig, *Spin Cycle: How Research Gets Used in Policy Debates—The Case of Charter Schools* (New York: Russell Sage Foundation, 2008), 219, https://www.jstor.org/stable/10.7758/9781610442855.

16. Henig, 223.

17. Kevin M. Esterling, *The Political Economy of Expertise* (Ann Arbor: University of Michigan Press, 2004), 45.

18. Esterling, 50; cf. Karen Bogenschneider, Elizabeth Day, and Emily Parrott, "Revisiting Theory on Research Use: Turning to Policymakers for Fresh Insights," *American Psychologist* 74, no. 7 (2019): 778–93, doi: 10.1037/amp0000460.

19. Rothman, *Something in Common.*

20. In categorizing IOs, Frederick Hess uses the term "mission-driven or ideological organizations" to describe those we refer to as hybrids. These organizations are indeed mission-driven, but we chose to call them hybrids to emphasize that how they use evidence shares some similarities with both translators/disseminators and advocates. Frederick M. Hess, ed., *When Research Matters: How Scholarship Influences Education Policy* (Cambridge, MA: Harvard Education Press, 2008), 247.

21. Hess, *When Research Matters.*

22. Sarah Reckhow, *Follow the Money: How Foundation Dollars Change Public School Politics* (New York: Oxford University Press, 2013), 27, doi: 10.1093/acprof:oso/9780199937738.001.0001.

23. Reckhow, 13, 143.

24. Reckhow, 2.

25. Michael J. Feuer, *The Rising Price of Objectivity: Philanthropy, Government, and the Future of Education Research* (Cambridge, MA: Harvard Education Press, 2016), 26–27. In discussing foundations as sponsors of research, Feuer makes a distinction between the large policy entrepreneurial institutions and several smaller ones, such as the Spencer and William T. Grant Foundations. They have continued to invest primarily in grants to researchers working on a broad range of education and youth development issues, even as they have become more targeted and strategic in the researcher-defined studies they fund.

26. In a 2011 interview in the *Wall Street Journal*, Bill Gates explained his reasons for supporting a uniform core curriculum. He argued that "it's ludicrous to think that multiplication in Alabama and multiplication in New York are really different . . . This is like having a common electrical system. It just makes sense." He continued, portraying common standards as a way for states to save money at a time when they faced budget shortfalls. "In terms of mathematics textbooks, why can't you have the scale of a national market? Right now, we have a Texas textbook that's different from a California textbook that's different from a Massachusetts textbook. That's very expensive." Jason L. Riley, "Was the $5 Billion Worth It?" *Wall Street Journal*, July 23, 2011, https://www.wsj.com/articles/SB10001424053111903554904576461571362279948.

27. For a discussion of Gates' funding of curriculum development and teacher supports in implementing the Common Core, see Vicki Phillips and Carina Wong, "Teaching to the Common Core by Design, Not Accident," *Phi Delta Kappan* 93, no. 7 (2012): 31–37, doi: 10.1177/003172171209300708.

28. Compilation by the authors from the websites of the Bill and Melinda Gates Foundation and funded organizations.

29. Although their grant-making in support of the CCSS and related initiatives was less than that of Gates, several other foundations also made major investments. For example, in addition to supporting the development of curriculum aligned with

the Common Core, the William & Flora Hewlett Foundation has funded a variety of research producers, translators and disseminators, and hybrids to focus on deeper learning, including its promotion and policy development, design of related curriculum and assessments, and provision of teacher professional development. Similarly, the Carnegie Corporation funded the National Research Council to develop the framework for the Next Generation Science Standards (NGSS), and then supported Achieve to work with states and the National Science Teaching Association (NSTA) to develop the standards based on the NRC frameworks. Subsequent Carnegie grants for implementing the NGSS, including the development of instructional materials, have been awarded to Achieve, NSTA, the NRC, and several science museums and universities.

30. Kingdon, *Agendas*, 179.
31. The distinction between political entrepreneurs and other advocates over the use of research should not be drawn too precisely. Evidence use by most policy actors is essentially a persuasive exercise, so its quality and rigor will often be shaped by the competing incentives of short-term rhetorical power versus future credibility. Political entrepreneurs are more sensitive to credibility considerations, but even policy advocates might sacrifice dramatic rhetorical claims for the credibility of research results, which, because they have been publicly vetted, are viewed as more credible than purely ideological arguments.

CHAPTER 4

1. The themes developed in this chapter have their origins in Lorraine M. McDonnell and M. Stephen Weatherford, "Evidence Use and the Common Core State Standards Movement: From Problem Definition to Policy Adoption," *American Journal of Education* 120, no. 1 (November 2013): 1–25, doi: 10.1086/673163; and Lorraine M. McDonnell and M. Stephen Weatherford, "Recognizing the Political in Implementation Research," *Educational Researcher* 45, no. 4 (2016): 233–42, doi: 10.3102/0013189X16649945.
2. John Kingdon, *Agendas, Alternatives, and Public Policies*, updated 2nd ed. (New York: Longman, 2011).
3. Kingdon, 110.
4. Deborah A. Stone, *Policy Paradox and Political Reason*, 3rd ed. (New York: W.W. Norton, 2012), 133.
5. Stone, 207.
6. Stone.
7. Frank R. Baumgartner and Bryan D. Jones, *Agendas and Instability in American Politics* (Chicago: University of Chicago Press, 1993).
8. Christina Wolbrecht and Michael T. Hartney, "'Ideas about Interests': Explaining the Changing Partisan Politics of Education," *Perspectives on Politics* 12, no. 3 (2014): 605, doi: 10.1017/S1537592714001613.

9. Policies are often portrayed as if-then statements that assume if a policy mandates or offers incentives for certain actions to be taken, the change will occur. These theories of action are essentially predictive causal statements, and usually decision-makers require some systematic, research-based evidence supporting the assumed link between policy and effects.

10. In 2007, the Hunt Institute requested that the NRC organize two workshops to examine available evidence on the ways in which standards-based accountability was currently functioning, criteria to use in evaluating common standards options, and the issues such an approach might raise. Although an NRC committee planned the workshop and commissioned papers, it was not intended to reach any conclusions or make any recommendations. However, the Hunt Institute drew on the research evidence presented at the workshops as an information source in advancing the case for common standards. James B. Hunt Jr. Institute for Educational Leadership, *Blueprint for Education Leadership*, vols. 1 and 2 (Durham, NC: June and October, 2008), http://www.hunt-institute.org/wp-content/uploads/2015/04/Blueprint_Number_1.pdf and http://www.hunt-institute.org/wp-content/uploads/2015/04/Blueprint_Number_2.pdf.

11. National Research Council, *Common Standards for K–12 Education? Considering the Evidence: Summary of a Workshop Series* (Washington, DC: National Academies Press, 2008), 15, doi: 10.17226/12462.

12. National Center for Education Statistics, *Mapping 2005 State Proficiency Standards onto the NAEP Scales*, NCES 2007–482 (Washington, DC: US Department of Education, 2007), https://nces.ed.gov/nationsreportcard/pdf/studies/2007482.pdf.

13. National Research Council, *Common Standards*, 23.

14. *Benchmarking for Success: Ensuring U.S. Students Receive a World-Class Education* (Washington, DC: NGA, CCSSO, and Achieve, 2008), http://www.corestandards.org/assets/0812BENCHMARKING.pdf.

15. Former governors Hunt and Wise were members of the group, as were Chester Finn Jr., the president of the Fordham Institute; Kati Haycock, the president of the Education Trust; and William Schmidt, a university distinguished professor at Michigan State and the director of the Trends in International Mathematics and Science Study (TIMSS). Schmidt is the academic most associated with promoting the need for national content standards, and functioned as a policy entrepreneur in advancing that argument.

16. Benchmarking for Success, 5.

17. Benchmarking for Success, 6.

18. Benchmarking for Success, 24.

19. The section on the strength of the Common Core evidence in chapter 2 analyzes the validity of the assumed relationship between academic standards and student learning outcomes.

20. David K. Cohen and Susan L. Moffitt, *The Ordeal of Equality: Did Federal Regulation*

Fix the Schools? (Cambridge, MA: Harvard University Press, 2009).

21. Margaret E. Goertz, "Standards-Based Reform: Lessons from the Past, Directions for the Future" (paper presented at Clio at the Table: A Conference on the Uses of History to Inform and Improve Education Policy, Brown University, Providence, RI, June 2007), http://citeseerx.ist.psu.edu/viewdoc/download?doi=10.1.1.184.3 306&rep=rep1&type=pdf; Diane Ravitch, *The Death and Life of the Great American School System: How Testing and Choice Are Undermining Education* (New York: Basic Books, 2010).

22. Although the systemic requirements and enabling conditions of standards policies were not given much prominence during the initial phase, policy entrepreneurs did acknowledge their role. For example, Governor Hunt noted in Congressional testimony, "standards need to be supported by an integrated system, including curriculum, assessment, instruction, teacher preparation, and professional development. Unless our efforts reach the on-the-ground activity of teaching and learning, they will have been in vain. Standards-based reform was meant to be systemic reform." *Strengthening America's Competitiveness Through Common Academic Standards, Hearing Before the Committee on Education and Labor,* US House of Representatives, 111th Cong., 1st sess. (April 29, 2009) (testimony of James B. Hunt Jr., former governor of North Carolina), https://www.govinfo.gov/content/pkg/CHRG-111hhrg48732/html/CHRG-111hhrg48732.htm.

23. National Research Council, *Common Standards,* 73.

24. Paul J. Quirk and Bruce Nesmith, "Reality-Based Policymaking Information, Advice, and Presidential Success," in *Governing at Home: The White House and Domestic Policymaking,* ed. Michael Nelson and Russell L. Riley (Lawrence: University Press of Kansas, 2011).

25. Kingdon, *Agendas.*

26. Forty-eight states signed a memorandum agreeing to participate in a process of developing a common core of state standards in ELA and mathematics and to support the development of common assessments to measure progress toward the standards.

27. Gary Mucciaroni and Paul Quirk, *Deliberative Choices: Debating Public Policy in Congress* (Chicago: University of Chicago Press, 2006), 24.

28. Steven Kelman, Making Public Policy: A Hopeful View of American Government (New York: Basic Books, 1987).

29. *Messaging Tool Kit* (Washington, DC: Common Core State Standards Initiative, 2010), http://programs.ccsso.org/link/CCSSI%20Toolkit%20Sept%202010.pdf.

30. Cynthia E. Coburn and Mary Kay Stein, eds., *Research and Practice in Education: Building Alliances, Bridging the Divide* (Lanham, MD: Rowman & Littlefield, 2010); Cynthia E. Coburn, William R. Penuel, and Kimberly E. Geil, "Research-Practice Partnerships at the District Level: A Strategy for Leveraging Research for Educational Improvement in School Districts" (New York: William T. Grant Foundation,

2013), https://wtgrantfoundation.org/library/uploads/2015/10/Research-Practice-Partnerships-at-the-District-Level.pdf.

31. David Mayhew, "Legislative Obstruction," *Perspectives on Politics* 8, no. 4 (December 2010): 1145–54, doi: 10.1017/S1537592710002203.

32. Kenneth Godwin, Scott H. Ainsworth, and Erik Godwin, *Lobbying and Policymaking: The Public Pursuit of Private Interests* (Thousand Oaks, CA: SAGE/CQ Press, 2013), doi: 10.4135/9781483349336; Burdett A. Loomis and Anthony J. Nownes, "Advocacy in an Era of Inequality," in *Interest Group Politics*, 9th ed., ed. Allan J. Cigler, Burdett A. Loomis, and Anthony J. Nownes (Thousand Oaks, CA: SAGE/ CQ Press, 2016), 363–78.

33. David Coleman and Susan Pimentel, *Revised Publishers' Criteria for the Common Core State Standards in English Language Arts and Literacy, Grades K–2* and *Grades 3–12* (Washington DC: National Governors Association et al., 2012), http://www .corestandards.org/assets/Publishers_Criteria_for_K–2.pdf and http://www.cores-tandards.org/assets/Publishers_Criteria_for_3–12.pdf; *K–8 Publishers' Criteria for the Common Core State Standards for Mathematics* (Washington, DC: National Governors Association et al., 2012), http://www.corestandards.org/assets/Math_ Publishers_Criteria_K–8_Summer%202012_FINAL.pdf; and *High School Publishers' Criteria for the Common Core State Standards for Mathematics* (Washington, DC: National Governors Association et al., 2013), http://www.corestandards.org/ assets/Math_Publishers_Criteria_HS_Spring%202013_FINAL.pdf.

34. Christina A. Samuels, "Districts Push for Texts Aligned to Common Core," *Education Week*, July 17, 2012, https://www.edweek.org/ew/articles/2012/07/18/36pub criteria.h31.html.

35. Vicki Phillips and Carina Wong, "Teaching to the Common Core by Design, Not Accident," *Phi Delta Kappan* 93, no. 7 (2012): 31–37, doi: 10.1177/003172171209300708.

36. Although surveys of faculty about the levels of mastery in mathematics and literacy that they expected of students beginning postsecondary education were a major source for the CCR design, higher education institutions and the organizations representing them had not been directly involved in development of the Common Core. However, once the states adopted the CCSS, several national organizations sought to include state higher education institutions in the implementation process. One example was the State Higher Education Executive Officers Association (SHEEO), which received grants from the Hewlett and Lumina Foundations to work with teams of K–12 SEA officials, higher education coordinating agency executives, and representatives of the largest state higher education institutions in seven states. Part of the initiative focused on establishing stronger collaborative communication networks. The hope was that building on these networks would lead to shared understandings of college readiness and eventually to better alignment of K–12 assessments and postsecondary entrance exams, and between high school graduation requirements and first-level postsecondary courses.

37. Morgan S. Polikoff, "How Well Aligned Are Textbooks to the Common Core Standards in Mathematics?" *American Educational Research Journal* 52, no. 6 (December 2015): 1185–211, doi: 10.3102/0002831215584435; Douglas Lee Lauen and S. Michael Gaddis, "Accountability Pressure, Academic Standards, and Educational Triage," *Educational Evaluation and Policy Analysis* 38, no. 1 (2016): 127–47, doi: 10.3102/0162373715598577; Lorraine M. McDonnell and M. Stephen Weatherford, "Organized Interests and the Common Core," *Educational Researcher* 42, no. 9 (December 2013): 488–97, doi: 10.3102/0013189X13512676; David M. Gamson, Xiaofei Lu, and Sarah Anne Eckert, "Challenging the Research Base of the Common Core State Standards: A Historical Reanalysis of Text Complexity," *Educational Researcher* 42, no. 7 (October 2013): 381–91, doi: 10.3102/0013189X13505684; Okhee Lee, Helen Quinn, and Guadalupe Valdés, "Science and Language for English Language Learners in Relation to Next Generation Science Standards and with Implications for Common Core State Standards for English Language Arts and Mathematics," *Educational Researcher* 42, no. 4 (May 2013): 223–33, doi: 10.3102/0013189X13480524; Gary L. Williamson, Jill Fitzgerald, and A. Jackson Stenner, "The Common Core State Standards' Quantitative Text Complexity Trajectory: Figuring Out How Much Complexity Is Enough," *Educational Researcher* 42, no. 2 (March 2013): 59–69, doi: 10.3102/0013189X12466695; Elfrieda H. Hiebert and Heidi Anne E. Mesmer, "Upping the Ante of Text Complexity in the Common Core State Standards: Examining Its Potential Impact on Young Readers," *Educational Researcher* 42, no. 1 (January 2013): 44–51, doi: 10.3102/0013189X12459802; William H. Schmidt and Richard T. Houang, "Curricular Coherence and the Common Core State Standards for Mathematics," *Educational Researcher* 41, no. 8 (November 2012): 294–308, doi: 10.3102/0013189X12464517; Paul Cobb and Kara Jackson, "Assessing the Quality of Common Core State Standards for Mathematics," *Educational Researcher* 40, no. 4 (May 2011): 183–85, doi: 10.3102/0013189X11409928; Andrew Porter et al., "Assessing the Common Core Standards: Opportunities for Improving Measures of Instruction," *Educational Researcher* 40, no. 4 (May 2011): 186–88, doi: 10.3102/0013189X11410232; Richard W. Beach, "Issues in Analyzing Alignment of Language Arts Common Core State Standards with State Standards," *Educational Researcher* 40, no. 4 (May 2011): 179–82, doi: 10.3102/0013189X11410055; and Andrew Porter et al., "Common Core Standards: The New U.S. Intended Curriculum," *Educational Researcher* 40, no. 3 (April 2011): 103–16, doi: 10.3102/0013189X11405038.
38. Polikoff, "How Well Aligned Are Textbooks?"
39. Emily M. Hodge, Serena J. Salloum, and Susanna L. Benko, "(Un)Commonly Connected: A Social Network Analysis of State Standards Resources for English/Language Arts," *AERA Open* 2, no. 4 (October 2016): 1–19, doi: 10.1177/2332858416674901.
40. Joan Herman, Scott Epstein, and Seth Leon, "Supporting Common Core

Instruction with Literacy Design Collaborative: A Tale of Two Studies," *AERA Open* 2, no. 3 (July 2016): 1–15, doi: 10.1177/2332858416655782.

41. Michael Q. McShane and Frederick Hess, "Flying Under the Radar? Analyzing Common Core Media Coverage" (Washington, DC: American Enterprise Institute, March 2014), https://www.aei.org/research-products/report/flying-under-the-radar-analyzing-common-core-media-coverage. Nationally representative surveys of registered voters, sponsored by Achieve and conducted in August 2011 and May 2012, found that 60 percent of those surveyed reported having seen, read, or heard nothing about the Common Core. *Growing Awareness, Growing Support: Teacher and Voter Understanding of the Common Core State Standards and Assessments* (Washington, DC: Achieve, 2012), https://www.achieve.org/publications/growing-awareness-growing-support-poll.

42. Patrick J. McGuinn, "Complicated Politics to the Core," *Phi Delta Kappan* 97, no. 1 (September 2015), 17, doi: 10.1177/0031721715602229.

43. Although the advocacy partners spent most of their conference calls discussing implementation strategies and political threats to the Common Core, they took seriously academic criticisms that claimed the standards had not adequately considered the full range of relevant research. One example was an op-ed in *Education Week* by Andrew Porter, then dean of the University of Pennsylvania Graduate School of Education and a respected curriculum researcher. Porter argued that an analysis comparing states' current mathematics and ELA standards with the CCSS, using the Surveys of Enacted Curriculum, showed that Common Core standards "do not represent a meaningful improvement over existing state standards," and that they had only "a somewhat greater emphasis on higher-order thinking." In their scheduled call one day after publication of the commentary, the participants wondered whether Porter's analysis was a valid way to look at standards. They also discussed who would have standing to respond, took issue with his use of "national curriculum" to characterize the CCSS, and agreed that talking points should be prepared in response.

What was clear from the conference call participants' discussion among themselves is that most of them had not read the research when it was published several months earlier in an academic journal, and that they were unsure of the methods Porter used or the basis on which to criticize his conclusions. Andrew C. Porter, "In Common Core, Little to Cheer About," *Education Week*, August 9, 2011, https://www.edweek.org/ew/articles/2011/08/10/37porter_ep.h30.html.

44. Lorraine M. McDonnell, "Assessing the Political Feasibility of Common Standards" (memo prepared for Workshop on Evaluating the Options for Common Standards, NRC Committee on State Standards in Education, Washington, DC, March 17, 2008).

45. Lorraine M. McDonnell, "Surprising Momentum: Spurring Education Reform in States and Localities," in *Reaching for a New Deal: Ambitious Governance, Economic*

Meltdown, and Polarized Politics in Obama's First Two Years, ed. Theda Skocpol and Lawrence R. Jacobs (New York: Russell Sage Foundation, 2011).

46. Jonathan Supovitz and Patrick McGuinn, "Interest Group Activity in the Context of Common Core Implementation," *Educational Policy* 33, no. 3 (July 2017): 453–85, doi: 10.1177/0895904817719516. An analysis of tweets for six months between September 2013 and March 2014 using *#commoncore* confirmed the differential use of social media by CCSS opponents and supporters. It found that 72 percent of those who sent the highest volume of tweets (transmitters) were opposed to the Common Core. About half of that group were from outside education and had taken positions on other issues such as antifederalism and privacy. The remainder were from individuals and organizations in education and opposed to the CCSS for education-related issues (such as being anti-testing, or considering the standards to be developmentally inappropriate). The researchers also found that opponents were more likely to use emotional appeals ("politicalspeak"), while CCSS supporters were more likely to base their claims on the merits of the evidence and the logic of the argument ("policyspeak"). Jonathan Supovitz, Alan Daly, and Miguel del Fresno, *#commoncore Project: How Social Media Is Changing the Politics of Education* (Philadelphia: Consortium for Policy Research in Education, February 23, 2015), http://repository.upenn.edu/hashtagcommoncore/1.

47. Ashley Jochim and Lesley Lavery, "The Evolving Politics of the Common Core: Policy Implementation and Conflict Expansion," *Publius: The Journal of Federalism* 45, no. 3 (Summer 2015): 380–404, doi: 10.1093/publius/pjv015.

48. William J. Bushaw and Shane J. Lopez, "Which Way Do We Go? The 45th Annual PDK/Gallup Poll of the Public's Attitudes Toward the Public Schools," *Phi Delta Kappan* 95, no. 1 (September 2013): 11, doi: 10.1177/003172171309500104; William J. Bushaw and Valerie J. Calderon, "Try It Again, Uncle Sam: The 46th Annual PDK/Gallup Poll of the Public's Attitudes Toward the Public Schools," *Phi Delta Kappan* 96, no. 1 (September 2014): 11, doi: 10.1177/0031721714547856.

49. Michael B. Henderson, Paul E. Peterson, and Martin West, "No Common Opinion on the Common Core," *Education Next* 15, no. 1 (Winter 2015): 10–11, https://www.educationnext.org/2014-ednext-poll-no-common-opinion-on-the-common-core.

50. Henderson, Peterson, and West, 12. The same survey found that K–12 teachers' support for the Common Core had also decreased from 76 percent in the 2013 survey to 46 percent in 2014, with opposition more than tripling from 12 to 40 percent. By 2014, teachers were better informed about the CCSS than the general public. The overwhelming majority answered two of the three knowledge questions correctly, but like the general public, most assumed incorrectly that the federal government would receive detailed data on individual students' test performance.

A year later, the American Teacher Panel (ATP), a nationally representative survey of K–12 teachers, found that large proportions of teachers in states that adopted the CCSS had misconceptions about what the Common Core called for in both mathematics and ELA content and classroom practice. V. Darleen Opfer, Julia H. Kaufman, and Lindsey E. Thompson, *Implementation of K–12 Standards for Mathematics and English Language Arts and Literacy: Findings from the American Teacher Panel* (Santa Monica, CA: RAND, 2016).

51. Henderson, Peterson, and West, 11.

52. Eric M. Patashnik and Julian E. Zelizer, "The Struggle to Remake Politics: Liberal Reform and the Limits of Policy Feedback in the Contemporary American State," *Perspectives on Politics* 11, no. 4 (December 2013): 1071–87, doi: 10.1017/S1537592713002831.

CHAPTER 5

1. Although this chapter focuses on the political conditions shaping implementation in each state and the differences among them, it is important to keep in mind that the transition from state policy to classroom practice shares similarities across states. Whether implementing the CCSS or other academic content standards, states must prepare frameworks to guide local districts and schools in designing curriculum; offer instructional materials and professional development opportunities for teachers or, alternatively, identify sources and providers whose products accurately reflect the standards; and develop assessments that reliably, validly, and fairly measure student mastery of the standards. How well and the manner in which states pursue these tasks depends on their capacity and political will.

2. Although it met the deadline to submit applications within the compressed time frame, California was not awarded a Race to the Top grant in either round one or two of the competition. One of the areas where it lost points was its lack of a state law that included student test scores as a criterion in a system of teacher and principal evaluations. Such an inclusion would have required local districts that agreed to participate in the Race to the Top application to renegotiate collective bargaining contracts with their teacher unions. In addition, the state lost points because its data system for tracking individual students had encountered problems and was not fully operational.

3. California Assessment of Academic Achievement, Program Provisions, California Education Code, section 60605.8(d) (2010), https://leginfo.legislature.ca.gov/faces/codes_displaySection.xhtml?lawCode=EDC&sectionNum=60605.8.

4. At the first meeting of the commission, David Coleman, one of the drafters of the ELA standards, explained how the commissioners should interpret the 15 percent rule:

   To address the "what is the 15 percent" question, he said you could add a standard, if you felt the addition gave the standards greater clarity. You could use a pencil to add, but you could never use the eraser—you could never take away from the CCSS.

5. John Fensterwald, "Yes to Common Core Plus 8th Grade Algebra," *The Educated Guess* (blog), July 16, 2010, http://theeducatedguess.org/2010/07/16/common-core-with-8th-grade-algebra-endorsed.

6. Five teacher members of the commission abstained on the mathematics standards vote because of their concern about the potential for tracking in algebra. As a CTA official explained:

> There were specific objections to the changes that were made to create the two math courses in the eighth grade. The teachers didn't believe that was the charge of the commission, to define math courses or to create this tracking in the standards of the eighth grade. It was not in the charge of the commission. That was a substantial departure from the legislative intent and the purpose that the CCSS was developed for. That was the reason for the abstention. As to whether it reflected the position of the CTA, it's both yes and no. While all of the teachers on the commission were CTA members and five of those teachers abstained, other teachers who didn't abstain also expressed the same reserve about tracking in eighth-grade math. The teachers have known about the problems of teaching math to students who aren't ready yet. And from their professional standpoint, it wasn't acceptable to push students into a course they don't have sufficient preparation for. But at the same time, the seventh-grade teachers are reluctant to make the judgment about who is ready and who is not. However, they call it, it is tracking. The results are not desirable and it was never a part of the responsibility of the commission, as dictated by the legislation, to rewrite certain parts of the CCSS.

7. The commission's staff director began the deliberations with the ELA standards, believing correctly that there would be greater agreement on them than on the mathematics standards. However, the commissioners chose to discuss the ELA standards at length, leaving less time for the mathematics standards.

8. *Common Core State Standards for English Language Arts and Literacy in History/Social Studies, Science, and Technical Subjects* (Washington, DC: National Governors Association and Council of Chief State School Officers, 2010), 6, http://www.core standards.org/assets/CCSSI_ELA%20Standards.pdf.

9. Although the CDE staff were not involved in the adoption process, California was one of the six states that the CCSSO and NGA standards writers had asked to conduct a formal review of the Common Core as it was being developed because their current standards were considered to be among the most rigorous in the country. The CDE staff prepared a "granular analysis" comparing the state standards with the CCSS. According to the CDE official who led the review:

> My main goal was to align with the statement that the CCSS would be "just as rigorous." Of course, you can't just get out the "rigor meter" and check this, but there are certain benchmarks—reading by the end of grade 3; communication skills—reading, writing, speaking; in math, prepare for higher math.

The previous evaluation of CA standards shows that we were weak in language arts, where the standards were not addressing vocabulary development, or the needs of special populations—for example, ELLs, or the transition from African American vernacular English. We also determined that there was an underemphasis on writing. We tried to resolve all that in the 2008 adoption of instructional materials. I was happy to see that the Common Core addressed those areas. It was as if they had begun with the California standards and built on that—not surprising given that the primary author of the ELA standards was Sue Pimentel, who wrote the 1997 California standards.

10. Several participants mentioned that the teachers on the commission were especially persuaded by the presentation of Hung-Hsi Wu, a UC Berkeley mathematician, who had been a strong supporter of the 1997 California mathematics standards, but who now viewed the CCSS as "the best hope for leading our students to a higher level of achievement." In his statement to the Commission, he outlined specific aspects of the standards that contributed to its mathematical coherence.

11. John Fensterwald, "Final Vote on Common Core Is Unanimous," *Thoughts on Public Education*, August 2, 2010, http://theeducatedguess.org/2010/08/02/final-vote-on-common-core-is-unanimous.

12. The reason for this dictate was explained by a longtime analyst of California education politics:

> The state legislature hemmed the board in; it didn't trust the board. Therefore, it was all up or down; you can't amend it . . . Maybe they tinkered with a few things they could tinker with, but they were hemmed in by the legislation. The state board–legislative relations were horrible.

13. Ted Mitchell, "Common Educational Standards for Common Good," *San Francisco Chronicle*, July 30, 2010, https://www.sfgate.com/opinion/openforum/article/Common-educational-standards-for-common-good-3180461.php

14. Mike W. Kirst, *The Common Core Meets State Policy: This Changes Almost Everything* (Stanford, CA: Policy Analysis for California Education, March 2013), https://edpolicyinca.org/sites/default/files/PACE_Common%20Core_Final.pdf.

15. Brown's view stemmed not only from a recognition of the limits of state government, but also from a belief in *subsidiarity*, a principle derived from Catholic social thought. It posits that central authorities should have a subsidiary function, performing only those tasks that cannot be competently handled by the smallest or least centralized authority. In essence, political decisions should be handled at the local level, if possible.

16. From a use of research evidence perspective, the LCFF is a unique policy. Its basic ideas were first proposed in a paper published in 2008 and coauthored by Kirst, former California secretary of education Alan Bersin, and then–Berkeley

Law professor Goodwin Liu (now an associate justice of the California Supreme Court). Five years later, under a different gubernatorial administration and a stronger economy, the LCFF was enacted. As Michael Kirst noted, "It's extremely rare in policy analysis that 80 percent of what you recommend is put into law. Usually, you hope policymakers will consider half or less." John Fensterwald, "Michael Kirst, Father of New School Funding Formula, Looks Back and at the Work Ahead," *EdSource*, June 12, 2013, https://edsource.org/2013/michael-kirst-father-of-new-school-funding-formula-looks-back-and-at-the-work-ahead/33408/33408.

17. Anecdotal evidence about the limited capacity of the CDE was subsequently verified by Susan Moffitt and her colleagues in a comprehensive study of state structures for instructional support in California. They found that the CDE had suffered significantly higher staff reductions during past state revenue downturns than other states, that these reductions had occurred disproportionately in parts of the agency focused on instructional support, and that average salaries of CDE subject-matter experts are lower than for those in equivalent positions in high enrollment county and district offices. Susan L. Moffitt et al., *State Structures for Instructional Support in California*, Getting Down to Facts II Technical Report (Stanford, CA: Stanford University, September 2018), https://gettingdowntofacts.com/sites/default/files/2018-09/GDTFII_Report_Moffitt_structures_0.pdf.

18. Jennifer A. O'Day, "A Window of Opportunity: The Politics and Policies of Common Core Implementation in California," in *Challenging Standards: Navigating Conflict and Building Capacity in the Era of the Common Core*, ed. Jonathan A. Supovitz and James P. Spillane (Lanham, MD: Rowman & Littlefield, 2015).

19. The CORE districts include: Fresno Unified, Garden Grove Unified, Los Angeles Unified, Long Beach Unified, Oakland Unified, Sacramento City Unified, San Francisco Unified, and Santa Ana Unified. The network is funded by the Stuart, Hewlett, Bechtel, and Gates Foundations. It has a research partnership with Policy Analysis for California Education (PACE) that allows the CORE districts to develop research questions in collaboration with PACE's university-based researchers, share data, and tailor reports to different audiences. https://coredistricts.org.

The California Collaborative on District Reform convenes researchers, educators, and policymakers three times a year to discuss evidence-based strategies to improve areas of district practice such as leadership, transitioning to the Common Core, and closing learning opportunity gaps among students. In addition, the Collaborative undertakes special projects, convenes working groups to advise on California policy initiatives, and prepares reports and policy briefs. It is housed at and staffed by the American Institutes for Research (AIR), and receives support from several foundations. https://cacollaborative.org.

20. Moffitt et al., *State Structures*; Susan L. Moffitt et al., *Frontlines Perspectives on Instructional Support in the Common Core Era*, Getting Down to Facts II Technical

Report (Stanford, CA: Stanford University, September 2018), https://gettingdown
tofacts.com/sites/default/files/2018-09/GDTFII_Report_Moffitt_standards.pdf;
Neil Finkelstein et al., *Insights on Standards Implementation in California's Schools*,
Getting Down to Facts II Technical Report (Stanford, CA: Stanford University, Sep-
tember 2018), https://gettingdowntofacts.com/sites/default/files/2018-09/GDTFII
_Report_Finkelstein.pdf.

21. Brentt Brown and Merrill Vargo, *Getting to the Core: How Early Implementers are
Approaching the Common Core in California* (Stanford, CA: PACE and Pivot Learning
Partners, February 2014), https://edpolicyinca.org/sites/default/files/PACE%20
Getting%20To%20The%20Core.pdf; Milbrey McLaughlin, Laura Glaab, and
Isabel Hilliger Carrasco, *Implementing Common Core State Standards in Califor-
nia: A Report from the Field* (Stanford, CA: PACE, June 2014), https://edpolicyinca
.org/publications/implementing-common-core-state-standards-california-report-
field; and Thomas Timar and Allison Carter, *Surprising Strengths and Substan-
tial Needs: Rural District Implementation of Common Core State Standards* (Stanford,
CA: PACE, June 2017), https://edpolicyinca.org/sites/default/files/Rural%20
District%20Implementation%20of%20CCSS.pdf.

22. Joel Knudson, Stephanie Hannan, and Jennifer O'Day, *Learning from the Past: Drawing on California's CLAS Experience to Inform Assessment of the Common Core* (San
Mateo: California Collaborative on District Reform, September 2012), https://
cacollaborative.org/sites/default/files/CA_Collaborative_CLAS.pdf.

23. By 2019, 64 percent of a representative sample of Californians reported that they
knew at least "a little" about the Common Core. After reading a brief description
of the policy, 51 percent said they favored it, a percentage that had increased from
2017. As at the national level, a higher proportion of Democrats (63 percent) support the CCSS, as compared with Republicans (32 percent) and Independents
(47 percent). The overwhelming majority of public school parents (70 percent)
favor the Common Core, and Latinos are more likely to favor it (64 percent) than
African Americans (44 percent), Asian Americans (55 percent), and Whites (40
percent). Mark Baldassare, et al., *Californians and Education*, PPIC Statewide Survey (San Francisco: Public Policy Institute of California, April 2019), https://www
.ppic.org/wp-content/uploads/ppic-statewide-survey-californians-and-education-
april-2019.pdf.

An earlier survey of Californians, in 2015, found that among those who
expressed opposition (29 percent of the sample), their view was strongly correlated with disapproval of President Obama, a belief that there is too much testing,
and several misconceptions about what the CCSS allows. Morgan S. Polikoff et al.,
"Who is Opposed to Common Core and Why?" *Educational Researcher* 45, no. 4
(May 2016): 263–66, doi: 10.3102/0013189X16651087.

24. John Fensterwald, "State Board of Education President Mike Kirst Announces
He'll Retire—and Reflects on Changes He Has Led," *EdSource*, May 9, 2018, https://

edsource.org/2018/state-board-of-education-president-mike-kirst-retires-and-reflects-on-changes-he-has-led/597625.

25. Michele McNeil and Alyson Klein, "California's Hopes Dashed for NCLB Waiver," *Education Week*, January 8, 2013, https://www.edweek.org/ew/articles/2013/01/09/15policy.h32.html.

26. Catherine Gewertz, "California in Testing Showdown with U.S. Department of Education," *Education Week*, September 10, 2013, https://www.edweek.org/ew/articles/2013/09/10/04california.h33.html; John Fensterwald, "Common Core Practice Test Would Replace State Math and English Tests Next Year," *EdSource*, September 4, 2013, https://edsource.org/2013/common-core-practice-test-would-replace-state-math-and-english-tests-next-year/38470/38470.

27. For an analysis of the reasons why California's approach to education reform differed from that of the Obama administration, see Charles Taylor Kerchner, "California: A K–12 Education Outlier," *Education Week*, February 25, 2014, https://www.edweek.org/ew/articles/2014/02/26/22kerchner.h33.html.

28. For an analysis of Putting Students First, see Paul Manna, Keenan Kelley, and Frederick M. Hess, *Implementing Indiana's "Putting Students First" Agenda: Early Lessons and Potential Futures* (Washington, DC: American Enterprise Institute, August 2012), https://www.aei.org/wp-content/uploads/2012/08/-implementing-indianas-putting-students-first-agenda-early-lessons-and-potential-futures_154113317564.pdf.

29. "About Us," Hoosiers Against Common Core, http://hoosiersagainstcommoncore.com/about-us-2.

30. In addition to the Chamber, other groups supported the Common Core. These included Stand for Children Indiana and the Indiana affiliate of Democrats for Education Reform. Although both these groups supported charter schools, they also sought to show that groups opposing the Common Core supported policies such as teaching creationism that liberals oppose. Andrew Ujifusa, "Common Core Supporters Firing Back," *Education Week*, May 14, 2013, https://www.edweek.org/ew/articles/2013/05/15/31standards_ep.h32.html.

31. Andrew Ujifusa, "Tony Bennett Says Common Core in Jeopardy in Indiana," *State EdWatch* (blog), Education Week, November 7, 2012, http://blogs.edweek.org/edweek/state_edwatch/2012/11/tony_bennett_says_common_core_in_jeopardy_in_indiana.html; Scott Elliott, "Five Theories for Why Tony Bennett Lost on Tuesday," *Indianapolis Star*, November 9, 2012.

Unlike in California, there were no statewide opinion polls measuring public support and opposition for the CCSS. The only statewide indicator was the 2012 SPI election, with a vote of 52 percent for Glenda Ritz and 48 percent for Tony Bennett. However, as with most elections, the Common Core was not the only issue influencing voters' decisions.

32. Liana Heitin Loewus, "Indiana's Draft vs. the Common Core: A Comparison of Math Standards," *Curriculum Matters* (blog), Education Week, March 12, 2014,

http://blogs.edweek.org/edweek/curriculum/2014/03/indianas_draft_vs_the_common_c.html.

33. *Strong Standards: A Review of Changes to State Standards Since the Common Core* (Washington, DC: Achieve, November 2017), https://www.achieve.org/strong-standards; Solomon Friedberg et al., *The State of State Standards Post-Common Core* (Washington, DC: Thomas B. Fordham Institute, 2018), https://fordhaminstitute .org/sites/default/files/publication/pdfs/%2808.22%29%20The%20State%20of %20State%20Standards%20Post-Common%20Core.pdf.

34. Erin Tuttle, "Side by Side Comparison of Indiana's 'New' K–12 Math Standards," Hoosiers Against Common Core, March 6, 2014, https://hoosiersagainstcommon core.com/side-side-comparison-indianas-new-k–12-math-standards.

35. Andrew Ujifusa, "Indiana Standards to Replace Common Core Greeted Skeptically," *Education Week*, March 4, 2014, https://www.edweek.org/ew/ articles/2014/03/05/23indiana.h33.html.

36. Steven Yaccino, "Tensions Rise as Indiana Schools Chief and Governor Clash Over New Agency," *New York Times*, December 8, 2013, https://www.nytimes .com/2013/12/09/us/politics/tensions-rise-as-indiana-schools-chief-and-governor-clash-over-new-agency.html.

37. Andrew Ujifusa, "Political, Policy Feuds Roil Indiana's K–12 Landscape," *Education Week*, March 10, 2014, https://www.edweek.org/ew/articles/2014/03/12/ 24indiana.h33.html.

38. In the 2016 election Glenda Ritz was defeated for a second term. Mike Pence was elected vice president in the Trump administration.

39. Scott Elliott, "The Basics of Indiana Academic Standards: A New Beginning," Chalkbeat, September 8, 2014, https://www.chalkbeat.org/posts/in/2014/09/08/ the-basics-of-indiana-academic-standards-a-new-beginning.

40. Amy Horton, "Statewide Implementation Plan: Indiana Academic Standards in E/LA and Mathematics" (slide presentation, Indiana Department of Education, 2014), https://www.doe.in.gov/sites/default/files/standards/standardspresentation visionprogressjuly2014.pdf.

41. Elliott, "The Basics of Indiana Academic Standards."

42. Massachusetts fourth- and eighth-grade students scored first or statistically tied for first place on every administration of the NAEP mathematics and reading tests between 2005 and 2017. Massachusetts participated, as a benchmarking entity, in the eighth-grade TIMSS assessment in 1999, 2007, and 2011. In the 2011 mathematics assessment, Massachusetts students tied with Japan for fifth place, falling behind only Korea, Singapore, Taipei, and Hong Kong in their scores. In science, Massachusetts tied for second place behind only Singapore. Not only did Massachusetts students score significantly above their US peers, but Massachusetts made statistically significant score gains over the four test administrations. The gain score in mathematics was the highest of any participating country or benchmarking

entity, and the second highest in science of all participants. Massachusetts Department of Elementary and Secondary Education, *2017 NAEP Reading and Mathematics: Summary of State Results* (Malden: Massachusetts DESE, May 2018), http://www.doe.mass.edu/mcas/natl-intl/naep/results/2017readingmath.docx; Massachusetts Department of Elementary and Secondary Education, *Trends in International Mathematics and Science Study (TIMSS) 2011: Summary of Massachusetts Results* (Malden: Massachusetts DESE, November 2013), http://www.doe.mass.edu/mcas/natl-intl/timss/2011timssSummary.docx.

43. "Report of the English Language Arts Review Panel on the Common Core and Massachusetts Standards," (internal report, Massachusetts DESE, July 2010).

44. "Findings of the Mathematics Common Core Review Panel," (internal report, Massachusetts DESE, June 2010), 1.

45. WestEd, Analysis of the Commonwealth of Massachusetts State Standards and the Common Core State Standards for English Language Arts and Mathematics (Boston: Massachusetts Business Alliance for Education, July 19, 2010), https://www.mbae.org/wp-content/uploads/2010/07/Report_MA-CCS-Analysis_071910_Final.rev_.pdf.

46. WestEd, *Analysis*, 9.

47. Tamar Lewin, "Many States Adopt National Standards for Their Schools," *New York Times*, July 21, 2010, https://www.nytimes.com/2010/07/21/education/21standards.html. The Pioneer Institute's executive director, Jim Stergios, also noted that the other groups providing evidence about the Common Core either had Gates Foundation funding or connections with those who developed the standards: "We're the only ones who had no dog in the fight."

48. James Vaznis, "State Panel Adopts US Academic Standards," *The Boston Globe*, July 22, 2010, http://archive.boston.com/news/education/k_12/mcas/articles/2010/07/22/state_panel_adopts_us_academic_standards.

49. Andrew Ujifusa, "Massachusetts' Mitch Chester on Common Core, Gov. Patrick's K-12 Plan," *State EdWatch* (blog), Education Week, January 28, 2013, https://blogs.edweek.org/edweek/state_edwatch/2013/01/massachusetts_mitch_chester_on_common_core_gov_patricks_k-12_plan.html.

50. However, DESE acknowledges that the majority of the model curriculum units, developed between 2011 and 2015, are no longer aligned with the state's 2017 revised curriculum frameworks, and only a subset have been updated.

51. The concept of *Understanding by Design* (UbD) is a framework for designing curriculum units and performance assessments based on "six facets of understanding": emphasizing students' ability to explain, interpret, apply, have perspective, empathize, and have self-knowledge about a given topic. UbD depends on "backwards design" (or "backwards planning"), segmented into three stages: 1) teachers identify the desired results by establishing the overall goal of the lessons based on CCSS, 2) teachers plan performance tasks and assessments to generate evidence

of understanding among students, and 3) teachers outline the road map that leads students to learn. Grant Wiggins and Jay McTighe, *Understanding by Design* (Alexandria, VA: ASCD, 2005).

52. Julia Marchand, Mary Nistler, and Matthew Welch, *Massachusetts Curriculum Frameworks Implementation Study: Phase 1 Findings* (Chicago: American Institutes for Research, September 2013), http://www.doe.mass.edu/research/reports/2013/09MA-CFIS-Phase1.docx; Julia Marchand et al., *2011 Massachusetts Curriculum Frameworks for English Language Arts and Mathematics Implementation Study: Final Report* (Chicago: American Institutes for Research, October 2014), http://www.doe.mass.edu/research/reports/2014/10MA-CFIS-Final.docx.

53. Massachusetts Department of Elementary and Secondary Education, "DESE VISTA Survey Project, 2018-2019," http://www.doe.mass.edu/research/vista/2019.

54. Morgan S. Polikoff and Shauna Campbell, *Adoption, Implementation, and Effects of Curriculum Materials*, DESE Policy Brief (Malden: Massachusetts Department of Elementary and Secondary Education, October 2018), http://www.doe.mass.edu/research/reports/2018/10curriculum-materials.docx.

55. See, for example, Thomas J. Kane et al., *Teaching Higher: Educators' Perspectives on Common Core Implementation* (Cambridge, MA: Center for Education Policy Research, February 2016), https://cepr.harvard.edu/files/cepr/files/teaching-higher-report.pdf; David Blazar et al., *Learning by the Book: Comparing Math Achievement Growth by Textbook in Six Common Core States* (Cambridge, MA: Center for Education Policy Research, March 2019), https://cepr.harvard.edu/files/cepr/files/cepr-curriculum-report_learning-by-the-book.pdf.

56. Kate Zernike, "Massachusetts's Rejection of Common Core Test Signals Shift in U.S.," *New York Times*, November 21, 2015, https://www.nytimes.com/2015/11/22/us/rejecting-test-massachusetts-shifts-its-model.html.

57. Andrew Ujifusa, "Two-Year Transition to Common-Core Tests Approved in Massachusetts," *State EdWatch* (blog), Education Week, November 19, 2013, http://blogs.edweek.org/edweek/state_edwatch/2013/11/two-year_transition_to_common-core_tests_approved_in_massachusetts.html.

58. End Common Core Massachusetts, https://www.endcommoncorema.com.

59. "Massachusetts Ending Common Core Education Standards Initiative (2016)," Ballotpedia, https://ballotpedia.org/Massachusetts_Ending_Common_Core_Education_Standards_Initiative_(2016).

60. Jeremy C. Fox, "Education Board Votes to Adopt Hybrid MCAS-PARCC Test," *Boston Globe*, December 2, 2015, https://www.bostonglobe.com/metro/2015/11/17/state-education-board-vote-whether-replace-mcas/aex1nGyBYZW2sucEW2o82L/story.html.

61. Gray v. Attorney General, SJC-12064 (Massachusetts Supreme Judicial Court 2016), https://cases.justia.com/massachusetts/supreme-court/2016-sjc-12064.pdf.

62. Abt Associates, *Massachusetts English Language Arts/Literacy and Mathematics Curriculum Frameworks Review: Final Report* (Boston, MA: Massachusetts Executive Office of Education, October 13, 2016), http://www.doe.mass.edu/bese/docs/fy2017/2016-10/spec-item1-ABTReport.pdf.

63. Michael Jonas, "Baker's Common Core Caution," *CommonWealth Magazine*, May 11, 2016, https://commonwealthmagazine.org/politics/bakers-common-core-caution.

64. *Race to the Top Tennessee Report: Year 1: School Year 2010–2011* (Washington, DC: US Department of Education, January 10, 2012), https://www2.ed.gov/programs/racetothetop/performance/tennessee-year-1.pdf.

65. Tennessee, with 444.2 points out of 500 possible, ranked second behind Delaware with 454.6 points.

66. Widmeyer Communications, "Gauging Attitudes on Tennessee Schools: Tennesseans are Cautiously Optimistic About K–12 Education" (Washington, DC: Widmeyer Communications, 2010).

67. Lauren Camera, "Tennessee on Dogged Path to Race to the Top Finish," *Education Week*, July 8, 2014, https://www.edweek.org/ew/articles/2014/07/09/36tennessee_ep.h33.html.

68. The collaboration between TDOE and Vanderbilt has continued under a different name. In October 2016, the Tennessee Education Research Alliance (TERA) was created to conduct research with practical implications for the state's major education strategies. Its focus areas include: early reading, reimagining state support for professional learning, driving improvement in low performing schools, and strengthening the state's education labor market: https://peabody.vanderbilt.edu/TERA.

69. *What We Heard: A Summary Report of Listening Sessions About Supporting Effective Teachers* (Franklin: United Ways of Tennessee, Fall 2010).

70. In their report assessing state structures for instructional support in California, Moffitt and her colleagues highlight the TDOE's Division of Research and Strategy as a model of how a state agency can be structured as an organization that connects timely data to the state's policy agenda, and that forms partnerships with other organizations to inform policy and practice. Moffitt et al., *State Structures*, 59–62.

71. Those supporting the Common Core noted that between 2011 and 2013, Tennessee's fourth graders had improved their NAEP scores in mathematics from forty-sixth to thirty-seventh among the states, and in reading, had improved from forty-first to thirty-first, and they attributed the transition to the Common Core as a primary reason. Although Tennessee was still in the bottom half of states, it was the fastest academically improving. In his 2014 State of the Union speech, President Obama acknowledged Tennessee's progress: "Teachers and principals in schools from Tennessee to Washington, DC, are making big strides in preparing students with skills for the new economy—problem solving, critical thinking,

science, technology, engineering, and math. Some of this change is hard ... But it's worth it and it's working." Barack Obama, "State of the Union Address," January 28, 2014, https://obamawhitehouse.archives.gov/the-press-office/2014/01/28/president-barack-obamas-state-union-address.

72. Joan Brasher, "Survey: Majority of Tennessee Teachers Oppose Common Core," *Research News @Vanderbilt*, September 24, 2014, https://news.vanderbilt.edu/2014/09/24/survey-common-core.

73. Although Haslam had been supportive of the Common Core since its adoption and believed in the idea of rigorous standards, he realized that opposition to it by a number of groups required rebranding. In a speech to the Tennessee Press Association in February 2015, he noted: "I just realized that fixing the brand is too hard. There's certainly hills you die on, but dying on a brand that people feel that way about, I don't think is smart." Grace Tatter, "Standards Review Committee or Repeal Common Core Committee? Tennessee Leaders Are Split," Chalkbeat, August 5, 2015, https://www.chalkbeat.org/posts/tn/2015/08/05/standards-review-committee-or-repeal-common-core-committee-tennessee-leaders-are-split.

74. Despite growing opposition, there were groups that continued to support the Common Core. One was Tennesseans for Student Success, which ran media campaigns, including placing an ad in the Nashville market that ran during the 2015 Super Bowl. Although the thirty-second commercial did not specifically mention the Common Core, it argued: "Some politicians want to drive us back to the days of lower standards, less accountability, and fewer choices for parents." The narrator then asked Tennesseans to "tell your legislators to focus on results—not rhetoric." The commercial was financed with assistance from a branch of the Tennessee Chamber of Commerce, and the group had received funding from the Gates Foundation. Grace Tatter, "Commercial About State Educational Standards Makes Super Bowl Splash," Chalkbeat, February 3, 2015, https://www.chalkbeat.org/posts/tn/2015/02/03/commercial-about-state-educational-standards-makes-super-bowl-splash.

75. The Standards Recommendation Committee was composed of ten members appointed by the Speaker of the Tennessee House of Representatives, the lieutenant governor, and the governor. Its charge was to review the revisions proposed by the committees appointed by the SBE.

76. Grace Tatter, "Most Common Core Standards Are Keepers, According to Tennessee's Public Review," Chalkbeat, May 14, 2015, https://www.chalkbeat.org/posts/tn/2015/05/14/most-common-core-standards-are-keepers-according-to-tennessees-public-review.

77. Grace Tatter, "At Long Last, Phase-Out of Common Core Is Official in Tennessee," Chalkbeat, April 15, 2016, https://chalkbeat.org/posts/tn/2016/04/15/at-long-last-phase-out-of-common-core-is-official-in-tennessee.

78. Reviews of the TAS by Achieve and the Fordham Institute reached somewhat different conclusions. Based on the extent to which the revised standards reflect

college and career ready expectations, Achieve found the mathematics standards to be strong in ten of eleven CCR expectations, and the ELA standards strong across all eight CCR expectations. In rating the TAS on content, rigor, clarity, and specificity, Fordham concluded that the revised mathematics standards are reasonably strong (seven out of ten, as compared with nine out of ten for the CCSS), but the Tennessee ELA standards are among the weakest they have evaluated (five out of ten). They found the standards to be vague in many places, with multiple points of redundancy where standards overlap with those for previous grade levels. Achieve, *Strong Standards*; Friedberg, *The State of State Standards*.

79. Marta W. Aldrich, "Common Core Is Out. Tennessee Academic Standards Are In. Here's How Teachers Are Prepping for the Change," Chalkbeat, June 26, 2017, https://www.chalkbeat.org/posts/tn/2017/06/26/common-core-is-out-tennessee-academic-standards-are-in-heres-how-teachers-are-prepping-for-the-change.

   In addition to preparing teachers for the third set of standards in eight years, the state faced another challenge. Like Indiana, Tennessee has encountered problems with its state assessment (TN Ready), leading *Education Week* to describe the state as "a poster child for the volatile testing atmosphere that's sweeping the country." Because of the breakdown of the testing contractor's online platform in 2016, the state canceled online testing and reverted to a paper-and-pencil format. In July 2019, Tennessee hired Pearson as its third testing contractor, which had previously been the contractor from 2003–14. Lauren Camera, "A Tennessee District Perseveres in Wake of Online-Testing Woes," *Education Week*, February 29, 2016, https://www.edweek.org/ew/articles/2016/02/29/a-tennessee-district-perseveres-in-wake-of.html.

CHAPTER 6

1. Carol S. Weissert and Daniel Sheller, "Learning from the States? Federalism and National Health Policy," *Public Administration Review* 68, no. S1 (Special Issue, "The Quest for High-Performance Federalism," December 2008): S162–S174, doi: 10.1111/j.1540-6210.2008.00986.x. Weissert and Sheller find that state authorities and experts on state policy testified five times more frequently in hearings on SCHIP than the average over other health legislation, and that the extent to which Congress translated state preferences into the enacted legislation was similarly exceptional.

2. We coded the testimony at all the hearings concerning SCHIP, beginning with the initial hearings regarding enactment (1997) and continuing through 2017 (a table in the appendix lists the hearings). Table 6.1 depicts the "Who" of evidence presentation. We counted each individual witness once. Some witnesses testified at more than one hearing, but this would not count as a different and hence additional use of evidence as long as the witness's organizational affiliation had not changed; the same individual speaking for a different organization was counted as

a new witness.

3. *Children's Access to Health Coverage, Hearing Before the Committee on Ways and Means, Subcommittee on Health*, US House of Representatives, 105th Cong., 1st sess. (April 8, 1997) (testimony of Patrick Purcell, analyst, Congressional Research Service), https://www.govinfo.gov/content/pkg/CHRG-105hhrg52730/pdf/CHRG-105hhrg52730.pdf.

4. State policymakers saw the potential conflict between the goals of covering all uninsured low-income children versus minimizing crowd-out. Observers agreed that families at the poverty line could not have afforded to buy coverage in the private market. But most uninsured children were in families whose income was just above the poverty line: too high to qualify for Medicaid, but too low to enable paying premiums for insurance in the private market. Expanding SCHIP to cover children in these families (for instance, setting the eligibility threshold at 200 or 250 percent of the poverty line) was necessary to achieving the goal of the program to extend health care to all low-income children. But obviously the trade-off would get steeper as family income increased. Conservatives in Congress, and lobbyists for organizations representing employers and insurance companies, insisted on minimizing crowd-out; liberals advocating expansion recognized the constraint but resisted the expectation that the private market should set the baseline. In the end, Sec 2101(a) of the Social Security Act, describing SCHIP, says provision of health assistance shall be "in an effective and efficient manner that is coordinated with other sources of health benefits coverage."

5. Virtually all (95 percent) the state-level testimony referred to current policy (compared to 41 percent, the average over federal administrators, group representatives, and academic experts), and over half (53 percent) the testimony from state representatives relied on professional judgment or practitioner experience (compared to 39 percent of federal administrators, group representatives, and academic experts).

6. *Improving the Health Status of Children, Hearing Before the Committee on Labor and Human Resources*, US Senate, 105th Cong., 1st sess. (April 18, 1997) (testimony of Howard Dean, governor of Vermont), https://babel.hathitrust.org/cgi/pt?id=mdp.39015042566599&view=1up&seq=3.

7. Sara Rosenbaum, Anne Markus, and Colleen Sonosky, "Public Health Insurance Design for Children: The Evolution from Medicaid to SCHIP," *Journal of Health and Biomedical Law* 1 (2004): 1–47, https://publichealth.gwu.edu/departments/healthpolicy/CHPR/downloads/Public_Health_Insurance_Design_for_Children.pdf. Rosenbaum, Markus, and Sonosky show that SCHIP was exceptional in mandating state discretion. They compare SCHIP to the two major social policy initiatives of the Clinton years, national health care reform and welfare reform. They point out that the structure and provisions of SCHIP resemble the block grant structure of welfare reform more closely than the comprehensive, top-down structure of

national health care reform; cf. Weissert and Sheller, "Learning from the States."

The balance of federal to state authority in SCHIP was innovative, and accounts for its bipartisan support in Congress and its popularity with state governments. Unlike Medicaid, CHIP is a block grant: total federal payments are capped, and a formula determines each state's annual allotment. On the other hand, CHIP is more generous: the federal government pays 70 percent of the costs of CHIP (in contrast, the federal government funded 57 percent, on average, of the costs of state Medicaid programs before the Affordable Care Act). States can design CHIP as a Medicaid expansion under Medicaid rules, or as a stand-alone program, or as a combination of the two—where each applies to different income levels. For programs separate from Medicaid, there is no legal entitlement to coverage, and states can charge premiums, require cost sharing by beneficiaries, and freeze enrollment in response to funding shortfalls.

8. *Implementation of the State Children's Health Insurance Program, Hearing Before the Committee on Finance*, US Senate, 106th Cong., 1st sess. (April 29, 1999) (remarks of Senator William Roth of Delaware, committee chair), https://www.finance.senate.gov/imo/media/doc/hrg106111.pdf.

9. *Health Coverage for Families Leaving Welfare, Hearing Before the Committee on Ways and Means, Subcommittee on Human Resources*, US House of Representatives, 106th Cong., 2nd sess. (May 16, 2000) (testimony of Marilyn Ellwood, senior researcher, Mathematica Policy Research), https://www.govinfo.gov/content/pkg/CHRG-106hhrg68979/pdf/CHRG-106hhrg68979.pdf. The disparity identified by the report resulted in amending Medicaid rules to align with SCHIP's.

10. *Implementation of the State Children's Health Insurance Program* (testimony of Barbara Edwards, deputy director for the Office of Medicaid, Ohio Department of Human Services).

11. *Health Coverage for Families Leaving Welfare* (testimony of Congressman Fortney Stark of California).

12. In counting the "What" (the types of evidence presented), we gave a positive score to each different type of evidence used in the testimony. Because the number of types of non-research-based evidence exceeded the number of types of research-based evidence, we counted up to two types of RBE evidence, and up to three types of non-RBE evidence. This counting rule factored out extraneous evidence that was mentioned in passing but not used in constructing or defending an argument.

13. *Children's Access to Health Coverage* (testimony of Jonathan Gruber, research fellow, National Bureau of Economic Research); *Increasing Children's Access to Healthcare, Hearing Before the Committee on Finance*, US Senate, 105th Cong., 1st sess. (April 30, 1997) (testimony of Barbara DeBuono, commissioner, New York State Department of Public Health), https://www.finance.senate.gov/imo/media/doc/hrg105-459.pdf.

14. *Health Coverage for Families Leaving Welfare* (testimony of Kathleen Gifford, assistant secretary, Indiana Office of Medicaid Policy and Planning).

15. *Improving the Health Status of Children* (testimony of Dr. Judith S. Palfrey, chief, division of general pediatrics, Children's Hospital, Boston).

16. *Improving the Health Status of Children* (testimony of Dr. Antoinette P. Eaton, American Academy of Pediatrics and the National Association of Children's Hospitals).

17. Medicaid and SCHIP reduced the proportion of uninsured low-income children by one-third from 1997 to 2005, during a period when employer-sponsored coverage declined and state budgets were stressed by the 2001 recession. Genevieve M. Kenney and Justin Yee, "SCHIP at a Crossroads: Experiences to Date and Challenges Ahead," *Health Affairs* 26, no. 2 (2007): 356–69, doi: 10.1377/hlthaff.26.2.356; Genevieve M. Kenney, "The Impacts of the State Children's Health Insurance Program on Children Who Enroll: Findings from Ten States," *Health Services Research* 42, no. 4 (2007): 1520–43, doi: 10.1111/j.1475-6773.2007.00707.x; and Pamela Herd and Donald P. Moynihan, *Administrative Burden: Policymaking by Other Means* (New York: Russell Sage Foundation, 2018), doi: 10.7758/9781610448789.

18. Jonathan B. Oberlander and Barbara Lyons, "Beyond Incrementalism? SCHIP and the Politics of Health Reform," *Health Affairs* 28, supplement 1 (March 2009), doi: 10.1377/hlthaff.28.3.w399.

19. Sarah K. Bruch, Myra Marx Ferree, and Joe Soss, "From Policy to Polity: Democracy, Paternalism, and the Incorporation of Disadvantaged Citizens," *American Sociological Review* 75, no. 2 (April 2010): 205–26, doi: 10.1177/0003122410363563; Suzanne Mettler, "The Policyscape and the Challenges of Contemporary Politics to Policy Maintenance," *Perspectives on Politics* 14, no. 2 (June 2016): 369–90, doi: 10.1017/S1537592716000074; and Suzanne Mettler, *The Submerged State: How Invisible Government Policies Undermine American Democracy* (Chicago: University of Chicago Press, 2011).

20. The coalition of interest groups supporting expansion included Families USA, America's Health Insurance Plans, the American Medical Association, Pharmaceutical Research and Manufacturers of America, and the Federation of American Hospitals. Robert Pear, "A Battle over Expansion of Children's Insurance," *New York Times*, July 9, 2007, https://www.nytimes.com/2007/07/09/washington/09child.html.

21. By dedicating to health care an increase in the cigarette tax, the program could be expanded to cover an estimated four million more children (in addition to the seven million enrolled currently) without worsening the deficit. Judith Feder, "Crowd-Out: The Politics of Health Reform," *Journal of Law, Medicine, and Ethics* 32, no. 3 (September 2004): 461–64, doi: 10.1111/j.1748-720X.2004.tb00158.x.

22. Changes in availability and affordability of health insurance in the private market had reversed the trend of gains attributable to SCHIP; after 2005, the number of uninsured children increased by more than a million. Donna Cohen Ross, Aleya Horn, and Caryn Marks, *Health Coverage for Children and Families in Medicaid and SCHIP: State Efforts Face New Hurdles* (Washington, DC: Kaiser Commission on Medicaid and the Uninsured, January 2008), https://www.kff.org/wp-content/

uploads/2013/01/7740.pdf.

23. The Kaiser Commission on Medicaid and the Uninsured authored several reports that surveyed the quantitative evidence and drew out the implications for program modification. On the gap between current coverage and SCHIP's goal of covering all low-income children, see John Holahan, Allison Cook, and Lisa Dubay, *Characteristics of the Uninsured: Who Is Eligible for Coverage and Who Needs Help Affording Coverage?* (Washington, DC: Kaiser Commission on Medicaid and the Uninsured, February 2007), https://www.kff.org/wp-content/uploads/2013/01/7613.pdf; on the expansion of state programs beyond federal funding levels, see Cindy Mann and Robin Rudowitz, *Financing Health Coverage: The State Children's Health Program Experience* (Washington, DC: Kaiser Commission on Medicaid and the Uninsured, February 2005), https://www.kff.org/wp-content/uploads/2013/01/financing-health-coverage-the-state-children-s-health-insurance-program-experience-issue-paper.pdf; on procyclical pattern of state revenues, see Donna Cohen Ross and Laura Cox, *Beneath the Surface: Barriers Threaten to Slow Progress on Expanding Health Coverage of Children and Families* (Washington, DC: Kaiser Commission on Medicaid and the Uninsured, October 2004), https://www.kff.org/wp-content/uploads/2013/01/beneath-the-surface-barriers-threaten-to-slow-progress-on-expanding-health-coverage-of-children-and-families-pdf.pdf; and Donna Cohen Ross and Laura Cox, *Out in the Cold: Enrollment Freezes in Six State Children's Health Insurance Programs Withhold Coverage from Eligible Children* (Washington, DC: Kaiser Commission on Medicaid and the Uninsured, December 2003), https://www.kff.org/wp-content/uploads/2013/01/out-in-the-cold-enrollment-freezes-in-six-state-children-s-health-insurance-programs-withhold-coverage-from-eligible-children.pdf.

    The Kaiser Family Foundation's Employer Health Benefits Annual Survey tracks employer health benefits and the costs of private health insurance. https://www.kff.org/health-costs/report/employer-health-benefits-annual-survey-archives.

24. Vernon Smith and Jason Cooke, *SCHIP Turns 10: An Update on Enrollment and the Outlook on Reauthorization from the Program's Directors* (Washington, DC: Kaiser Commission on Medicaid and the Uninsured, May 2007).

25. Margo Rosenbach et al., *Implementation of the State Children's Health Insurance Program: Synthesis of State Evaluations* (Cambridge, MA: Mathematica Policy Research, March 2003), https://www.cms.gov/Research-Statistics-Data-and-Systems/Statistics-Trends-and-Reports/Reports/downloads/rosenbach_2003_5.pdf; Craig Volden, "States as Policy Laboratories: Emulating Success in the Children's Health Insurance Program," *American Journal of Political Science* 50, no. 2 (April 2006): 294–312, doi: https://doi.org/10.1111/j.1540-5907.2006.00185.x; Rosenbach et al., *Implementation*; and Oberlander and Lyons, "Beyond Incrementalism."

26. *CHIP at 10: A Decade of Covering Children, Hearing Before the Committee on Finance, Subcommittee on Health Care*, US Senate, 109th Cong., 2nd sess. (July 25, 2006)

(testimony of Mark McLellan, administrator, Centers for Medicare and Medicaid), https://www.finance.senate.gov/imo/media/doc/31961.pdf; *CHIP Program from the States' Perspective, Hearing Before the Committee on Finance, Subcommittee on Health Care*, US Senate, 109th Cong., 2nd sess. (November 16, 2006) (testimony of Ann Clemency Kohler, director, New Jersey Division of Medical Assistance and Health Services), https://www.finance.senate.gov/imo/media/doc/32112.pdf.

27. *Children's Health Insurance Program in Action: A State's Perspective on CHIP, Field Hearing Before the Committee on Finance*, US Senate, 110th Cong., 1st sess. (Billings, MT, April 4, 2007) (testimony of Melissa Anderson, self-employed business owner), https://www.finance.senate.gov/imo/media/doc/430211.pdf; *Covering the Uninsured Through the Eyes of a Child, Hearing Before the Committee on Energy and Commerce, Subcommittee on Health*, US House of Representatives, 110th Cong., 1st sess. (February 14, 2007) (testimony of Kathy Mingledorff, volunteer, March of Dimes), https://www.govinfo.gov/content/pkg/CHRG-110hhrg35598/pdf/CHRG-110hhrg35598.pdf.

28. *The Future of CHIP: Improving the Health of America's Children, Hearing Before the Committee on Finance*, US Senate, 110th Cong., 1st sess. (February 1, 2007) (testimony of Sonny Perdue, governor of Georgia), https://www.finance.senate.gov/imo/media/doc/41339.pdf.

29. *Covering Uninsured Kids: Reversing Progress Already Made, Hearing Before the Committee on Energy and Commerce, Subcommittee on Health*, US House of Representatives, 110th Cong., 2nd sess. (February 26, 2008) (testimony of Chris Gregoire, governor of Washington), https://www.govinfo.gov/content/pkg/CHRG-110hhrg49370/pdf/CHRG-110hhrg49370.pdf.

30. Quoted in David Stout, "Bush Vetoes Children's Health Bill," *New York Times*, October 3, 2007, https://www.nytimes.com/2007/10/03/washington/03cnd-veto.html.

31. All states were covering children in families earning 200 percent of the federal poverty level, and most states covered children from families earning up to 250 percent of FPL. The Centers for Medicare and Medicaid Services had approved every proposal by states to raise the threshold to 250 percent of FPL. The increase to 300 percent of FPL responded to both experience and research showing that expanding coverage to moderate-income children had the effect of promoting enrollment among already eligible children. Julie L. Hudson, Thomas M. Selden, and Jessica S. Banthin, "The Impact of SCHIP on Insurance Coverage of Children," *Inquiry* 42, no. 3 (August 2005): 232–54, doi: 10.5034/inquiryjrnl_42.3.232; *Covering Uninsured Children: The Impact of the August 17th CHIP Directive, Hearing Before the Committee on Finance, Subcommittee on Health Care*, US Senate, 110th Cong., 2nd sess. (April 9, 2008) (testimony of Alan Weil, executive director, National Academy for State Health Policy), https://www.finance.senate.gov/imo/media/doc/55851.pdf; and Cohen Ross, Horn, and Marks, *Health Coverage for Children and Families*.

32. Dennis G. Smith, "Directive to State Health Officials," Department of Health and Human Services, Centers for Medicare and Medicaid Services, Center for Medicaid and State Operations (August 17, 2007), https://downloads.cms.gov/cmsgov/archived-downloads/SMDL/downloads/SHO081707.pdf.

33. The Urban Institute had calculated that for every 1 percent increase in the unemployment rate, 700,000 children and 1.7 million adults lose their employer-based coverage. Stan Dorn et al., *Medicaid, SCHIP and Economic Downturn: Policy Challenges and Policy Responses* (Washington, DC: Kaiser Commission on Medicaid and the Uninsured, April 2008), https://www.kff.org/wp-content/uploads/2013/01/7770.pdf.

34. In his State of the Union speech, President Bush had linked SCHIP reauthorization to his goal of reining in spending, and during the early months of the year, the White House had tried to mobilize congressional support for expanding the program through tax breaks. The CMS directive specified administrative barriers to minimize crowd-out, including waiting periods, cost sharing (via premiums and co-pays) that would raise the SCHIP cost to approximate private coverage, and monitoring the family's health insurance status at the time of application. The directive also stated approval would be denied if the number of children insured through private employers decreased by more than two percentage points over the previous five years.

35. *Covering Uninsured Kids: Reversing Progress Already Made.*

36. *H.R. 5998, The Protecting Children's Health Coverage Act of 2008, Hearing Before the Committee on Energy and Commerce, Subcommittee on Health*, US House of Representatives, 110th Cong., 2nd sess. (May 15, 2008), testimony of Peter Orszag, Congressional Budget Office, https://www.govinfo.gov/content/pkg/CHRG-110hhrg54777/pdf/CHRG-110hhrg54777.pdf.

37. *Covering Uninsured Children: The Impact of the August 17th CHIP Directive* (testimony of Nina Owcharenko, senior policy analyst, Heritage Foundation).

38. *Covering Uninsured Children: The Impact of the August 17th CHIP Directive* (testimony of Alan Weil).

39. *Covering Uninsured Kids: Missed Opportunities for Moving Forward, Hearing Before the Committee on Energy and Commerce, Subcommittee on Health*, US House of Representatives, 110th Cong., 2nd sess. (January 29, 2008) (testimony of Chris Peterson, health care financing specialist, Congressional Research Service), https://www.govinfo.gov/content/pkg/CHRG-110hhrg48375/pdf/CHRG-110hhrg48375.pdf.

40. David Stout, "Bush Vetoes Children's Health Bill"; Michael Abramowitz and Jonathan Weisman, "Bush Vetoes Health Measure," *Washington Post*, October 4, 2007, http://www.washingtonpost.com/wp-dyn/content/article/2007/10/03/AR2007100300116.html.

41. Oberlander and Lyons, "Beyond Incrementalism," 11.

42. Bush summed up his objection in a speech to a business group in Lancaster, Pennsylvania, accusing the bill's backers of trying to "federalize health care." After the veto, the President signaled that he would sign a stopgap measure, and Congress

passed an extension for one year that maintained the funding level; the legislation also changed the name of the program to CHIP from SCHIP.

43. Robert D. Benford and David A. Snow, "Framing Processes and Social Movements: An Overview and Assessment," *Annual Review of Sociology* 26 (August 2000): 611–39, doi: 10.1146/annurev.soc.26.1.611; Thomas E. Mann and Norman J. Ornstein, *It's Even Worse Than It Was: How the American Constitutional System Collided with the New Politics of Extremism* (New York: Basic Books, 2016). Mann and Ornstein map the history of the increasing polarization over social welfare policy.

44. Pear, "A Battle over Expansion"; John K. Iglehart, "The Fate of SCHIP—Surrogate Marker for Health Care Ideology?" *New England Journal of Medicine* 357, no. 21 (November 22, 2007): 2104–7, doi: 10.1056/NEJMp0706881; and Genevieve M. Kenney, *The Failure of SCHIP Reauthorization: What Next?*" (Washington, DC: Urban Institute, March 2008), https://www.urban.org/sites/default/files/publication/31541/411628-The-Failure-of-SCHIP-Reauthorization-What-Next-.PDF.

45. William T. Gormley Jr., *Voices for Children: Rhetoric and Public Policy* (Washington, DC: Brookings Institution, 2012). Chapters 2 and 3, especially, summarize this transformation from the perspective of policies directed at children. As Gormley explains, the shift to justifying social programs on the basis of material gains to recipients, and aggregating those individual gains to judge the program's payoff to society, entailed moving from moral philosophy to economics as the source of concepts and theories. It was facilitated by the rise of economic analysis in the paradigm of policy studies, but gained momentum from the rightward ideological shift of Republicans in Congress and in the White House.

46. In the first hearing, Professor Jonathan Gruber of MIT discussed his own research on the correlation of health insurance to outcomes. *Children's Access to Health Coverage*, (testimony of Jonathan Gruber); Kathleen N. Lohr et al., "Use of Medical Care in the RAND Health Insurance Experiment," *Medical Care* 24, no. 9, supplement (September 1986): S72–S78, https://www.rand.org/pubs/reports/R3469.html.

47. Jonathan B. Oberlander, "The Partisan Divide—the McCain and Obama Plans for U.S. Health Care Reform," *New England Journal of Medicine* 359 (August 21, 2008): 781–84, doi: 10.1056/NEJMp0804659.

48. In peer-reviewed articles, researchers investigated in detail the state programs in Florida, New York, and Pennsylvania (see Peter G. Szilagyi, Mark A. Schuster, Tina L. Cheng, "The Scientific Evidence for Child Health Insurance," *Academic Pediatrics* 9, no. 1 (January 2009), doi: 10.1016/j.acap.2008.12.002), measuring the correlations among access, use, and outcomes. RAND researchers carried out a multiyear investigation of the impacts of SCHIP in California. Michael Seid et al., "The Impact of Realized Access to Care on Health-Related Quality of Life: A Two-Year Prospective Cohort Study of Children in the California State Children's Health Insurance Program," *Journal of Pediatrics* 149, no. 3 (October 2006): 354–61, doi: 10.1016/j.jpeds.2006.04.024.

49. Reviews of the literature include the Institute of Medicine, Committee on Consequences of Uninsurance, *Health Insurance Is a Family Matter* (Washington, DC: National Academies Press, 2002), doi: 10.17226/10503; Szilagyi et al., "Scientific Evidence," 4–6; and Aimee E. Jeffrey and Paul W. Newacheck, "Role of Insurance for Children with Special Health Care Needs: A Synthesis of the Evidence," *Pediatrics* 118, no. 4 (October 2006): 1027–38, doi: 10.1542/peds.2005-2527.

   A methodologically demanding meta-analysis of hundreds of studies of the health effects of program expansions since 1997 was published shortly after reauthorization. Embry M. Howell and Genevieve M. Kenney, "The Impact of the Medicaid/ CHIP Expansions on Children: A Synthesis of the Evidence," *Medical Care Research and Review* 69, no 4 (August 2012): 372–96, doi: 10.1177/1077558712437245.

50. James J. Heckman, "Microdata, Heterogeneity and the Evaluation of Public Policy," (Nobel Prize Lecture, Stockholm, Sweden, December 8, 2000), https://www .nobelprize.org/prizes/economic-sciences/2000/heckman/lecture; James J. Heckman, "Building Bridges Between Structural and Program Evaluation Approaches to Evaluating Policy" (NBER Working Paper No. 16110, National Bureau of Economic Research, Cambridge, MA, June 2010), https://www.nber.org/papers/ w16110.

51. Pedro Carneiro and James Heckman, "Human Capital Policy" (NBER Working Paper No. 9495, National Bureau of Economic Research, Cambridge, MA, February 2003), 5, 7, https://www.nber.org/papers/w9495.

52. See, for instance, the following hearings: *The Future of CHIP* (February 1, 2007); *Covering the Uninsured Through the Eyes of a Child* (February 14, 2007 and March 1, 2007); *Protecting Children's Health Coverage Act of 2008* (May 15, 2008).

53. *Covering Uninsured Kids: Reversing Progress Already Made* (testimony of Deval Patrick, governor of Massachusetts). Although not available to Congress when the renewal of CHIP was considered, the authoritative meta-analysis of the hundreds of relevant studies, by Howell and Kenney (see note 49), sets out a logical map of the implementation and effect of CHIP (they distinguish among eligibility, enrollment, use, and health status), and provides estimates of the impact of expanding health insurance availability for children. Cf. Laura R. Wherry, Genevieve M. Kenney, and Benjamin D. Sommers, "The Role of Public Health Insurance in Reducing Child Poverty," *Academic Pediatrics* 16, no. 3 supplement (April 2016): S98–S104, doi: 10.1016/j.acap.2015.12.011.

54. For instance, Dr. Jeanne Lambrew (Georgetown Public Health) frames her testimony around the value of public investments in children. James J. Heckman, Alan B. Krueger, and Benjamin M. Friedman, *Inequality in America: What Role for Human Capital Policies?* (Cambridge, MA: MIT Press, 2004). Heckman, Krueger, and Friedman's analysis observes evidence of lasting individual impacts (e.g., maintaining good health in childhood was correlated with going farther in school, reduced crime, and higher earnings), that are then aggregated to determine the impact on

the economy and the public (e.g., increased youth access to preventive care saved on taxpayer-supported health care expenditures for the indigent and reduced the use of emergency room treatment for chronic conditions).

A RAND research review mentioned in testimony by Massachusetts governor Deval Patrick emphasized the investment character of social policies directed to children. Lynn A. Karoly, M. Rebecca Kilburn, and Jill S. Cannon, *Children at Risk: Consequences for School Readiness and Beyond* (Santa Monica, CA: RAND Corporation, 2005), https://www.rand.org/pubs/research_briefs/RB9144.html.

55. This counts not only individuals but witnesses from grassroots groups representing low-income citizens.

56. *The Future of CHIP: Improving the Health of America's Children* (testimony of Kim Lee Bedford, Craig Bedford, and Job Bedford).

57. *Covering the Uninsured Through the Eyes of a Child* (March 1, 2007) (testimony of Dr. Lolita McDavid, National Association of Children's Hospitals).

58. On November 7, 2009, the House passed H.R. 3962, the Affordable Health Care for America Act, expanding Medicaid. Carl Hulse and Robert Pear, "Sweeping Health Care Plan Passes House," *The New York Times*, November 7, 2009, https://www.nytimes.com/2009/11/08/health/policy/08health.html.

This intraparty debate was finessed in the final version of ACA, which extended CHIP to 2015, increased federal matching payments to the states, and required the states to maintain current eligibility thresholds for children through 2019.

59. Inconsistencies included ACA's creation of multiple sources of coverage targeted to people depending on their ages and incomes, which made for difficulties in maintaining continuity of coverage; and the "family glitch," which wrote into law a mistakenly narrow definition of affordable employer-sponsored insurance, leaving many families without affordable coverage for children. Julie L. Hudson and Salam Abdus, "Coverage and Care Consequences for Families in Which Children Have Mixed Eligibility for Public Insurance," *Health Affairs* 34, no. 8 (August 2015): 1340–48, doi: 10.1377/hlthaff.2015.0128, citing reports to Congress by the Medicaid and CHIP Payment and Access Commission (MACPAC) in 2014 and 2015.

60. Sara Rosenbaum and Genevieve M. Kenney, "The Search for a National Child Health Coverage Policy," *Health Affairs* 33, no. 12 (December 2014): 2125–35, doi: 10.1377/hlthaff.2014.0906. ACA extended CHIP funding to September 2015; the authorization for CHIP (and new rules for state programs) was extended to 2019.

61. After Republicans won congressional majorities in 2010, they clashed with the White House over the budget, immigration, debt ceiling, and especially ACA; by 2015, House Republicans had voted some fifty times to repeal ACA; the 112th and 113th Congresses (2011–12 and 2013–14) were the least productive in the modern period; CHIP's champions, Senators Ted Kennedy (D-MA) and Jay Rockefeller (D-WV) and Representative Henry Waxman (D-CA), were gone, and the increasing ideological extremism of the Republican Party suggested that CHIP's

unusual degree of federalism and its block grant structure might not be conserva-tive enough to attract GOP support. On the history of polarization in US politics, see Mann and Ornstein, *It's Even Worse Than It Was*; Byron E. Shafer, *The Amer-ican Political Pattern: Stability and Change, 1932–2016* (Lawrence: University Press of Kansas, 2016); David Mayhew, "Legislative Obstruction," *Perspectives on Poli-tics* 8, no. 4 (December 2010): 1145–54, doi: 10.1017/S1537592710002203; Sean M. Theriault, *The Gingrich Senators: The Roots of Partisan Warfare in Congress* (New York: Oxford University Press, 2013); Theda Skocpol and Alexander Hertel-Fer-nandez, "The Koch Network and Republican Party Extremism," *Perspectives on Politics* 14, no. 3 (September 2016): 681–99, doi: 10.1017/S1537592716001122; and Martin Gilens and Benjamin I. Page, "Testing Theories of American Politics: Elites, Interest Groups, and Average Citizens," *Perspectives on Politics* 12, no. 3 (September 2014): 564–81, doi: 10.1017/S1537592714001595.

62. Rockefeller was not standing for election in November 2014.

63. Two reports evaluated CHIP and concluded that it was a "success in nearly every area examined." Mary Harrington and Genevieve M. Kenney et al., *CHIPRA Man-dated Evaluation of the Children's Health Insurance Program: Final Findings* (Ann Arbor MI: Mathematica Policy Research and Urban Institute, August 1, 2014), https://aspe .hhs.gov/report/chipra-mandated-evaluation-childrens-health-insurance-program-final-findings; *June 2014 Report to the Congress on Medicaid and CHIP* (Washing-ton, DC: Medicaid and CHIP Payment and Access Commission (MACPAC), June 2014), https://www.macpac.gov/wp-content/uploads/2015/01/2014-06-13_MAC PAC_Report.pdf.

64. *The Children's Health Insurance Program: Protecting America's Children and Families, Hearing Before the Committee on Finance, Subcommittee on Health Care*, US Senate, 113th Cong., 2nd sess. (September 16, 2014), https://www.govinfo.gov/content/ pkg/CHRG-113shrg94479/pdf/CHRG-113shrg94479.pdf.

65. Republicans Upton and Hatch and Democrats Wyden and Waxman jointly requested that governors weigh in on CHIP. Forty-two states responded and thirty-seven governors (including nineteen Republicans) explicitly backed renewal of funding. Sophia Duong, *Summary: Governors' Letters to Congress on the Future of CHIP* (Washington, DC: Georgetown University Health Policy Institute, Center for Children and Families, December 2014), https://ccf.georgetown.edu/wp-content/ uploads/2015/02/Gov-letters-summary-125-updated-211.pdf; Jonathan Weisman "Brighter Economy Raises Odds of Action in Congress," *New York Times*, December 5, 2014, https://www.nytimes.com/2014/12/06/business/economy/brighter-economy-raises-odds-of-action-in-congress.html.

66. Jonathan Oberlander et al., "In the Affordable Care Act's Shadow: The Fate of the Children's Health Insurance Program," *Health Affairs* 35, no. 10 (October 2016): 1835–41, doi: 10.1377/hlthaff.2016.0226. The changes included abandon-ing the ACA's maintenance of effort provision, allowing states to increase the

administrative barriers to enrolling for CHIP, cutting the federal matching rate for children between 250 and 300 percent FPL, and eliminating the funding for children whose families earned more than 300 percent FPL. See Orrin Hatch, Fred Upton, and Joe Pitts, *Discussion Draft: Extending Funding for the State Children's Health Insurance Program*, US House of Representatives, Committee on Energy and Commerce, 114th Cong., 1st sess. (February 24, 2015), https://www.finance.senate.gov/imo/media/doc/SCHIP%20Discussion.pdf; Hillary Rodham Clinton and Bill Frist, "Save the Children's Insurance," *New York Times*, February 12, 2015, https://www.nytimes.com/2015/02/13/opinion/hillary-clinton-and-bill-frist-on-health-care-for-americas-kids.html.

67. The SGR originated in 1997's Balanced Budget Act. See Mary Agnes Carey, "FAQ on Medicare Doctor Pay: Why Is It So Hard to Fix?" Kaiser Health News, February 27, 2013, https://khn.org/news/faq-doc-fix.

68. The trade for SGR reform explains the immediate vote, but CHIP retained many political advantages: it is directed toward a sympathetic population; it is relatively cheap compared to other social programs; states (including Republican governors) are supportive; and it began well before ACA, so that supporters could make the case separate from the partisan divide over Obamacare. Robert Pear, "Senate Approves a Bill on Changes to Medicare," *New York Times*, April 14, 2015, https://www.nytimes.com/2015/04/15/us/politics/senate-approves-a-bill-on-changes-to-medicare.html.

69. *Examining the Extension of Safety Net Health Programs, Hearing Before the Committee on Energy and Commerce, Subcommittee on Health*, US House of Representatives, 115th Cong., 1st sess. (June 23, 2017) (opening statement by Representative Michael Burgess of Texas), https://www.govinfo.gov/content/pkg/CHRG-115hhrg28525/pdf/CHRG-115hhrg28525.pdf.

70. *Examining the Extension of Safety Net Health Programs* (testimony of Michael Holmes, CEO, Cook Area Health Services; Jami Snyder, associate commissioner, Texas Health and Human Services Commission; and Cindy Mann, partner, Manatt Health).

71. *The Children's Health Insurance Program: The Path Forward, Hearing Before the Committee on Finance*, US Senate, 115th Cong., 1st sess. (September 7, 2017) (opening statements by Senator Orrin Hatch of Utah and Senator Ron Wyden of Oregon), https://www.govinfo.gov/content/pkg/CHRG-115shrg31255/pdf/CHRG-115shrg31255.pdf.

72. *The Children's Health Insurance Program: The Path Forward* (testimony of Leanna George, mother of a CHIP recipient; Linda Nablo, chief deputy director, Virginia Department of Medical Assistance Services; and Anne Schwartz, executive director, MACPAC).

73. Robert Pear, "Deal Struck to Extend Financing for Children's Health Program," *New York Times*, September 12, 2017, https://www.nytimes.com/2017/09/12/us/politics/childrens-health-insurance-program-chip-deal-hatch-wyden.html.

74. David Leonhardt, "Taking Health Care from Kids," *New York Times*, December 21, 2017, https://www.nytimes.com/2017/12/21/opinion/tax-bill-chip.html; Abby Goodnough and Robert Pear, "The CHIP Program Is Beloved: Why Is Its Funding in Danger?," *New York Times*, December 5, 2017, https://www.nytimes.com/2017/12/05/health/childrens-health-insurance-program.html; and Tricia Brooks, "CHIP Funding Has Been Extended, What's Next for Children's Health Coverage?," *Health Affairs Blog*, January 30, 2018, https://www.healthaffairs.org/do/10.1377/hblog20180130.116879/full. The gridlock between the White House and Congress meant that CHIP funding lapsed for more than three months. Most states covered the shortfall with carryover funds from FY2017, but on December 22, 2017, Congress passed a continuing resolution that appropriated the money needed to carry the states until the longer-term extension was approved. The six-year extension (in Hatch-Wyden) is explained by the fact that the tax package eliminated the ACA's individual mandate and modified the marketplace for insurance. Because these changes made it more expensive to insure children in the marketplace rather than CHIP, the CBO calculated that extending CHIP would save money; the breakeven point would come after six years.

75. E. Scott Adler and John D. Wilkerson, *Congress and the Politics of Problem Solving* (New York: Cambridge University Press, 2012).

76. The political science literature on social welfare programs makes clear that this trait is a dramatic departure from the norm. Cf. Bruch, Ferree, and Soss, "From Policy to Polity"; and Suzanne Mettler and Joe Soss, "The Consequences of Public Policy for Democratic Citizenship: Bridging Policy Studies and Mass Politics," *Perspectives on Politics* 2, no. 1 (March 2004): 55–73, doi: 10.1017/S1537592704000623.

77. Although the elevation of the states' authority vis-à-vis the federal government in CHIP doubtless appealed—as an abstraction—to politicians of both parties, this property rankled with national policymakers when some states used their discretion to deviate from the party's preferences. For instance, liberal members of Congress pushed to have CHIP eligibility thresholds relaxed; conservative members pushed against this, and additionally insisted that state programs give precedence to the private insurance market. President George W. Bush's 2007 vetoes of CHIP reauthorization were motivated, in part, by the attempt to punish states that had expanded eligibility; President Obama succeeded in implementing national standards in the ACA's maintenance of effort mandate.

78. David K. Cohen and Susan L. Moffitt, *The Ordeal of Equality: Did Federal Regulation Fix the Schools?* (Cambridge, MA: Harvard University Press, 2009).

79. Eric Patashnik, *Reforms at Risk: What Happens After Major Policy Changes Are Enacted* (Princeton, NJ: Princeton University Press, 2008).

80. Mann and Ornstein, *It's Even Worse Than It Was*; Jennifer L. Hochschild and Katherine Levine Einstein, *Do Facts Matter? Information and Misinformation in American Politics* (Norman: University of Oklahoma Press, 2015); Gordon Gauchat,

"Politicization of Science in the Public Sphere: A Study of Public Trust in the United States, 1974 to 2010," *American Sociological Review* 77, no. 2 (April 2012): 167–87, doi: 10.1177/0003122412438225; Alexander Hertel-Fernandez, "Who Passes Business's 'Model Bills'? Policy Capacity and Corporate Influence in U.S. State Politics," *Perspectives on Politics* 12, no. 3 (September 2014): 582–602, doi: 10.1017/S1537592714001601; and Julian E. Zelizer, "Seizing Power: Conservatives and Congress Since the 1970s," in *The Transformation of American Politics: Activist Government and the Rise of Conservatism*, ed. Paul Pierson and Theda Skocpol (Princeton, NJ: Princeton University Press, 2007).

CHAPTER 7

1. Teresa Watanabe, "California Groups Demand UC Drop the SAT, Alleging it Illegally Discriminates Against Disadvantaged Students," *Los Angeles Times*, October 29, 2019, https://www.latimes.com/california/story/2019-10-29/california-groups-demand-uc-drop-the-sat-saying-they-illegally-discriminate-against-disadvantaged-students.

Six weeks after sending the letter, two lawsuits were filed on behalf of the Compton Unified School District, four students, and six community organizations. Consistent with the letter, the lawsuit argued that UC is violating California civil rights law by requiring applicants to take either the SAT or the ACT. Teresa Watanabe, "UC Violates Civil Rights of Disadvantaged Students by Requiring SAT for Admission, Lawsuit Says," *Los Angeles Times*, December 11, 2019, https://www.latimes.com/california/story/2019-12-10/uc-violates-civil-rights-of-disadvantaged-students-by-requiring-sat-for-admission-lawsuit-alleges.

2. Teresa Watanabe, "Will UC Schools Drop Their SAT Scores Requirement?" *Los Angeles Times*, October 2, 2019, https://www.latimes.com/california/story/2019-10-02/uc-sat-test-optional.

3. Watanabe, "Will UC Schools?"

4. Michal Kurlaender and Kramer Cohen, *Predicting College Success: How Do Different High School Assessments Measure Up?* (Stanford, CA: Policy Analysis for California Education, March 2019), https://edpolicyinca.org/sites/default/files/R_Kurlaender_Mar-2019.pdf. Although Kurlaender's research suggests a feasible alternative to the SAT and ACT, more research would be necessary to ascertain how altering Smarter Balanced from what is now a low-stakes test for students to a high-stakes admission test would affect student performance and the validity of the test.

5. These innovations fall into three successive approaches, the first focusing on translation and transmission: Baruch Fischhoff and Alex L. Davis, "Communicating Scientific Uncertainty," *Proceedings of the National Academy of Sciences* 111, supplement 4 (September 2014): 13664–71, doi: 10.1073/pnas.1317504111; Meredith I. Honig and Cynthia E. Coburn, "EvidenceBased Decision Making in School

District Central Offices: Toward a Policy and Research Agenda," *Educational Policy* 22, no. 4 (July 2008): 578–608, doi: 10.1177/0895904807307067; and Diane Massell and Margaret E. Goertz, "State Education Department Acquisition and Use of Research in School Improvement" (paper presented at the Annual Meeting of the American Educational Research Association, Vancouver, BC, Canada, April 16, 2012).

The second approach considers the role of intermediaries: Karen Bogenschneider and Thomas J. Corbett, *Evidence-Based Policy Making: Insights from Policy-Minded Researchers and Research-Minded Policymakers* (New York: Routledge, 2010); Christopher Lubienski, Janelle Scott, and Elizabeth DeBray, "The Rise of Intermediary Organizations in Knowledge Production, Advocacy, and Educational Policy," *Teachers College Record* (July 22, 2011), https://www.academia.edu/5087738/The_Rise_of_Intermediary_Organizations_in_Knowledge_Production_Advocacy_and_Education_Policy; and Robert B. Schwartz and Susan M. Kardos, "Research-Based Evidence and State Policy," in *The Role of Research in Educational Improvement*, ed. John D. Bransford et al. (Cambridge, MA: Harvard Education Press, 2009), 47–66.

The last approach highlights the purposeful construction of networks of researchers and policymakers: Anthony S. Bryk, "Accelerating How We Learn to Improve," *Educational Researcher* 44, no. 9 (December 2015): 467–77, doi: 10.3102/0013189X15621543; Cynthia E. Coburn and William R. Penuel, "Research–Practice Partnerships in Education: Outcomes, Dynamics, and Open Questions," *Educational Researcher* 45, no. 1 (January 2016): 48–54, doi: 10.3102/0013189X16631750; and "About Research-Practice Partnerships," William T. Grant Foundation (website), https://rpp.wtgrantfoundation.org/about.

For reviews of the literature, see *To Secure Knowledge: Social Science Partnerships for the Common Good* (Brooklyn, NY: Social Science Research Council, 2018), https://www.ssrc.org/to-secure-knowledge; and M. Stephen Weatherford, "The Research–Policy Connection: Communicating Versus Using" (unpublished manuscript, Department of Political Science, University of California, Santa Barbara, 2017).

6. Terry M. Moe, "Political Institutions: The Neglected Side of the Story," *Journal of Law, Economics, and Organization* 6 (April 1990): 213–53, https://www.jstor.org/stable/764990.

7. Through a variety of strategies, the Trump administration significantly lessened the role of science in federal policymaking by reducing agency budgets, canceling research projects, transferring technical staff, and enacting regulations at odds with research results. Agencies dealing with the environment and public health have been especially vulnerable as the administration responded to mining and oil and gas interests. Although it has severely diminished some agencies, the administration cannot entirely abolish organizational structures established by Congress. Brad Plumer and Coral Davenport, "Science Under Attack: How Trump Is

Sidelining Researchers and Their Work," *New York Times*, December 28, 2019, https://www.nytimes.com/2019/12/28/climate/trump-administration-war-on-science.html.

8. National Research Council, Committee on the Use of Social Science Knowledge in Public Policy, *Using Science as Evidence in Public Policy*, ed. Kenneth Prewitt, Thomas A. Schwandt, and Miron L. Straf (Washington, DC: National Academies Press, 2012), doi: 10.17226/13460.

APPENDIX

1. We gathered data about the groups involved in the Common Core process from several sources, including the group's website and publications and coverage in specialized education media and national media.

2. Dataverse is described at https:/dataverse.org/about. The URL for the interview guides is https://dataverse.harvard.edu/dataset.xhtml?persistentId=doi:10.7910/DVN/M4LM4Z.

3. Coding was done by graduate student research assistants, under supervision of the PIs. The coding instructions and their application were established by training over several iterations, beginning with a detailed discussion of the project, the focus on evidence and purposive evidence use, and the coding scheme. The RA coded several documents and then discussed ambiguities and problem cases with the PIs or an experienced coder. The inter-coder reliability typically started out at above 0.8, rising to over 0.9 after discussion and experience. We used Dedoose, a software application developed for multimethod investigation of documentary data, to compute inter-coder reliability and to analyze the documents.

4. For examples, see Jonathan Supovitz, Alan Daly, and Miguel del Fresno, *#commoncore Project: How Social Media Is Changing the Politics of Education* (Philadelphia: Consortium for Policy Research in Education, February 23, 2015), http://repository.upenn.edu/hashtagcommoncore/1; and Christina Wolbrecht and Michael T. Hartney, "'Ideas about Interests': Explaining the Changing Partisan Politics of Education," *Perspectives on Politics* 12, no. 3 (September 2014): 603–30.

References

Abramowitz, Michael, and Jonathan Weisman. "Bush Vetoes Health Measure." *Washington Post*, October 4, 2007. http://www.washingtonpost.com/wp-dyn/content/article/2007/10/03/AR2007100300116.html.

Abt Associates. *Massachusetts English Language Arts/Literacy and Mathematics Curriculum Frameworks Review: Final Report*. Boston, MA: Massachusetts Executive Office of Education, October 13, 2016. http://www.doe.mass.edu/bese/docs/fy2017/2016-10/spec-item1-ABTReport.pdf.

Achieve. *Comparing the Common Core State Standards in Mathematics and NCTM's Curriculum Focal Points*. Washington, DC: Achieve, 2010. https://www.achieve.org/files/CCSSandFocalPoints.pdf.

Achieve. *Growing Awareness, Growing Support: Teacher and Voter Understanding of the Common Core State Standards and Assessments*. Washington, DC: Achieve, 2012. https://www.achieve.org/publications/growing-awareness-growing-support-poll.

Achieve. *Out of Many, One: Toward Rigorous Common Core Standards from the Ground Up*. Washington, DC: Achieve, 2008. https://www.achieve.org/files/OutofManyOne.pdf.

Achieve. *Ready or Not: Creating a High School Diploma That Counts*. Washington, DC: Achieve, 2004. https://www.achieve.org/files/ReadyorNot.pdf.

Achieve. *Strong Standards: A Review of Changes to State Standards Since the Common Core*. Washington, DC: Achieve, 2017. https://www.achieve.org/strong-standards.

Achieve and the Education Trust. *Making College and Career Readiness the Mission for High Schools*. Washington, DC: Acheive and the Education Trust, 2008. https://www.achieve.org/files/MakingCollegeandCareerReadinesstheMissionfor HighSchool.pdf.

ACT. *Affirming the Goal: Is College and Career Readiness an Internationally Competitive Standard?* Iowa City, IA: ACT, 2011. https://eric.ed.gov/?id=ED520009.

ACT. *Reading Between the Lines: What the ACT Reveals About College Readiness in Reading*. Iowa City, IA: ACT, January 1, 2006. https://eric.ed.gov/?id=ED490828.

ACT. *2009 National Curriculum Survey Report*. Iowa City, IA: ACT, January 20, 2010. http://www.act.org/content/dam/act/unsecured/documents/NationalCurriculum Survey2009.pdf.

Adler, E. Scott, and John D. Wilkerson. *Congress and the Politics of Problem Solving*. New York: Cambridge University Press, 2012.

Aldrich, Marta W. "Common Core Is Out. Tennessee Academic Standards Are In. Here's How Teachers Are Prepping for the Change." Chalkbeat, June 26, 2017. https://www.chalkbeat.org/posts/tn/2017/06/26/common-core-is-out-tennessee-academic-standards-are-in-heres-how-teachers-are-prepping-for-the-change.

All4Ed. *Common Standards: The Time Is Now*. Washington, DC: All4Ed, 2009. https://all4ed.org/reports-factsheets/common-standards-the-time-is-now.

American Federation of Teachers. "Core Standards." AFT website, April 15, 2010. https://www.aft.org/news/core-standards.

American Federation of Teachers. "ELL Forum Stresses Alignment of State Standards." AFT website, October 21, 2010. https://www.aft.org/news/ell-forum-stresses-alignment-state-standards.

American Federation of Teachers. *The Instructional Demands of Standards-Based Reform*. Washington, DC: AFT, June 24, 2009. https://www.aft.org/sites/default/files/instructionaldemands0609.pdf.

American Institutes for Research. *Informing Grades 1–6 Mathematics Standards Development: What Can Be Learned from High-Performing Hong Kong, Korea, and Singapore*. Washington, DC: AIR, December 2009. https://www.air.org/sites/default/files/downloads/report/MathStandards_0.pdf.

Amos, Jason. "Nationalize the Schools (. . . A Little)!: Report Calls for National Standards, Increased Federal Role in Education." *Straight A's: Public Education Policy and Progress* 8, no. 6 (March 24, 2008). https://all4ed.org/articles/nationalize-the-schools-a-little-report-calls-for-national-standards-increased-federal-role-in-education.

Baldassare, Mark, Dean Bonner, Alyssa Dykman, and Rachel Ward. *Californians and Education*. PPIC Statewide Survey. San Francisco: Public Policy Institute of California, April 2019. https://www.ppic.org/wp-content/uploads/ppic-statewide-survey-californians-and-education-april-2019.pdf.

Ballotpedia. "Massachusetts Ending Common Core Education Standards Initiative (2016)." https://ballotpedia.org/Massachusetts_Ending_Common_Core_Education_Standards_Initiative_(2016).

Baumgartner, Frank R., and Bryan D. Jones. *Agendas and Instability in American Politics*. Chicago: University of Chicago Press, 1993.

Beach, Richard W. "Issues in Analyzing Alignment of Language Arts Common Core State Standards with State Standards." *Educational Researcher* 40, no. 4 (May 2011): 179–82. doi: 10.3102/0013189X11410055.

Beland, Daniel. "Ideas and Social Policy: An Institutionalist Perspective." *Social Policy and Administration* 39, no. 1 (2005): 1–18. doi: 10.1111/j.1467-9515.2005.00421.x.

Benford, Robert D., and David A. Snow. "Framing Processes and Social Movements: An Overview and Assessment." *Annual Review of Sociology* 26 (August 2000): 611–39. doi: 10.1146/annurev.soc.26.1.611.

Blazar, David, Thomas J. Kane, Douglas Staiger, Dan Goldhaber, Rachel Hitch, Michal Kurlaender, Blake Heller, et al. *Learning by the Book: Comparing Math Achievement Growth by Textbook in Six Common Core States*. Cambridge, MA: Center for Education Policy Research, March 2019. https://cepr.harvard.edu/files/cepr/files/cepr-curriculum-report_learning-by-the-book.pdf.

Boaz, Annette, Huw Davies, Alec Fraser, and Sandra Nutley, eds. *What Works Now? Evidence-Informed Policy and Practice*. London: Policy Press, 2019.

Bogenschneider, Karen, and Thomas J. Corbett. *Evidence-Based Policy Making: Insights from Policy-Minded Researchers and Research-Minded Policymakers*. New York: Routledge, 2010.

Bogenschneider, Karen, Elizabeth Day, and Emily Parrott. "Revisiting Theory on Research Use: Turning to Policymakers for Fresh Insights." *American Psychologist* 74, no. 7 (2019): 778–93. doi: 10.1037/amp0000460.

Bomer, Randy, and Beth Maloch. "Relating Policy to Research and Practice: The Common Core Standards." *Language Arts* 89, no. 1 (September 2011). https://secure.ncte.org/library/NCTEFiles/Resources/Journals/LA/0891–sep2011/LA089Research.pdf.

Brady, Henry E., and David Collier, eds. *Rethinking Social Inquiry: Diverse Tools, Shared Standards*. 2nd ed. Lanham, MD: Rowman & Littlefield, 2010.

Brasher, Joan. "Survey: Majority of Tennessee Teachers Oppose Common Core." *Research News @Vanderbilt*, September 24, 2014. https://news.vanderbilt.edu/2014/09/24/survey-common-core.

Brooks, Tricia. "CHIP Funding Has Been Extended, What's Next for Children's Health Coverage?" *Health Affairs Blog*, January 30, 2018. https://www.healthaffairs.org/do/10.1377/hblog20180130.116879/full.

Brown, Brentt, and Merrill Vargo. *Getting to the Core: How Early Implementers are Approaching the Common Core in California*. Stanford, CA: PACE and Pivot Learning Partners, February 2014. https://edpolicyinca.org/sites/default/files/PACE%20Getting%20To%20The%20Core.pdf.

Bruch, Sarah K., Myra Marx Ferree, and Joe Soss. "From Policy to Polity: Democracy, Paternalism, and the Incorporation of Disadvantaged Citizens." *American Sociological Review* 75, no. 2 (April 2010): 205–26. doi: 10.1177/0003122410363563.

Bryk, Anthony S. "Accelerating How We Learn to Improve." *Educational Researcher* 44, no. 9 (December 2015): 467–77. doi: 10.3102/0013189X15621543.

Bushaw, William J., and Valerie J. Calderon. "Try It Again, Uncle Sam: The 46th Annual PDK/Gallup Poll of the Public's Attitudes Toward the Public Schools." *Phi Delta Kappan* 96, no. 1 (September 2014). doi: 10.1177/0031721714547856.

Bushaw, William J., and Shane J. Lopez. "Which Way Do We Go? The 45th Annual PDK/Gallup Poll of the Public's Attitudes Toward the Public Schools." *Phi Delta Kappan* 95, no. 1 (September 2013). doi: 10.1177/003172171309500104.

California Assessment of Academic Achievement, Program Provisions. California Education Code, section 60605.8(d) (2010). https://leginfo.legislature.ca.gov/faces/

codes_displaySection.xhtml?lawCode=EDC&sectionNum=60605.8.

Camera, Lauren. "A Tennessee District Perseveres in Wake of Online-Testing Woes." *Education Week*, February 29, 2016. https://www.edweek.org/ew/articles/2016/02/29/a-tennessee-district-perseveres-in-wake-of.html.

Camera, Lauren. "Tennessee on Dogged Path to Race to the Top Finish." *Education Week*, July 8, 2014. https://www.edweek.org/ew/articles/2014/07/09/36tennessee_ep.h33.html.

Campbell, John L. "Ideas, Politics, and Public Policy." *Annual Review of Sociology* 28 (2002): 21–38. doi: 10.1146/annurev.soc.28.110601.141111.

Caplan, Nathan. "The Two-Communities Theory and Knowledge Utilization." *American Behavioral Scientist* 22, no. 3 (1979): 459–70. doi: 10.1177/000276427902200308.

Carey, Mary Agnes. "FAQ on Medicare Doctor Pay: Why Is It So Hard to Fix?" Kaiser Health News, February 27, 2013. https://khn.org/news/faq-doc-fix.

Carneiro, Pedro, and James Heckman. "Human Capital Policy." NBER Working Paper No. 9495. National Bureau of Economic Research, Cambridge, MA, February 2003. https://www.nber.org/papers/w9495.

Chubb, John E., and Terry M. Moe. *Politics, Markets, and America's Schools*. Washington, DC: Brookings Institution, 1990.

Clements, Douglas. "What Do We Know About Content and Curriculum." In *Research in Mathematics Education: Where Do We Go from Here?* Conference proceedings. Washington, DC: Michigan State University Institute for Research on Mathematics and Science Education, 2011.

Clinton, Hillary Rodham, and Bill Frist. "Save the Children's Insurance." *New York Times*, February 12, 2015. https://www.nytimes.com/2015/02/13/opinion/hillary-clinton-and-bill-frist-on-health-care-for-americas-kids.html.

Cobb, Paul, and Kara Jackson. "Assessing the Quality of Common Core State Standards for Mathematics." *Educational Researcher* 40, no. 4 (May 2011): 183–85. doi: 10.3102/0013189X11409928.

Coburn, Cynthia E., and William R. Penuel. "Research-Practice Partnerships in Education: Outcomes, Dynamics, and Open Questions." *Educational Researcher* 45, no. 1 (January 2016): 48–54. doi: 10.3102/0013189X16631750.

Coburn, Cynthia E., William R. Penuel, and Kimberly E. Geil. "Research-Practice Partnerships: A Strategy for Leveraging Research for Educational Improvement in School Districts." New York: William T. Grant Foundation, 2013. https://wtgrant foundation.org/library/uploads/2015/10/Research-Practice-Partnerships-at-the-District-Level.pdf.

Coburn, Cynthia E., and Mary K. Stein. "Key Lessons About the Relationship Between Research and Practice." In *Research and Practice in Education: Building Alliances, Bridging the Divide*, edited by Cynthia Coburn and Mary K. Stein, 201–26. Lanham, MD: Rowman & Littlefield, 2010.

Coburn, Cynthia E., and Mary K. Stein, eds. *Research and Practice in Education: Building Alliances, Bridging the Divide.* Lanham, MD: Rowman & Littlefield, 2010.

Coburn, Cynthia E., and Joan E. Talbert. "Conceptions of Evidence Use in School Districts: Mapping the Terrain." *American Journal of Education* 112 (2006): 469–95. doi: 10.1086/505056.

Cohen, David K., and Heather C. Hill. *Learning Policy: When State Education Reform Works.* New Haven, CT: Yale University Press, 2001.

Cohen, David K., and Susan L. Moffitt. *The Ordeal of Equality: Did Federal Regulation Fix the Schools?* Cambridge, MA: Harvard University Press, 2009.

Cohen, David K., and James P. Spillane. "Policy and Practice: The Relations Between Governance and Instruction." *Review of Research in Education* 18 (1992): 3–49. doi: 10.2307/1167296.

Cohen Ross, Donna, and Laura Cox. *Beneath the Surface: Barriers Threaten to Slow Progress on Expanding Health Coverage of Children and Families.* Washington, DC: Kaiser Commission on Medicaid and the Uninsured, October 2004. https://www.kff .org/wp-content/uploads/2013/01/beneath-the-surface-barriers-threaten-to-slow-progress-on-expanding-health-coverage-of-children-and-families-pdf.pdf.

Cohen Ross, Donna, and Laura Cox. *Out in the Cold: Enrollment Freezes in Six State Children's Health Insurance Programs Withhold Coverage from Eligible Children.* Washington, DC: Kaiser Commission on Medicaid and the Uninsured, December 2003. https://www.kff.org/wp-content/uploads/2013/01/out-in-the-cold-enrollment-freezes-in-six-state-children-s-health-insurance-programs-withhold-coverage-from-eligible-children.pdf.

Cohen Ross, Donna, Aleya Horn, and Caryn Marks. *Health Coverage for Children and Families in Medicaid and SCHIP: State Efforts Face New Hurdles.* Washington, DC: Kaiser Commission on Medicaid and the Uninsured, January 2008. https://www.kff .org/wp-content/uploads/2013/01/7740.pdf.

Coleman, David, and Susan Pimentel. *Revised Publishers' Criteria for the Common Core State Standards in English Language Arts and Literacy, Grades K–2 and Grades 3–12.* Washington DC: NGA, CCSSO, Achieve, Council of the Great City Schools, and NASBE, 2012. http://www.corestandards.org/assets/Publishers_Criteria_for_K–2. pdf and http://www.corestandards.org/assets/Publishers_Criteria_for_3-12.pdf.

Common Core State Standards Initiative. *"Messaging Tool Kit."* Washington, DC: CCSSI, 2010. http://programs.ccsso.org/link/CCSSI%20Toolkit%20Sept%202010.pdf.

Coulson, Andrew J. "The Case Against National School Standards." Cato Institute, August 14, 2009. https://www.cato.org/publications/commentary/case-against-national-school-standards.

Council of Chief State School Officers. *SEC Content Analysis of Standards.* Washington, DC: CCSSO, October 12, 2010. https://files.eric.ed.gov/fulltext/ED543314.pdf.

Council of Chief State School Officers and the National Governors Association. *Reactions to the March 2010 Draft Common Core State Standards: Highlights and Themes*

from the Public Feedback. Washington, DC: CCSSO and NGA, 2010. http://www
.corestandards.org/assets/k-12-feedback-summary.pdf.

Darling-Hammond, Linda, and Ray Pecheone. *Developing an Internationally Comparable Balanced Assessment System That Supports High-Quality Learning*. Princeton, NJ: Educational Testing Services, March 2010. https://www.ets.org/Media/Research/pdf/Darling-HammondPechoneSystemModel.pdf.

Daro, Phil, Frederic A. Mosher, and Tom Corcoran. *Learning Trajectories in Mathematics: A Foundation for Standards, Curriculum, Assessment, and Instruction*. CPRE Research Report # RR-68. Philadelphia: Consortium for Policy Research in Education, 2011. doi: 10.12698/cpre.2011.rr68.

Davies, Huw T.O., Sandra M. Nutley, and Peter C. Smith. *What Works? Evidence-Based Policy and Practice in Public Service*. London: Policy Press, 2000.

Donovan, M. Suzanne, Alexandra K. Wigdor, and Catherine E. Snow, eds. *Strategic Education Research Partnership*. Washington, DC: National Academies Press, 2003.

Dorn, Stan, Bowen Garrett, John Holahan, and Aimee Williams. *Medicaid, SCHIP and Economic Downturn: Policy Challenges and Policy Responses*. Washington, DC: Kaiser Commission on Medicaid and the Uninsured, April 2008. https://www.kff.org/wp-content/uploads/2013/01/7770.pdf.

Duong, Sophia. *Summary: Governors' Letters to Congress on the Future of CHIP*. Washington, DC: Georgetown University Health Policy Institute, Center for Children and Families, December 2014. https://ccf.georgetown.edu/wp-content/uploads/2015/02/Gov-letters-summary-125-updated-211.pdf.

Elliott, Scott. "The Basics of Indiana Academic Standards: A New Beginning." Chalkbeat, September 8, 2014. https://www.chalkbeat.org/posts/in/2014/09/08/the-basics-of-indiana-academic-standards-a-new-beginning.

Elliott, Scott. "Five Theories for Why Tony Bennett Lost on Tuesday." *Indianapolis Star*, November 9, 2012.

End Common Core Massachusetts. https://www.endcommoncorema.com.

Esterling, Kevin M. *The Political Economy of Expertise*. Ann Arbor: University of Michigan Press, 2004.

Feder, Judith. "Crowd-Out: The Politics of Health Reform." *Journal of Law, Medicine, and Ethics* 32, no. 3 (September 2004): 461–64. doi: 10.1111/j.1748-720X.2004.tb00158.x.

Fensterwald, John. "Common Core Practice Test Would Replace State Math and English Tests Next Year." *EdSource*, September 4, 2013. https://edsource.org/2013/common-core-practice-test-would-replace-state-math-and-english-tests-next-year/38470/38470.

Fensterwald, John. "Final Vote on Common Core Is Unanimous." *Thoughts on Public Education*, August 2, 2010. http://theeducatedguess.org/2010/08/02/final-vote-on-common-core-is-unanimous.

Fensterwald, John. "Michael Kirst, Father of New School Funding Formula, Looks Back and at the Work Ahead." *EdSource*, June 12, 2013. https://edsource.org/2013/

michael-kirst-father-of-new-school-funding-formula-looks-back-and-at-the-work-ahead/33408/33408.

Fensterwald, John. "State Board of Education President Mike Kirst Announces He'll Retire—and Reflects on Changes He Has Led." *EdSource*, May 9, 2018. https://edsource.org/2018/state-board-of-education-president-mike-kirst-retires-and-reflects-on-changes-he-has-led/597625.

Fensterwald, John. "Yes to Common Core Plus 8th Grade Algebra." *The Educated Guess* blog, July 16, 2010. http://theeducatedguess.org/2010/07/16/common-core-with-8th-grade-algebra-endorsed.

Feuer, Michael J. *The Rising Price of Objectivity: Philanthropy, Government, and the Future of Education Research.* Cambridge, MA: Harvard Education Press, 2016.

Finkelstein, Neil, Reino Makkonen, Rebecca Perry, Francesca Delgado, Clay Willis, Pam Spycher, and Kim Austin. *Insights on Standards Implementation in California's Schools.* Getting Down to Facts II Technical Report. Stanford, CA: Stanford University, September 2018. https://gettingdowntofacts.com/sites/default/files/2018-09/GDTFII_Report_Finkelstein.pdf.

Fischhoff, Baruch, and Alex L. Davis. "Communicating Scientific Uncertainty." *Proceedings of the National Academy of Sciences* 111, supplement 4 (September 2014): 13664–71. doi: 10.1073/pnas.1317504111.

Fox, Jeremy C. "Education Board Votes to Adopt Hybrid MCAS-PARCC Test." *Boston Globe*, December 2, 2015. https://www.bostonglobe.com/metro/2015/11/17/state-education-board-vote-whether-replace-mcas/aex1nGyBYZW2sucEW2o82L/story.html.

Friedberg, Solomon, Diane Barone, Juliana Belding, Andrew Chen, Linda Dixon, Francis (Skip) Fennell, Douglas Fisher, Nancy Frey, Roger Howe, and Tim Shanahan. *The State of State Standards Post-Common Core.* Washington, DC: Thomas B. Fordham Institute, 2018. https://fordhaminstitute.org/sites/default/files/publication/pdfs/%2808.22%29%20The%20State%20of%20State%20Standards%20Post-Common%20Core.pdf.

Gamoran, Adam. "Evidence-Based Policy in the Real World: A Cautionary View." *Annals of the American Academy of Political and Social Science* 678 (2018): 180–91. doi: 10.1177/0002716218770138.

Gamson, David M., Xiaofei Lu, and Sarah Anne Eckert. "Challenging the Research Base of the Common Core State Standards: A Historical Reanalysis of Text Complexity." *Educational Researcher* 42, no. 7 (October 2013): 381–91. doi: 10.3102/0013189X13505684.

Gauchat, Gordon. "Politicization of Science in the Public Sphere: A Study of Public Trust in the United States, 1974 to 2010." *American Sociological Review* 77, no. 2 (April 2012): 167–87. doi: 10.1177/0003122412438225.

George, Alexander L., and Andrew Bennett. *Case Studies and Theory Development in the Social Sciences.* Cambridge, MA: MIT Press, 2005.

Gerring, John. *Social Science Methodology: A Unified Framework*. New York: Cambridge University Press, 2011.

Gerring, John. "What Is a Case Study and What Is It Good For?" *American Political Science Review* 98, no. 2 (2004): 341–54, https://www.jstor.org/stable/4145316.

Gewertz, Catherine. "Academics Find Common Standards Fit for College: But Academics Maintain Some Skills are Missing." *Education Week*, August 25, 2011. https://www.edweek.org/ew/articles/2011/08/25/02collegeready_ep.h31.html.

Gewertz, Catherine. "Aligning Standards and Curriculum Begets Questions." *Education Week*, May 18, 2010. https://www.edweek.org/ew/articles/2010/05/19/32common-curric_ep.h29.html.

Gewertz, Catherine. "Both Value and Harm Seen in K–3 Common Standards." *Education Week*, April 7, 2010. https://www.edweek.org/ew/articles/2010/04/07/28common.h29.html.

Gewertz, Catherine. "California in Testing Showdown with U.S. Department of Education." *Education Week*, September 10, 2013. https://www.edweek.org/ew/articles/2013/09/10/04california.h33.html.

Gewertz, Catherine. "Union Details Teacher Influence on Common Standards." *Curriculum Matters* (blog), Education Week, April 16, 2010. https://blogs.edweek.org/edweek/curriculum/2010/04/union_details_teacher_influenc.html.

Gilens, Martin, and Benjamin I. Page. "Testing Theories of American Politics: Elites, Interest Groups, and Average Citizens." *Perspectives on Politics* 12, no. 3 (September 2014): 564–81. doi: 10.1017/S1537592714001595.

Godwin, Kenneth, Scott H. Ainsworth, and Erik Godwin. *Lobbying and Policymaking: The Public Pursuit of Private Interests*. Thousand Oaks, CA: SAGE/CQ Press, 2013. doi: 10.4135/9781483349336.

Goertz, Margaret E. "Standards-Based Reform: Lessons from the Past, Directions for the Future." Paper presented at Clio at the Table: A Conference on the Uses of History to Inform and Improve Education Policy, Brown University, Providence, RI, June 2007. http://citeseerx.ist.psu.edu/viewdoc/download?doi=10.1.1.184.3306&rep=rep1&type=pdf.

Goodnough, Abby, and Robert Pear, "The CHIP Program Is Beloved: Why Is Its Funding in Danger?" *New York Times*, December 5, 2017, https://www.nytimes.com/2017/12/05/health/childrens-health-insurance-program.html.

Goodson, Barbara D. "Evidence at the Crossroads Pt. 5: Improving Implementation Research." 2015. http://wtgrantfoundation.org/evidence-at-the-crossroads-pt-5-improving-implementation-research.

Gormley, William T., Jr. *Voices for Children: Rhetoric and Public Policy*. Washington, DC: Brookings Institution, 2012.

Gray v. Attorney General, SJC-12064. Massachusetts Supreme Judicial Court, 2016. https://cases.justia.com/massachusetts/supreme-court/2016-sjc-12064.pdf.

Harrington, Mary, and Genevieve M. Kenney et al. *CHIPRA Mandated Evaluation of the*

Children's Health Insurance Program: Final Findings. Ann Arbor, MI: Mathematica Policy Research and Urban Institute, August 1, 2014. https://aspe.hhs.gov/report/chipra-mandated-evaluation-childrens-health-insurance-program-final-findings.

Hart, Beth, Elaine Carman, Danielle Luisier, and Natasha Vasavada. *Common Core State Standards Alignment.* College Board Research Report no. 2011–8. Washington, DC: College Board, 2011. http://secure-media.collegeboard.org/digitalServices/pdf/research/RR2011-8.pdf.

Haskins, Ron, and Jon Baron. *Building the Connection Between Policy and Evidence: The Obama Evidence-Based Initiatives.* Washington, DC: Brookings Institution, September 7, 2011. https://www.brookings.edu/research/building-the-connection-between-policy-and-evidence-the-obama-evidence-based-initiatives.

Haskins, Ron, and Greg Margolis. *Show Me the Evidence.* Washington, DC: Brookings Institution, 2014.

Hatch, Orrin, Fred Upton, and Joe Pitts. *Discussion Draft: Extending Funding for the State Children's Health Insurance Program.* Washington, DC: US House of Representatives, Committee on Energy and Commerce, 114th Cong., 1st sess., February 24, 2015. https://www.finance.senate.gov/imo/media/doc/SCHIP%20Discussion.pdf.

Heckman, James J. "Building Bridges Between Structural and Program Evaluation Approaches to Evaluating Policy." NBER Working Paper 16110. Cambridge, MA: National Bureau of Economic Research, June 2010. https://www.nber.org/papers/w16110.

Heckman, James J. "Microdata, Heterogeneity and the Evaluation of Public Policy." Nobel Prize Lecture, Stockholm, Sweden, December 8, 2000. https://www.nobelprize.org/prizes/economic-sciences/2000/heckman/lecture.

Heckman, James J., Alan B. Krueger, and Benjamin M. Friedman. *Inequality in America: What Role for Human Capital Policies?* Cambridge, MA: MIT Press, 2004.

Heclo, Hugh. *Modern Social Politics in Britain and Sweden: From Relief to Income Maintenance.* New Haven, CT: Yale University Press, 1974.

Heitin Loewus, Liana. "Indiana's Draft vs. the Common Core: A Comparison of Math Standards." *Curriculum Matters* blog, Education Week, March 12, 2014. http://blogs.edweek.org/edweek/curriculum/2014/03/indianas_draft_vs_the_common_c.html.

Henderson, Michael B., Paul E. Peterson, and Martin West. "No Common Opinion on the Common Core." *Education Next* 15, no. 1 (Winter 2015): 9–19. https://www.educationnext.org/2014-ednext-poll-no-common-opinion-on-the-common-core.

Henig, Jeffrey R. *Spin Cycle: How Research Gets Used in Policy Debates—The Case of Charter Schools.* New York: Russell Sage Foundation, 2008. https://www.jstor.org/stable/10.7758/9781610442855.

Herd, Pamela, and Donald P. Moynihan. *Administrative Burden: Policymaking by Other Means.* New York: Russell Sage Foundation, 2018. doi: 10.7758/9781610448789.

Herman, Joan, Scott Epstein, and Seth Leon. "Supporting Common Core Instruction with Literacy Design Collaborative: A Tale of Two Studies." *AERA Open* 2, no. 3 (July 2016): 1–15. doi: 10.1177/2332858416655782.

Hertel-Fernandez, Alexander. "Who Passes Business's 'Model Bills'? Policy Capacity and Corporate Influence in U.S. State Politics." *Perspectives on Politics* 12, no. 3 (September 2014): 582–602. doi: 10.1017/S1537592714001601.

Hess, Frederick M., ed. *When Research Matters: How Scholarship Influences Education Policy.* Cambridge, MA: Harvard Education Press, 2008.

Hiebert, Elfrieda H., and Heidi Anne E. Mesmer. "Upping the Ante of Text Complexity in the Common Core State Standards: Examining Its Potential Impact on Young Readers." *Educational Researcher* 42, no. 1 (January 2013): 44–51. doi: 10.3102/0013189X12459802.

Hochschild, Jennifer L., and Katherine Levine Einstein. *Do Facts Matter? Information and Misinformation in American Politics.* Norman: University of Oklahoma Press, 2015.

Hochschild, Jennifer L., and Nathan Scovronick. *The American Dream and the Public Schools.* New York: Oxford University Press, 2003.

Hodge, Emily M., Serena J. Salloum, and Susanna L. Benko. "(Un)Commonly Connected: A Social Network Analysis of State Standards Resources for English/Language Arts." *AERA Open* 2, no. 4 (October 2016): 1–19. doi: 10.1177/2332858416674901.

Holahan, John, Allison Cook, and Lisa Dubay. *Characteristics of the Uninsured: Who Is Eligible for Coverage and Who Needs Help Affording Coverage?* Washington, DC: Kaiser Commission on Medicaid and the Uninsured, February 2007. https://www.kff.org/wp-content/uploads/2013/01/7613.pdf.

Honig, Meredith I., and Cynthia E. Coburn. "Evidence-Based Decision Making in School District Central Offices: Toward a Policy and Research Agenda." *Educational Policy,* 22, no. 4 (July 2008): 578–608. doi: 10.1177/0895904807307067.

Hoosiers Against Common Core. "About Us." Hoosiers Against Common Core website. http://hoosiersagainstcommoncore.com/about-us-2.

Horton, Amy. "Statewide Implementation Plan: Indiana Academic Standards in ELA and Mathematics." Slide presentation, Indiana Department of Education, 2014. https://www.doe.in.gov/sites/default/files/standards/standardspresentationvisionprogressjuly2014.pdf.

Howell, Embry M., and Genevieve M. Kenney. "The Impact of the Medicaid/CHIP Expansions on Children: A Synthesis of the Evidence." *Medical Care Research and Review* 69, no 4 (August 2012): 372–96). doi: 10.1177/1077558712437245.

Hudson, Julie L., and Salam Abdus. "Coverage and Care Consequences for Families in Which Children Have Mixed Eligibility for Public Insurance." *Health Affairs* 34, no. 8 (August 2015): 1340–48. doi: 10.1377/hlthaff.2015.0128.

Hudson, Julie L., Thomas M. Selden, and Jessica S. Banthin. "The Impact of SCHIP on Insurance Coverage of Children." *Inquiry* 42, no. 3 (August 2005): 232–54. doi: 10.5034/inquiryjrnl_42.3.232.

Hulse, Carl, and Robert Pear. "Sweeping Health Care Plan Passes House." *The New York Times.* November 7, 2009. https://www.nytimes.com/2009/11/08/health/policy/08health.html.

Iglehart, John K. "The Fate of SCHIP—Surrogate Marker for Health Care Ideology?" *New England Journal of Medicine* 357, no. 21 (November 22, 2007): 2104–7. doi: 10.1056/NEJMp0706881.

Institute for Mathematics and Education. "Progressions Documents for the Common Core Math Standards." Tucson: University of Arizona, 2013. http://ime.math .arizona.edu/progressions.

Institute of Medicine, Committee on Consequences of Uninsurance. *Health Insurance Is a Family Matter*. Washington, DC: National Academies Press, 2002. doi: 10.17226/10503.

James B. Hunt Jr. Institute for Educational Leadership. *"Blueprint for Education Leadership*, vols. 1 and 2." Policy briefs. Durham, NC: , June and October, 2008. http:// www.hunt-institute.org/wp-content/uploads/2015/04/Blueprint_Number_1.pdf and http://www.hunt-institute.org/wp-content/uploads/2015/04/Blueprint_ Number_2.pdf.

Jeffrey, Aimee E., and Paul W. Newacheck. "Role of Insurance for Children with Special Health Care Needs: A Synthesis of the Evidence." *Pediatrics* 118, no. 4 (October 2006): 1027–38. doi: 10.1542/peds.2005–2527.

Jochim, Ashley, and Lesley Lavery. "The Evolving Politics of the Common Core: Policy Implementation and Conflict Expansion." *Publius: The Journal of Federalism* 45, no. 3 (Summer 2015): 380–404. doi: 10.1093/publius/pjv015.

Jonas, Michael. "Baker's Common Core Caution." *CommonWealth Magazine*, May 11, 2016. https://commonwealthmagazine.org/politics/bakers-common-core-caution.

Kaiser Family Foundation. "The Kaiser Family Foundation's Employer Health Benefits Annual Survey Archives." KFF website, September 25, 2019. https://www.kff.org/ health-costs/report/employer-health-benefits-annual-survey-archives.

Kane, Thomas J., Antoniya M. Owens, William H. Marinell, Daniel R. C. Thal, and Douglas O. Staiger. *Teaching Higher: Educators' Perspectives on Common Core Implementation*. Cambridge, MA: Center for Education Policy Research, February 2016. https://cepr.harvard.edu/files/cepr/files/teaching-higher-report.pdf.

Kaplan, Abraham. *The Conduct of Inquiry: Methodology for Behavioral Science*. San Francisco: Chandler, 1964.

Karoly, Lynn A., M. Rebecca Kilburn, and Jill S. Cannon. *Children at Risk: Consequences for School Readiness and Beyond*. Santa Monica, CA: RAND Corporation, 2005. https://www.rand.org/pubs/research_briefs/RB9144.html.

Kelman, Steven. *Making Public Policy: A Hopeful View of American Government*. New York: Basic Books, 1987.

Kenney, Genevieve M. *The Failure of SCHIP Reauthorization: What Next?* Washington, DC: Urban Institute, March 2008. https://www.urban.org/sites/default/files/ publication/31541/411628-The-Failure-of-SCHIP-Reauthorization-What-Next-.PDF.

Kenney, Genevieve M. "The Impacts of the State Children's Health Insurance Program on Children Who Enroll: Findings from Ten States." *Health Services Research* 42, no. 4 (2007): 1520–43. doi: 10.1111/j.1475-6773.2007.00707.x.

Kenney, Genevieve M., and Justin Yee. "SCHIP at a Crossroads: Experiences to Date and Challenges Ahead." *Health Affairs* 26, no. 2 (2007): 356–69. doi: 10.1377/hlthaff.26.2.356.

Kerchner, Charles Taylor. "California: A K–12 Education Outlier." *Education Week*, February 25, 2014. https://www.edweek.org/ew/articles/2014/02/26/22kerchner.h33.html.

King, Gary, Robert O. Keohane, and Sidney Verba. *Designing Social Inquiry: Scientific Inference in Qualitative Research*. Princeton, NJ: Princeton University Press, 1994.

Kingdon, John. *Agendas, Alternatives, and Public Policies*. Updated 2nd ed. New York: Longman, 2011.

Kirst, Mike W. *The Common Core Meets State Policy: This Changes Almost Everything*. Stanford, CA: Policy Analysis for California Education, March 2013. https://edpolicyinca.org/sites/default/files/PACE_Common%20Core_Final.pdf.

Klein, Alyson. "Critics Pan Obama Plan to Tie Title I to Standards." *Education Week*, February 26, 2010. https://www.edweek.org/ew/articles/2010/02/26/23esea_ep-2.h29.html.

Klein, Alyson. "Federal Role Touchy in Standards Push." *Education Week*, September 1, 2010. https://www.edweek.org/ew/articles/2010/09/01/02policy.h30.html.

Klein, Alyson. "In Standards Push, Lawmakers Cheer States' Initiative." *Education Week*, May 13, 2009. https://www.edweek.org/ew/articles/2009/05/13/31standards-2.h28.html.

Knudson, Joel, Stephanie Hannan, and Jennifer O'Day. *Learning from the Past: Drawing on California's CLAS Experience to Inform Assessment of the Common Core*. San Mateo: California Collaborative on District Reform, September 2012. https://cacollaborative.org/sites/default/files/CA_Collaborative_CLAS.pdf.

Kosar, Kevin. *Failing Grades: The Federal Politics of Education Standards*. Boulder, CO: Lynne Rienner, 2005.

Kurlaender, Michal, and Kramer Cohen. *Predicting College Success: How Do Different High School Assessments Measure Up?* Stanford, CA: Policy Analysis for California Education, March 2019. https://edpolicyinca.org/sites/default/files/R_Kurlaender_Mar-2019.pdf.

La Raza. *Raising the Bar: Implementing Common Core Standards for Latino Student Success*. Washington, DC: National Council of La Raza, 2012. publications.unidosus.org/bitstream/handle/123456789/371/raisingthebar.pdf.

Lauen, Douglas Lee, and S. Michael Gaddis. "Accountability Pressure, Academic Standards, and Educational Triage." *Educational Evaluation and Policy Analysis* 38, no. 1 (2016): 127–47. doi: 10.3102/0162373715598577.

Lee, Okhee, Helen Quinn, and Guadalupe Valdés. "Science and Language for English Language Learners in Relation to Next Generation Science Standards and with Implications for Common Core State Standards for English Language Arts and Mathematics." *Educational Researcher* 42, no. 4 (May 2013): 223–33. doi: 10 .3102/0013189X13480524.

Leonhardt, David "Taking Health Care from Kids." *New York Times*, December 21, 2017. https://www.nytimes.com/2017/12/21/opinion/tax-bill-chip.html.

Levitt, Barbara, and James G. March. "Organizational Learning." *Annual Review of Sociology* 14 (1988): 319–38. doi: 10.1146/annurev.so.14.080188.001535.

Lewin, Tamar. "Many States Adopt National Standards for Their Schools." *New York Times*, July 21, 2010. https://www.nytimes.com/2010/07/21/education/ 21standards.html.

Lohr, Kathleen N., Robert H. Brook, Caren Kamberg, George A. Goldberg, Arleen Leibowitz, Joan Keesey, David Reboussin, and Joseph P. Newhouse. "Use of Medical Care in the RAND Health Insurance Experiment." *Medical Care* 24, no. 9, supplement (September 1986): S72–S78, https://www.rand.org/pubs/reports/R3469.html.

Long, Cindy. "Here Come the Common Core Standards." *NEAToday* blog. National Education Association, March 17, 2011. http://neatoday.org/2011/05/17/here-come-the-common-core-standards-2.

Loomis, Burdett A., and Anthony J. Nownes. "Advocacy in an Era of Inequality." In *Interest Group Politics*, 9th ed., Edited by Allan J. Cigler, Burdett A. Loomis, and Anthony J. Nownes, 363–78. Thousand Oaks, CA: SAGE/CQ Press, 2016.

Loveless, Tom. *How Well Are American Students Learning?* Washington, DC: Brown Center on Education Policy, Brookings Institution, 2012.

Lubienski, Christopher, Janelle Scott, and Elizabeth DeBray. "The Rise of Intermediary Organizations in Knowledge Production, Advocacy, and Educational Policy." *Teachers College Record* (July 22, 2011). https://www.academia.edu/5087738/The_ Rise_of_Intermediary_Organizations_in_Knowledge_Production_Advocacy_and_ Education_Policy.

Majone, Giandomenico. *Evidence, Argument, and Persuasion in the Policy Process*. New Haven, CT: Yale University Press, 1989.

Mann, Cindy, and Robin Rudowitz. *Financing Health Coverage: The State Children's Health Program Experience*. Washington, DC: Kaiser Commission on Medicaid and the Uninsured, February 2005. https://www.kff.org/wp-content/uploads/2013/ 01/financing-health-coverage-the-state-children-s-health-insurance-program-experience-issue-paper.pdf.

Mann, Thomas E., and Norman J. Ornstein. *It's Even Worse Than It Was: How the American Constitutional System Collided with the New Politics of Extremism*. New York: Basic Books, 2016.

Manna, Paul. *School's In: Federalism and the National Education Agenda*. Washington, DC: Georgetown University Press, 2006.

Manna, Paul, Keenan Kelley, and Frederick M. Hess. *Implementing Indiana's "Putting Students First" Agenda: Early Lessons and Potential Futures*. Washington, DC: American Enterprise Institute, August 2012. https://www.aei.org/wp-content/

uploads/2012/08/-implementing-indianas-putting-students-first-agenda-early-lessons-and-potential-futures_154113317564.pdf.

Mansbridge, Jane J., ed. *Beyond Self-Interest*. Chicago: University of Chicago Press, 1990.

Marchand, Julia, Mary Nistler, and Matthew Welch. *Massachusetts Curriculum Frameworks Implementation Study: Phase 1 Findings*. Chicago: American Institutes for Research, September 2013. http://www.doe.mass.edu/research/reports/2013/09MA-CFIS-Phase1.docx.

Marchand, Julia, Matthew Welch, Mary Nistler, Janet Levings, and Christine Paulson. *2011 Massachusetts Curriculum Frameworks for English Language Arts and Mathematics Implementation Study: Final Report*. Chicago: American Institutes for Research, October 2014. http://www.doe.mass.edu/research/reports/2014/10MA-CFIS-Final.docx.

Massachusetts Department of Elementary and Secondary Education. "DESE VISTA Survey Project, 2018–2019." http://www.doe.mass.edu/research/vista/2019.

Massachusetts Department of Elementary and Secondary Education. "Findings of the Mathematics Common Core Review Panel." Internal report, Massachusetts DESE, June 2010.

Massachusetts Department of Elementary and Secondary Education. "Report of the English Language Arts Review Panel on the Common Core and Massachusetts Standards." Internal report, Massachusetts DESE, July 2010.

Massachusetts Department of Elementary and Secondary Education. *Trends in International Mathematics and Science Study (TIMSS) 2011: Summary of Massachusetts Results*. Malden: Massachusetts DESE, November 2013. http://www.doe.mass.edu/mcas/natl-intl/timss/2011timssSummary.docx.

Massachusetts Department of Elementary and Secondary Education. *2017 NAEP Reading and Mathematics: Summary of State Results*. Malden: Massachusetts DESE, May 2018. http://www.doe.mass.edu/mcas/natl-intl/naep/results/2017readingmath.docx.

Massell, Diane, and Margaret E. Goertz. "State Education Department Acquisition and Use of Research in School Improvement." Paper presented at the Annual Meeting of the American Educational Research Association, Vancouver, B.C., Canada, April 16, 2012.

May, Peter J. "Policy Learning and Failure." *Journal of Public Policy* 12, no. 4 (October 1992): 331–54. doi: 10.1017/S0143814X00005602.

Mayhew, David. "Legislative Obstruction." *Perspectives on Politics* 8, no. 4 (December 2010): 1145–54. doi: 10.1017/S1537592710002203.

McDermott, Kathryn A., *High-Stakes Reform: The Politics of Educational Accountability*. Washington, DC: Georgetown University Press, 2011.

McDonnell, Lorraine M. "Assessing the Political Feasibility of Common Standards." Memo prepared for Workshop on Evaluating the Options for Common Standards, NRC Committee on State Standards in Education. Washington, DC, March 17, 2008.

McDonnell, Lorraine M. "Educational Accountability and Policy Feedback." *Educational Policy* 27, no. 2 (March 2013): 170–89. doi: 10.1177/0895904812465119.

McDonnell, Lorraine M. "Opportunity to Learn as a Research Concept and a Policy Instrument." *Educational Evaluation and Policy Analysis* 17, no. 3 (September 1995): 305–22. doi: 10.3102/01623737017003305.

McDonnell, Lorraine M. *Politics, Persuasion, and Educational Testing.* Cambridge, MA: Harvard University Press, 2004.

McDonnell, Lorraine M. "Repositioning Politics in Education's Circle of Knowledge." *Educational Researcher* 38, no. 6 (August 2009): 417–27. doi: 10.3102/0013189X09342584.

McDonnell, Lorraine M. "Surprising Momentum: Spurring Education Reform in States and Localities." In *Reaching for a New Deal: Ambitious Governance, Economic Meltdown, and Polarized Politics in Obama's First Two Years,* edited by Theda Skocpol and Lawrence R. Jacobs. New York: Russell Sage Foundation, 2011.

McDonnell, Lorraine M., and M. Stephen Weatherford. "Evidence Use and the Common Core State Standards Movement: From Problem Definition to Policy Adoption." *American Journal of Education* 120, no. 1 (November 2013): 1–25. doi: 10.1086/673163.

McDonnell, Lorraine M., and M. Stephen Weatherford. "Organized Interests and the Common Core." *Educational Researcher* 42, no. 9 (December 2013): 488–97. doi: 10.3102/0013189X13512676.

McDonnell, Lorraine M., and M. Stephen Weatherford. "Recognizing the Political in Implementation Research." *Educational Researcher* 45, no. 4 (2016): 233–42. doi: 10.3102/0013189X16649945.

McGuinn, Patrick J. "Complicated Politics to the Core." *Phi Delta Kappan* 97, no. 1 (September 2015). doi: 10.1177/0031721715602229.

McGuinn, Patrick J. *No Child Left Behind and the Transformation of Federal Education Policy, 1965–2005.* Lawrence: University Press of Kansas, 2006.

McLaughlin, Milbrey, Laura Glaab, and Isabel Hilliger Carrasco. *Implementing Common Core State Standards in California: A Report from the Field.* Stanford, CA: PACE, June 2014. https://edpolicyinca.org/publications/implementing-common-core-state-standards-california-report-field.

McNeil, Michele, and Alyson Klein. "California's Hopes Dashed for NCLB Waiver." *Education Week,* January 8, 2013. https://www.edweek.org/ew/articles/2013/01/09/15policy.h32.html.

McShane, Michael Q., and Frederick Hess. "Flying Under the Radar? Analyzing Common Core Media Coverage." Washington, DC: American Enterprise Institute, March 2014. https://www.aei.org/research-products/report/flying-under-the-radar-analyzing-common-core-media-coverage.

Medicaid and CHIP Payment and Access Commission. *June 2014 Report to the Congress on Medicaid and CHIP.* Washington, DC: MACPAC, June 2014. https://www.macpac.gov/wp-content/uploads/2015/01/2014-06-13_MACPAC_Report.pdf.

Mehta, Jal. *The Allure of Order.* New York: Oxford University Press, 2013.

Mettler, Suzanne. "The Policyscape and the Challenges of Contemporary Politics to Policy Maintenance." *Perspectives on Politics* 14, no. 2 (June 2016): 369–90. doi: 10.1017/S1537592716000074.

Mettler, Suzanne. *The Submerged State: How Invisible Government Policies Undermine American Democracy*. Chicago: University of Chicago Press, 2011.

Mettler, Suzanne, and Joe Soss. "The Consequences of Public Policy for Democratic Citizenship: Bridging Policy Studies and Mass Politics." *Perspectives on Politics* 2, no. 1 (March 2004): 55–73. doi: 10.1017/S1537592704000623.

Mintrom, Michael. *Policy Entrepreneurs and School Choice*. Washington, DC: Georgetown University Press, 2000.

Mitchell, Ted. "Common Educational Standards for Common Good." *San Francisco Chronicle*, July 30, 2010. https://www.sfgate.com/opinion/openforum/article/Common-educational-standards-for-common-good-3180461.php.

Moe, Terry M. "Political Institutions: The Neglected Side of the Story." *Journal of Law, Economics, and Organization* 6 (April 1990): 213–53. https://www.jstor.org/stable/764990.

Moffitt, Susan L., Matthew J. Lyddon, Domingo Morel, Michaela Krug O'Neill, Kelly B. Smith, Cadence Willse, and David K. Cohen. *State Structures for Instructional Support in California*, Getting Down to Facts II Technical Report. Stanford, CA: Stanford University, September 2018. https://gettingdowntofacts.com/sites/default/files/2018-09/GDTFII_Report_Moffitt_structures_0.pdf.

Moffitt, Susan L., Matthew J. Lyddon, Michaela Krug O'Neill, Kelly B. Smith, Marie Schenk, Cadence Willse, and David K. Cohen. *Frontlines Perspectives on Instructional Support in the Common Core Era*, Getting Down to Facts II Technical Report. Stanford, CA: Stanford University, September 2018. https://gettingdowntofacts.com/sites/default/files/2018-09/GDTFII_Report_Moffitt_standards.pdf.

Mucciaroni, Gary, and Paul Quirk. *Deliberative Choices: Debating Public Policy in Congress*. Chicago: University of Chicago Press, 2006.

National Academy of Education. *Recommendations Regarding Research Priorities: An Advisory Report to the National Educational Research Policy and Priorities Board*. Washington, DC: National Academy of Education, 1999.

National Center for Education Statistics. *Mapping 2005 State Proficiency Standards onto the NAEP Scales*. NCES 2007-482. Washington, DC: US Department of Education, 2007. https://nces.ed.gov/nationsreportcard/pdf/studies/2007482.pdf.

National Education Association. "NEA Comments on K–12 Common Core Standards Draft." News release. Washington, DC: NEA, March 1, 2010.

National Governors Association and Council of Chief State School Officers. "Appendix A: Research Supporting Key Elements of the Standards." In *Common Core State Standards for English Language Arts and Literacy in History/Social Studies, Science, and Technical Subjects*. Washington, DC: NGA and CCSSO, 2010. http://www.corestandards.org/assets/Appendix_A.pdf.

National Governors Association and Council of Chief State School Officers. *Common Core State Standards for English Language Arts and Literacy in History/Social Studies, Science, and Technical Subjects.* Washington, DC: NGA and CCSSO, 2010. http://www.corestandards.org/assets/CCSSI_ELA%20Standards.pdf.

National Governors Association and Council of Chief State School Officers. *Reaching Higher: The Common Core State Standards Validation Committee.* Washington, DC: NGA and CCSSO, 2010.

National Governors Association, Council of Chief State School Officers, and Achieve. *Benchmarking for Success: Ensuring U.S. Students Receive a World-Class Education.* Washington, DC: NGA, CCSSO, and Achieve, 2008. http://www.corestandards.org/assets/0812BENCHMARKING.pdf.

National Governors Association, Council of Chief State School Officers, Achieve, Council of the Great City Schools, and National Association of State Boards of Education. *High School Publishers' Criteria for the Common Core State Standards for Mathematics.* Washington, DC: NGA, CCSSO, Achieve, Council of the Great City Schools, and NASBE, 2013. http://www.corestandards.org/assets/Math_Publishers_Criteria_HS_Spring%202013_FINAL.pdf.

National Governors Association, CCSSO, Achieve, Council of the Great City Schools, and NASBE. *K-8 Publishers' Criteria for the Common Core State Standards for Mathematics.* Washington, DC: NGA, CCSSO, Achieve, Council of the Great City Schools, and NASBE, 2012. http://www.corestandards.org/assets/Math_Publishers_Criteria_K-8_Summer%202012_FINAL.pdf.

National Parent Teacher Association. *Equal Education for All.* Washington, DC: PTA, March 1, 2010.

National Research Council, Committee on the Use of Social Science Knowledge in Public Policy. *Using Science as Evidence in Public Policy,* edited by Kenneth Prewitt, Thomas A. Schwandt, and Miron L. Straf. Washington, DC: National Academies Press, 2012. doi: 10.17226/13460.

National Research Council. *Common Standards for K-12 Education? Considering the Evidence: Summary of a Workshop Series.* Washington, DC: National Academies Press, 2008. doi: 10.17226/12462.

O'Day, Jennifer A. "A Window of Opportunity: The Politics and Policies of Common Core Implementation in California." In *Challenging Standards: Navigating Conflict and Building Capacity in the Era of the Common Core,* edited by Jonathan A. Supovitz and James P. Spillane. Lanham, MD: Rowman & Littlefield, 2015.

O'Day, Jennifer A., and Marshall A. Smith. "Systemic School Reform." In *Designing Coherent Education Policy: Improving the System,* edited by Susan H. Fuhrman. San Francisco: Jossey-Bass, 1993.

Obama, Barack. "State of the Union Address." January 28, 2014. https://obamawhitehouse.archives.gov/the-press-office/2014/01/28/president-barack-obamas-state-union-address.

Oberlander, Jonathan B. "The Partisan Divide—the McCain and Obama Plans for US Health Care Reform." *New England Journal of Medicine* 359 (August 21, 2008): 781–84. doi: 10.1056/NEJMp0804659.

Oberlander, Jonathan B., David K. Jones, Steven Spivack, Philip M. Singer. "In the Affordable Care Act's Shadow: The Fate of the Children's Health Insurance Program." *Health Affairs* 35, no. 10 (October 2016): 1835–41. doi: 10.1377/hlthaff.2016.0226.

Oberlander, Jonathan B., and Barbara Lyons. "Beyond Incrementalism? SCHIP and the Politics of Health Reform." *Health Affairs* 28, supplement 1 (March 2009). doi: 10.1377/hlthaff.28.3.w399.

Opfer, V. Darleen, Julia H. Kaufman, and Lindsey E. Thompson. *Implementation of K–12 Standards for Mathematics and English Language Arts and Literacy: Findings from the American Teacher Panel.* Santa Monica, CA: RAND, 2016.

Patashnik, Eric M., *Reforms at Risk: What Happens After Major Policy Changes Are Enacted.* Princeton, NJ: Princeton University Press, 2008.

Patashnik, Eric M., and Julian E. Zelizer. "The Struggle to Remake Politics: Liberal Reform and the Limits of Policy Feedback in the Contemporary American State." *Perspectives on Politics* 11, no. 4 (December 2013): 1071–87. doi: 10.1017/S1537592713002831.

Pear, Robert. "A Battle over Expansion of Children's Insurance." *New York Times*, July 9, 2007. https://www.nytimes.com/2007/07/09/washington/09child.html.

Pear, Robert. "Deal Struck to Extend Financing for Children's Health Program." *New York Times*, September 12, 2017. https://www.nytimes.com/2017/09/12/us/politics/childrens-health-insurance-program-chip-deal-hatch-wyden.html.

Pear, Robert. "Senate Approves a Bill on Changes to Medicare." *New York Times*, April 14, 2015. https://www.nytimes.com/2015/04/15/us/politics/senate-approves-a-bill-on-changes-to-medicare.html.

Pearson, P. David, and Elfrieda H. Hiebert. "Understanding the Common Core State Standards." In *Teaching with the Common Core State Standards for English Language Arts, PreK–2,* edited by Lesley Mandel Morrow, Timothy Shanahan, and Karen K. Wixson. New York: Guilford Press, 2012.

Phillips, Vicki. "More Is Not Better." *Education Week*, September 30, 2009. https://www.edweek.org/ew/articles/2009/09/30/05phillips_ep.h29.html.

Phillips, Vicki, and Carina Wong. "Teaching to the Common Core by Design, Not Accident." *Phi Delta Kappan* 93, no. 7 (2012): 31–37. doi: 10.1177/003172171209300708.

Pierson, Paul. "When Effect Becomes Cause: Policy Feedback and Political Change." *World Politics* 45, no. 4 (1993): 595–628. doi: 10.2307/2950710.

Plumer, Brad, and Coral Davenport. "Science Under Attack: How Trump Is Sidelining Researchers and Their Work." *New York Times*, December 28, 2019. https://www.nytimes.com/2019/12/28/climate/trump-administration-war-on-science.html.

Polikoff, Morgan S. "How Well Aligned Are Textbooks to the Common Core Standards in Mathematics?" *American Educational Research Journal* 52, no. 6 (December 2015): 1185–211. doi: 10.3102/0002831215584435.

Polikoff, Morgan S., and Shauna Campbell. *Adoption, Implementation, and Effects of Curriculum Materials.* DESE Policy Brief. Malden: Massachusetts Department of Elementary and Secondary Education, October 2018. http://www.doe.mass.edu/research/reports/2018/10curriculum-materials.docx.

Polikoff, Morgan S., Tenice Hardaway, Julie A. Marsh, and David N. Plank. "Who is Opposed to Common Core and Why?" *Educational Researcher* 45, no. 4 (May 2016): 263–66. doi: 10.3102/0013189X16651087.

Porter, Andrew C. "In Common Core, Little to Cheer About." *Education Week*, August 9, 2011. https://www.edweek.org/ew/articles/2011/08/10/37porter_ep.h30.html.

Porter, Andrew C., Jennifer McMaken, Jun Hwang, and Rui Yang. "Assessing the Common Core Standards: Opportunities for Improving Measures of Instruction." *Educational Researcher* 40, no. 4 (May 2011):186–88. doi: 10.3102/0013189X11410232.

Porter, Andrew C., Jennifer McMaken, Jun Hwang, and Rui Yang. "Common Core Standards: The New U.S. Intended Curriculum." *Educational Researcher* 40, no. 3 (April 2011): 103–16. doi: 10.3102/0013189X11405038.

Quirk, Paul J., and Bruce Nesmith. "Reality-Based Policymaking Information, Advice, and Presidential Success." In *Governing at Home: The White House and Domestic Policymaking*, edited by Michael Nelson and Russell L. Riley. Lawrence: University Press of Kansas, 2011.

Ravitch, Diane. *The Death and Life of the Great American School System: How Testing and Choice Are Undermining Education.* New York: Basic Books, 2010.

Reckhow, Sarah. *Follow the Money: How Foundation Dollars Change Public School Politics.* New York: Oxford University Press, 2013. doi: 10.1093/acprof:oso/9780199937738.001.0001.

Reich, Robert B., ed. *The Power of Public Ideas.* Cambridge, MA: Ballinger, 1988.

Rhodes, Jesse. *An Education in Politics: The Origins and Evolution of No Child Left Behind.* Ithaca, NY: Cornell University Press, 2012.

Riley, Jason L. "Was the $5 Billion Worth It?" *Wall Street Journal*, July 23, 2011. https://www.wsj.com/articles/SB10001424053111903554904576461571362279948.

Rosenbach, Margo, Marilyn Ellwood, Carol Irvine, Cheryl Young, Wendy Conroy, Brian Quinn, and Megan Kell. *Implementation of the State Children's Health Insurance Program: Synthesis of State Evaluations.* Cambridge, MA: Mathematica Policy Research, March 2003. https://www.cms.gov/Research-Statistics-Data-and-Systems/Statistics-Trends-and-Reports/Reports/downloads/rosenbach_2003_5.pdf.

Rosenbaum, Sara, and Genevieve M. Kenney. "The Search for a National Child Health Coverage Policy." *Health Affairs* 33, no. 12 (December 2014): 2125–35. doi: 10.1377/hlthaff.2014.0906.

Rosenbaum, Sara, Anne Markus, and Colleen Sonosky. "Public Health Insurance Design for Children: The Evolution from Medicaid to SCHIP." *Journal of Health and Biomedical Law* 1 (2004): 1–47. https://publichealth.gwu.edu/departments/healthpolicy/CHPR/downloads/Public_Health_Insurance_Design_for_Children.pdf.

Rothman, Robert. *Something in Common: The Common Core Standards and the Next Chapter in American Education.* Cambridge, MA: Harvard Education Press, 2011.

Samuels, Christina A. "Districts Push for Texts Aligned to Common Core." *Education Week,* July 17, 2012. https://www.edweek.org/ew/articles/2012/07/18/36pubcriteria.h31html.

Samuels, Christina A. "Special Educators Look to Tie IEPs to Common Core." *Education Week,* December 27, 2010. https://www.edweek.org/ew/articles/2010/12/27/15iep_ep.h30.html.

Sawchuk, Stephen. "Common Standards Judged Better Than Most States." *Education Week,* July 21, 2010. https://www.edweek.org/ew/articles/2010/07/21/37fordham.h29.html.

Schmidt, William H., Leland S. Cogan, and Curtis C. McKnight. "Equality of Educational Opportunity: Myth or Reality in U.S. Schooling?" *American Educator* 34, no. 4 (2011). https://www.aft.org/sites/default/files/periodicals/Schmidt_1.pdf.

Schmidt, William H., and Richard T. Houang. "Curricular Coherence and the Common Core State Standards for Mathematics." *Educational Researcher* 41, no. 8 (November 2012): 294–308. doi: 10.3102/0013189X12464517.

Schmidt, William H., and Adam Maier. "Opportunity to Learn." In *Handbook of Education Policy Research,* edited by Gary Sykes, Barbara Schneider, and David N. Plank, 541–59. New York: Routledge, 2009.

Schwartz, Robert B., and Susan M. Kardos. "Research-Based Evidence and State Policy." In *The Role of Research in Educational Improvement,* edited by John D. Bransford, Deborah J. Stipek, Nancy J. Vye, Louis M. Gomez, and Diana Lam (Cambridge, MA: Harvard Education Press, 2009), 47–66.

Seid, Michael, James W. Varni, Lesley Cummings, and Matthias Schonlau. "The Impact of Realized Access to Care on Health-Related Quality of Life: A Two-Year Prospective Cohort Study of Children in the California State Children's Health Insurance Program." *Journal of Pediatrics* 149, no. 3 (October 2006): 354–61. doi: 10.1016/j.jpeds.2006.04.024.

Shafer, Byron E. *The American Political Pattern: Stability and Change, 1932–2016.* Lawrence: University Press of Kansas, 2016.

Sheingate, Adam. "Political Entrepreneurship, Institutional Change, and American Development." *Studies in American Political Development* 17, no. 2 (2003): 185–203. doi: 10.1017/S0898588X03000129.

Skocpol, Theda, and Alexander Hertel-Fernandez. "The Koch Network and Republican Party Extremism." *Perspectives on Politics* 14, no. 3 (September 2016): 681–99. doi: 10.1017/S1537592716001122.

Smith, Dennis G. "Directive to State Health Officials." Department of Health and Human Services, Centers for Medicare and Medicaid Services, Center for

Medicaid and State Operations. August 17, 2007. https://downloads.cms.gov/cms-gov/archived-downloads/SMDL/downloads/SHO081707.pdf.

Smith, Vernon, and Jason Cooke. *SCHIP Turns 10: An Update on Enrollment and the Outlook on Reauthorization from the Program's Directors.* Washington, DC: Kaiser Commission on Medicaid and the Uninsured, May 2007.

Social Science Research Council. *To Secure Knowledge: Social Science Partnerships for the Common Good.* Brooklyn, NY: SSRC, 2018. https://www.ssrc.org/to-secure-knowledge.

Stergios, Jim. "National Standards Will Define Local Curricula." Pioneer Institute, November 21, 2011. https://pioneerinstitute.org/education/national-standards-will-define-local-curricula.

Stergios, Jim. "Questioning the Convergence on National Standards." Pioneer Institute, November 23, 2010. https://pioneerinstitute.org/education/questioning-the-convergence-on-national-standards.

Stone, Deborah A. *Policy Paradox and Political Reason.* 3rd ed. New York: W.W. Norton, 2012.

Stout, David. "Bush Vetoes Children's Health Bill." *New York Times*, October 3, 2007. https://www.nytimes.com/2007/10/03/washington/03cnd-veto.html.

Supovitz, Jonathan, Alan Daly, and Miguel del Fresno. *#commoncore Project: How Social Media Is Changing the Politics of Education.* Philadelphia: Consortium for Policy Research in Education, February 23, 2015. http://repository.upenn.edu/hashtagcommoncore/1.

Supovitz, Jonathan, and Patrick McGuinn. "Interest Group Activity in the Context of Common Core Implementation." *Educational Policy* 33, no. 3 (July 2017): 453–85. doi: 10.1177/0895904817719516.

Szilagyi, Peter G., Mark A. Schuster, and Tina L. Cheng. "The Scientific Evidence for Child Health Insurance." *Academic Pediatrics* 9, no. 1 (January 2009). doi: 10.1016/j.acap.2008.12.002.

Sztajn, Paola, Jere Confrey, P. Holt Wilson, and Cynthia Edgington. "Learning Trajectory Based Instruction: Toward a Theory of Teaching." *Educational Researcher* 41, no. 5 (June 2012). doi: 10.3102/0013189X12442801.

Tatter, Grace. "At Long Last, Phase-Out of Common Core Is Official in Tennessee." Chalkbeat, April 15, 2016. https://chalkbeat.org/posts/tn/2016/04/15/at-long-last-phase-out-of-common-core-is-official-in-tennessee.

Tatter, Grace. "Commercial About State Educational Standards Makes Super Bowl Splash." Chalkbeat, February 3, 2015. https://www.chalkbeat.org/posts/tn/2015/02/03/commercial-about-state-educational-standards-makes-super-bowl-splash.

Tatter, Grace. "Most Common Core Standards Are Keepers, According to Tennessee's Public Review." Chalkbeat, May 14, 2015. https://www.chalkbeat.org/posts/tn/2015/05/14/most-common-core-standards-are-keepers-according-to-tennessees-public-review.

Tatter, Grace. "Standards Review Committee or Repeal Common Core Committee? Tennessee Leaders Are Split." Chalkbeat, August 5, 2015. https://www.chalkbeat .org/posts/tn/2015/08/05/standards-review-committee-or-repeal-common-core-committee-tennessee-leaders-are-split.

"Tennessee Gov. Haslam Says 'Immoral' Education Gaps Must Be Closed." *Commercial Appeal* (Memphis, TN). August 11, 2011.

Theriault, Sean M. *The Gingrich Senators: The Roots of Partisan Warfare in Congress.* New York: Oxford University Press, 2013.

Thomas, Paul L. "Why Common Standards Won't Work." *Education Week,* August 9, 2010. https://www.edweek.org/ew/articles/2010/08/11/37thomas.h29.html.

Timar, Thomas, and Allison Carter. *Surprising Strengths and Substantial Needs: Rural District Implementation of Common Core State Standards.* Stanford, CA: PACE, June 2017 . https://edpolicyinca.org/sites/default/files/Rural%20District%20Implementation %20of%20CCSS.pdf.

Tseng, Vivian, and Sandra Nutley. "Building the Infrastructure to Improve the Use and Usefulness of Research in Education." In *Using Research Evidence in Education: From Schoolhouse Door to Capitol Hill,* edited by Kara S. Finnigan and Alan J. Daly, 163–75. New York: Springer, 2014.

Tuttle, Erin. "Side by Side Comparison of Indiana's 'New' K–12 Math Standards." Hoosiers Against Common Core, March 6, 2014. https://hoosiersagainstcommoncore .com/side-side-comparison-indianas-new-k-12-math-standards.

Ujifusa, Andrew. "Common Core Supporters Firing Back." *Education Week,* May 14, 2013. https://www.edweek.org/ew/articles/2013/05/15/31standards_ep.h32.html.

Ujifusa, Andrew. "Indiana Standards to Replace Common Core Greeted Skeptically." *Education Week,* March 4, 2014. https://www.edweek.org/ew/articles/2014/ 03/05/23indiana.h33.html.

Ujifusa, Andrew. "Massachusetts' Mitch Chester on Common Core, Gov. Patrick's K–12 Plan." *State EdWatch* blog, Education Week, January 28, 2013. https://blogs .edweek.org/edweek/state_edwatch/2013/01/massachusetts_mitch_chester_on_ common_core_gov_patricks_k-12_plan.html.

Ujifusa, Andrew. "Political, Policy Feuds Roil Indiana's K–12 Landscape." *Education Week,* March 10, 2014. https://www.edweek.org/ew/articles/2014/03/12/24indiana.h33 .html.

Ujifusa, Andrew. "Tony Bennett Says Common Core in Jeopardy in Indiana." *State EdWatch* (blog), Education Week, November 7, 2012. http://blogs.edweek.org/ edweek/state_edwatch/2012/11/tony_bennett_says_common_core_in_jeopardy_in_ indiana.html.

Ujifusa, Andrew. "Two-Year Transition to Common-Core Tests Approved in Massachusetts." *State EdWatch* blog, Education Week, November 19, 2013. http://blogs .edweek.org/edweek/state_edwatch/2013/11/two-year_transition_to_common-core_ tests_approved_in_massachusetts.html.

United Ways of Tennessee. *What We Heard: A Summary Report of Listening Sessions about Supporting Effective Teachers.* Franklin: United Ways of Tennessee, Fall 2010.

US Congress, House of Representatives, Committee on Education and Labor, *Improving our Competitiveness: Common Core Education Standards,* 111th Cong., 1st sess., December 8, 2009. https://www.govinfo.gov/content/pkg/CHRG-111hhrg53732/pdf/CHRG-111hhrg53732.pdf.

US Congress, House of Representatives, Committee on Education and Labor, *Strengthening America's Competitiveness Through Common Academic Standards,* 111th Cong., 1st sess., April 29, 2009. https://www.govinfo.gov/content/pkg/CHRG-111hhrg48732/pdf/CHRG-111hhrg48732.pdf.

US Congress, House of Representatives, Committee on Energy and Commerce, Subcommittee on Health, *Covering the Uninsured Through the Eyes of a Child,* 110th Cong., 1st sess., February 14 and March 1, 2007. https://www.govinfo.gov/content/pkg/CHRG-110hhrg35598/pdf/CHRG-110hhrg35598.pdf.

US Congress, House of Representatives, Committee on Energy and Commerce, Subcommittee on Health, *Covering Uninsured Kids: Missed Opportunities for Moving Forward,* 110th Cong., 2nd sess., January 29, 2008. https://www.govinfo.gov/content/pkg/CHRG-110hhrg48375/pdf/CHRG-110hhrg48375.pdf.

US Congress, House of Representatives, Committee on Energy and Commerce, Subcommittee on Health, *Covering Uninsured Kids: Reversing Progress Already Made,* 110th Cong., 2nd sess., February 26, 2008. https://www.govinfo.gov/content/pkg/CHRG-110hhrg49370/pdf/CHRG-110hhrg49370.pdf.

US Congress, House of Representatives, Committee on Energy and Commerce, Subcommittee on Health, *Examining the Extension of Safety Net Health Programs,* June 23, 2017. https://www.govinfo.gov/content/pkg/CHRG-115hhrg28525/pdf/CHRG-115hhrg28525.pdf.

US Congress, House of Representatives, Committee on Energy and Commerce, Subcommittee on Health, *H.R. 5998, The Protecting Children's Health Coverage Act of 2008,* 110th Cong., 2nd sess., May 15, 2008. https://www.govinfo.gov/content/pkg/CHRG-110hhrg54777/pdf/CHRG-110hhrg54777.pdf.

US Congress, House of Representatives, Committee on Ways and Means, Subcommittee on Health, *Children's Access to Health Coverage,* 105th Cong., 1st sess., April 8, 1997. https://www.govinfo.gov/content/pkg/CHRG-105hhrg52730/pdf/CHRG-105hhrg52730.pdf.

US Congress, House of Representatives, Committee on Ways and Means, Subcommittee on Human Resources, *Health Coverage for Families Leaving Welfare,* 106th Cong., 2nd sess., May 16, 2000. https://www.govinfo.gov/content/pkg/CHRG-106hhrg68979/pdf/CHRG-106hhrg68979.pdf.

US Congress, Senate, Committee on Finance, *Children's Health Insurance Program in Action: A State's Perspective,* 110th Cong., 1st sess., April 4, 2007. https://www

.finance.senate.gov/imo/media/doc/430211.pdf.

US Congress, Senate, Committee on Finance, *The Children's Health Insurance Program: The Path Forward*, 115th Cong., 1st sess., September 7, 2017. https://www.govinfo .gov/content/pkg/CHRG-115shrg31255/pdf/CHRG-115shrg31255.pdf.

US Congress, Senate, Committee on Finance, *The Future of CHIP: Improving the Health of America's Children*, 110th Cong., 1st sess., February 1, 2007. https://www.finance .senate.gov/imo/media/doc/41339.pdf.

US Congress, Senate, Committee on Finance, *Implementation of the State Children's Health Insurance Program*, 106th Cong., 1st sess., April 29, 1999. https://www .finance.senate.gov/imo/media/doc/hrg106111.pdf.

US Congress, Senate, Committee on Finance, *Increasing Children's Access to Healthcare*, 105th Cong., 1st sess., April 30, 1997. https://www.finance.senate.gov/imo/media/ doc/hrg105-459.pdf.

US Congress, Senate, Committee on Finance, Subcommittee on Health Care, *The Children's Health Insurance Program: Protecting America's Children and Families*, 113th Cong., 2nd sess., September 16, 2014. https://www.govinfo.gov/content/pkg/ CHRG-113shrg94479/pdf/CHRG-113shrg94479.pdf.

US Congress, Senate, Committee on Finance, Subcommittee on Health Care, *CHIP at 10: A Decade of Covering Children*, 109th Cong., 2nd sess., July 25, 2006. https:// www.finance.senate.gov/imo/media/doc/31961.pdf.

US Congress, Senate, Committee on Finance, Subcommittee on Health Care, *CHIP Program from the States' Perspective*, 109th Cong., 2nd sess., November 16, 2006. https://www.finance.senate.gov/imo/media/doc/32112.pdf.

US Congress, Senate, Committee on Finance, Subcommittee on Health, *Covering Uninsured Children: The Impact of the August 17th CHIP Directive*, 110th Cong., 2nd sess., April 9, 2008. https://www.finance.senate.gov/imo/media/doc/55851.pdf.

US Congress, Senate, Committee on Labor and Human Resources, *Improving the Health Status of Children*, 105th Cong., 1st sess., April 18, 1997. https://babel.hathitrust.org/ cgi/pt?id=mdp.39015042566599&view=1up&seq=3.

US Department of Education. *Race to the Top Tennessee Report: Year 1: School Year 2010– 2011*. Washington, DC: US Department of Education, January 10, 2012. https:// www2.ed.gov/programs/racetothetop/performance/tennessee-year-1.pdf.

Valencia, Sheila W., P. David Pearson, and Karen K. Wixson. *Assessing and Tracking Progress in Reading Comprehension*. Paper commissioned by the Center for K–12 Assessment and Performance Management, Educational Testing Service, Princeton, NJ, April 2011. http://www.ets.org/Media/Research/pdf/TCSA_Symposium_ Final_Paper_Valencia_Pearson_Wixson.pdf.

Vaznis, James. "State Panel Adopts US Academic Standards." *The Boston Globe*, July 22, 2010. http://archive.boston.com/news/education/k_12/mcas/articles/2010/07/22/ state_panel_adopts_us_academic_standards.

Volden, Craig. "States as Policy Laboratories: Emulating Success in the Children's

Health Insurance Program." *American Journal of Political Science* 50, no. 2 (April 2006): 294–312. doi: https://doi.org/10.1111/j.1540-5907.2006.00185.x.

Watanabe, Teresa. "California Groups Demand UC Drop the SAT, Alleging it Illegally Discriminates Against Disadvantaged Students." *Los Angeles Times*, October 29, 2019. https://www.latimes.com/california/story/2019-10-29/california-groups-demand-uc-drop-the-sat-saying-they-illegally-discriminate-against-disadvantaged-students.

Watanabe, Teresa. "UC Violates Civil Rights of Disadvantaged Students by Requiring SAT for Admission, Lawsuit Alleges." *Los Angeles Times*, December 11, 2019. https://www.latimes.com/california/story/2019-12-10/uc-violates-civil-rights-of-disadvantaged-students-by-requiring-sat-for-admission-lawsuit-alleges.

Watanabe, Teresa. "Will UC Schools Drop Their SAT Scores Requirement?" *Los Angeles Times*, October, 2, 2019. https://www.latimes.com/california/story/2019-10-02/uc-sat-test-optional.

Weatherford, M. Stephen. "The Research–Policy Connection: Communicating Versus Using." Unpublished manuscript, Department of Political Science, University of California, Santa Barbara, 2017.

Weaver, R. Kent. *Ending Welfare as We Know It*. Washington, DC: Brookings Institution, 2000.

Weisman, Jonathan. "Brighter Economy Raises Odds of Action in Congress." *New York Times*, December 5, 2014. https://www.nytimes.com/2014/12/06/business/economy/brighter-economy-raises-odds-of-action-in-congress.html.

Weissert, Carol S., and Daniel Sheller. "Learning from the States? Federalism and National Health Policy." *Public Administration Review* 68, no. S1 (Special Issue, "The Quest for High-Performance Federalism," December 2008): S162–S174. doi: 10.1111/j.1540-6210.2008.00986.x.

"We Need National Reading Standards." *Boston Globe*, June 12, 2007.

WestEd. *Analysis of the Commonwealth of Massachusetts State Standards and the Common Core State Standards for English Language Arts and Mathematics*. Boston: Massachusetts Business Alliance for Education, July 19, 2010. https://www.mbae.org/wp-content/uploads/2010/07/Report_MA-CCS-Analysis_071910_Final.rev_.pdf.

WestEd. *R&D Alert: Academic Literacy for Adolescents*. San Francisco, CA: WestEd, October 10, 2011.

Wherry, Laura R., Genevieve M. Kenney, and Benjamin D. Sommers. "The Role of Public Health Insurance in Reducing Child Poverty." *Academic Pediatrics* 16, no. 3 supplement (April 2016): S98–S104. doi: 10.1016/j.acap.2015.12.011.

Whitehurst, Grover J. *"Don't Forget Curriculum."* Brown Center Letters on Education. Washington, DC: Brookings Institution, 2009. https://www.brookings.edu/research/dont-forget-curriculum.

Widmeyer Communications. "Gauging Attitudes on Tennessee Schools: Tennesseans are Cautiously Optimistic About K-12 Education." Washington, DC: Widmeyer

Communications, 2010.

Wiggins, Grant, and Jay McTighe. *Understanding by Design*. Alexandria, VA: ASCD, 2005.

Williamson, Gary L., Jill Fitzgerald, and A. Jackson Stenner. "The Common Core State Standards' Quantitative Text Complexity Trajectory: Figuring Out How Much Complexity Is Enough." *Educational Researcher* 42, no. 2 (March 2013). doi: 10.3102/0013189X12466695.

William T. Grant Foundation. "About Research-Practice Partnerships." Grant Foundation website. https://rpp.wtgrantfoundation.org/about.

Wolbrecht, Christina, and Michael T. Hartney. "'Ideas about Interests': Explaining the Changing Partisan Politics of Education." *Perspectives on Politics* 12, no. 3 (2014): 605. doi: 10.1017/S1537592714001613.

Yaccino, Steven. "Tensions Rise as Indiana Schools Chief and Governor Clash Over New Agency." *New York Times*, December 8, 2013. https://www.nytimes.com/2013/12/09/us/politics/tensions-rise-as-indiana-schools-chief-and-governor-clash-over-new-agency.html.

Yin, Robert K. *Case Study Research: Design and Methods*. 4th ed. Thousand Oaks, CA: Sage Publications, 2009.

Zelizer, Julian E. "Seizing Power: Conservatives and Congress Since the 1970s." In *The Transformation of American Politics: Activist Government and the Rise of Conservatism*, edited by Paul Pierson and Theda Skocpol. Princeton, NJ: Princeton University Press, 2007.

Zernike, Kate. "Massachusetts's Rejection of Common Core Test Signals Shift in U.S." *New York Times*, November 21, 2015. https://www.nytimes.com/2015/11/22/us/rejecting-test-massachusetts-shifts-its-model.html.

Acknowledgments

AS POLITICAL SCIENTISTS committed to studying K–12 education, we have often felt like missionaries bringing concepts and research from our discipline to the study of education policy. This book is an example of that effort, and made possible because of colleagues supportive of interdisciplinary research. We are grateful to Vivian Tseng, Kimberly DuMont, Robert Granger, and Adam Gamoran of the William T. Grant Foundation, who have not only funded our research on evidence use in the development of the Common Core, and funded the preparation of this book, but have also welcomed us and our political science perspective into the intellectual community they have built around the study of research-based evidence in youth policy and practice. We have learned much from their wide-ranging initiatives and the annual convenings of grantees and users of their research.

Our understanding of evidence use and the Common Core was greatly enhanced by all the participants in the process who generously shared their knowledge and experience with us. We hope that our analysis has given full voice to their views on the role of evidence in education policymaking.

Obtaining the data analyzed in this book depended on the work of a skilled group of graduate research assistants: Lisa Argyle, Cecilia Farfán-Méndez, Sam Fontaine, Jeanette Yih Harvie, and Kristoffer Smemo at the University of California Santa Barbara, and Stephanie E. Dean, Ashley Clark Perry, and Lindsay Shouldis at the Hunt Institute. We have also benefited from the enthusiastic assistance of a group of UC Santa Barbara undergraduates who took advantage of UCSB's commitment to their full participation in the university's research endeavors: Bruce Arao, Alex Cortez, Marika Fain, Marcus Loiseau, Arlene Perez, Mabel Pérez, Gabriela Romo, Jenna Zendarski, and Kimberly Zilles.

For more than a year, Caroline Chauncey, editor in chief of the Harvard Education Press, has guided us through the writing of this book. Throughout the process, she has been gracious and encouraging while nudging us along with insightful comments and gentle prods.

Finally, this book is dedicated to our grandsons, Colin and Theo Weatherford, who have shown us again and again that children's natural curiosity is really about using the evidence they have collected in many different forms from the world around them.

About the Authors

LORRAINE M. MCDONNELL is a professor emerita of political science at the University of California, Santa Barbara. Prior to coming to UCSB, she was a senior political scientist at RAND. Her research focuses on the politics of elementary and secondary education policies and their institutional effects. In recent studies, she has examined the politics of student standards and testing, particularly their historical role in federal policy and the policy feedback they generate among political interest groups, and has used them as a lens for understanding the role of research and other evidence in policy decisions. Her publications have focused on a range of topics, including teacher unions, the education of immigrant students, and the role of citizen deliberation. She served for seven years on the National Research Council's Board on Testing and Assessment, and was a member of the NRC's Advisory Committee for the Division of the Behavioral and Social Sciences and Education. She is a past president of the American Educational Research Association and a member of the National Academy of Education.

M. STEPHEN WEATHERFORD is a professor emeritus of political science at the University of California, Santa Barbara, a former associate dean of social science and chair of the political science department. His research has been supported by the National Science Foundation and private foundations, and has ranged over questions of representation, political trust, political economy and the politics of education policy. His writings have focused on presidential leadership in economic policy, the way presidents' economic understanding set the agenda, and how presidents have drawn on research and policy ideas in seeking to persuade Congress and the public to support their national goals. On education, his research has investigated the school desegregation controversies of 1970s and 1980s, how parents and local activists have sought to employ deliberative processes to influence the governance of public K–12 education, and the way formal research and other evidence is integrated into the educational policy process.

Index